Measurement guide
— conversion approximate

Centimetres to inches
1 cm.	=	*0.39 in.*
5 cm.	=	c.2 in.
10 cm.	=	3.9 in.
30 cm.	=	11.8 in.
50 cm.	=	19.7 in.
100 cm.	=	39.4 in.

Inches to centimetres
1 in.	=	*2.54 cm.*
		(25.4 mm.)
3 in.	=	7.6 cm.
6 in.	=	15.2 cm.
12 in.	=	30.4 cm.

Metres to feet
1 m.	=		*3.28 ft.*
5 m.	=		16.4 ft.
10 m.	=	c.	33 ft.
30 m.	=	c.	100 ft.
50 m.	=	c.	165 ft.
100 m.	=	c.	330 ft.
500 m.	=	c.	1,650 ft.
1,000 m.	=	c.	3,300 ft.
1,200 m.	=	c.	4,000 ft.
1,500 m.	=	c.	5,000 ft.
1,850 m.	=	c.	6,000 ft.
2,000 m.	=	c.	6,500 ft.
2,200 m.	=	c.	7,200 ft.
2,450 m.	=	c.	8,000 ft.
2,800 m.	=	c.	9,200 ft.

0 — 1 — 2 — 3 — 4 — 5 — 6 — 7 — 8 — 9 — 10 — 11 — 12 — 13 — 14 — 15 — 16 — 17 — 18 — 19 — 20

EX·LIBRIS

WILLIAM G.
HARVEY

TREES
OF KENYA

**TIM NOAD and
ANN BIRNIE**

TREES
OF KENYA

TIM NOAD and
ANN BIRNIE

Illustrations by
Ann Birnie

Published by
T.C. Noad and A. Birnie,
P.O. Box 40034, Nairobi, Kenya.

© 1989 T.C. Noad and A. Birnie

Phototypesetting and colour separation by
Kul Graphics Limited, P.O. Box 18095, Nairobi.

Colour printing by Prudential Printers Limited
Printed litho by General Printers Limited

Printed and produced entirely in Kenya

First edition November 1989
Second (hardback) edition October 1990

ISBN NO 9966—848—95—9

What would the world be, once bereft
Of wet and of wildness? Let them be left,
O let them be left, wildness and wet;
Long live the weeds and the wilderness yet.

—Gerald Manley Hopkins

This book is dedicated to Acacia Deborah Werikhe, who was born in 1988, and through her to the next generation upon whom the future of Kenya will rest.

Acacia's father Michael, Kenya's famous Rhino Man, has walked countless miles through Kenya and across Europe to appeal to the world to help us save the rhino and its wild habitat.

On World Environment Day 1989 the name of Michael Werikhe was added to UNEP's Global Roll of Honour, in recognition of his dedication to the cause of preserving the environment.

INTRODUCTION

RECOGNITION is a giant step towards conservation, and the aim of this book is to give people who are not specialists the pleasure and satisfaction of being able to recognise the trees they see around them.

This book is a field guide, not a botanical text-book. It includes most of the common trees of Kenya, and covers both indigenous and exotic species, meaning trees introduced from other countries. However, the 300 or so species described covers less than a quarter of the trees that may be encountered somewhere in this diverse and beautiful country, and many species that are locally prominent, often in drier areas or at the coast, have therefore had to be omitted. The main emphasis is on the trees of the Nairobi area, with a selection of outstanding trees from other parts of Kenya.

The line drawings illustrating each species will help with identification. The text is arranged to complement the drawings, and although the descriptions are detailed, botanical terms have been kept to a minimum. The measurements given are guidelines, because many variations will be found; for instance, young leaves are often much larger than mature leaves, and a tree near water may be much taller than its counterpart in a dry area.

No key has been attempted, because the botanical detail required makes it impossible to devise a key simple enough to be helpful to the non-botanist. A key is in any event probably of value only where all species have been included, which is well beyond the scope of this book.

Classification and naming of trees

Like all plants, trees are grouped in botanical families and occasionally plants which are not strictly trees have been included to help the reader to understand the family pattern. Even the experts disagree on the correct order of these families, and the alphabetical order in this book is used simply for convenience.

The way trees have been named by botanists is best explained by taking an example from the text.

(continued)

MORACEAE	:	the family, grouping together genera with major characteristics in common. The family name is usually formed by adding -*aceae* to the name of one genus in the family, often the genus considered to be the most typical. In this example the family is named after the Mulberry genus Morus.
Ficus	:	the genus, grouping together closely related plants of different species. It is often best to learn the name of the genus first, and leave the other details until later.
Ficus thonningii	:	the species, which is the basic unit of classi-fication. No two species are identical.

The name given to the species may indicate an important characteristic (such as *'salutaris'*, meaning health-giving), or may indicate its origin *('africana', 'abyssinica')* or may be a Latinized version of the name of the botanist who first described it *('hildebrandtii', 'battiscombei').* |
| *(Ficus eriocarpa)* | : | a synonym, or a previous name which has now been superseded. These are included, in smaller print, to help cross-reference to other publi-cations. |
| **Wild Fig, Strangler Fig**)
Mugumo (Kikuyu)) | | common names, where they exist. This is a problem area, and is discussed further in the following paragraph. |

Tree names

Because people ask about 'common' names — by which they usually mean a name in their own language — the prominence given to Latin names needs a little explanation.

The great advantage of the Latin names is their absolute precision. They identify the tree worldwide, regardless of language or dialect, and with practice they quickly become familiar. A common name like 'Flame Tree' may be simple to remember, but it will mean one species to a person from Kisumu, another to someone from Thika and a third to someone living at the coast — let alone a visitor from overseas.

Most of Kenya's indigenous trees never acquired English names, probably because they were so unfamiliar to early visitors from Europe. Some were given names by association with trees from the northern hemisphere, but the result is often misleading: thus, the Pencil Cedar is not really a cedar, the Meru Oak is not an oak and the Whistling Pine does not belong to the pine family.

Many trees have tribal names because of their local use and importance, but these names often cover more than one species. A complete list of local names would be unmanageable, and the common names included in this book are mainly restricted to the Kikuyu names for trees in the Nairobi area.

Medicinal and poisonous properties.

Valuable medicinal properties are attributed to many trees, and references to these have been included in the text for the sake of interest. However, research is at a relatively early state, and by no means all the claims made in traditional medicine have been verified. No one should experiment outside a laboratory, because it is certain that many of the chemicals involved are highly poisonous.

The trees of Kenya, particularly the invaluable indigenous trees, are part of our national heritage. They belong to the whole community, and the urgent need for conservation and re-planting has priority at the highest levels. The spread of knowledge and interest, and the awareness of trees as a valuable natural resource, is essential to the preservation of that heritage.

Nairobi
October 1989

Tim Noad
Ann Birnie

NOTES ON PLANTING TREES

The notes that follow are to help people who are not expert gardeners to plant trees successfully, and to encourage 'social' planting in gardens, villages, roadsides and shambas as a way of helping to make good the depletion of natural forests.

The techniques of plantation forestry, germination from seed and planting in arid areas are dealt with in other specialised publications. So is agroforestry, the integration of crops with multi-purpose trees that enrich the soil, which is probably the single most important discipline for the future of agriculture in Africa.

Choice of trees

On a garden scale, it is easiest to buy seedlings or young trees from a nursery. The practical notes in the text will help with the choice of species; trees indigenous to the area should be preferred, partly because they are the most likely to succeed, and partly because to many eyes they have an attraction unrivalled by the faster-growing exotics.

Preparation

A good deep hole, ideally a metre across by a metre deep, should be dug some weeks before planting. Too small a hole may cramp the roots and stunt the tree. The hole should be square and not round, because roots take the line of least resistance: in hard ground they will grow round and round inside a circular hole, but in a square hole they will force their way down through the corners, which helps to avoid roots coming to the surface as the tree matures.

When the hole is re-filled, very poor soil should be replaced or mixed with better soil. The soil should be tamped down at regular intervals, and a shallow catchment area should be left at the top. A thorough soaking will then wet the soil to the bottom of the hole and exclude pockets of air; if water is not available, it is best to wait until 100 mm. of rain has fallen. The most successful time for planting out is after the start of the long rains, although never when the site is actually flooded.

Planting

The soil in the hole will subside, and the hole should be slightly over-filled, leaving a depression at the top for the new tree. Care must be taken not to disturb the soil around the roots as the nursery container is cut away; the tree must be tamped firmly in place and if necessary loosely staked.

Compost and watering

The effectiveness of adding compost or fertiliser is debatable. Fresh manure will burn the roots, but well-matured compost may help growth in poorer soils, although it may encourage termites. It is probably best just to add a few handfuls of bone meal to the soil as the hole is re-filled.

Unless rainfall is adequate, watering will be necessary if the tree is to survive. A good soaking once a week is much better than light daily watering, which only encourages roots to come to the surface.

LIST OF CONTENTS

Introduction

Notes on planting trees

Acknowledgements

Descriptive text and illustrations:

Note: the enormous pod-bearing family LEGUMINOSAE is treated under the three sub-family headings shown above, namely

CAESALPINIOIDEAE	Cassia sub-family
MIMOSOIDEAE	Acacia sub-family
PAPILIONOIDEAE	Pea sub-family

Selected bibliography
Glossary
Index

ACKNOWLEDGEMENTS

The authors would like to record their grateful thanks to the staff of the East African Herbarium in Nairobi for their generous assistance with research and information, particularly Christine Kabuye who kindly undertook the final checking, Dr. Henk Beentje and Geoffrey Mungai.

Our thanks also to many other individuals for help with research, inspiration and general critical appreciation, in particular Gaye Aikman, Jim Birnie, Joseph Cheruyiot, Charles Dewhurst, Dick and Louise Fordyce, Serena Gledhill, Tom and Joan Grumbley, John Karmali, Hon. Mwai Kibaki, Festus Kiogora, Peter Leech, Githuku Macharia, Margaret May, Fleur Ng'weno, Sarah Noad, Sheila Norman, Carin Parfitt, Dee Raymer, Anne Robertson, Sue Silvester, Mary Sinclair, Eleanor Thompson, Ros Trail, Francis Wanyeki and John Wright.

Willing help and encouragement over artwork and layout has been given by Phil Galley, Helen Nunn, Elizabeth Robinson, Christina Willis and Peps Heasman; some of whose original illustrations have been included.

Too numerous to mention individually are the many people who have allowed us to visit their gardens, farms and nurseries in many parts of Kenya to gather material. Our thanks and appreciation go out to all of them.

Our special thanks go to Victoria Ndesandjo, who has typed the numerous drafts and re-drafts with tireless accuracy throughout the long course of production of this book.

We would like to record our appreciation to Kul Bhakoo and his staff for their untiring efforts in the preparation of the manuscript and artwork.

Finally, the authors are deeply indebted to Dicky and Jytte Evans and their company Homegrown (Kenya) Limited, without whose generous involvement and financial support publication of this book could not have been undertaken.

The second edition of 'Trees of Kenya' has been produced in hardback, and incorporates minor corrections and improvements. In particular, a number of Kikuyu tree names have been revised, and the authors are grateful to Norman Gachathi, author of 'Kikuyu Botanical Dictionary', for his help and advice in this respect.

ANACARDIACEAE   Mango family

A worldwide but mainly tropical family of about 600 trees, shrubs and vines which includes a number of ornamental trees such as the South American Pepper tree *Schinus molle,* and a number of species producing commercially valuable fruit and nuts, such as the cashew, pistachio and mango.

Most members of the family have resinous tissues, although the leaves are not gland-dotted. In some species the resin is an important source of tannin, and in others it is used for mastic or gum, turpentine and varnish: the resin of *Rhus verniciflua,* the Varnish Tree from China and Japan, is the basis of all oriental lacquer work. Sometimes the resin is poisonous, as in the Poison Ivy *Rhus radicans* and the Poison Sumac or Poison Elder *Toxicodendron vernix* from North America. A similar poison is found in the fruit walls of the cashew nut.

Members of this family in Kenya include *Anacardium, Mangifera, Ozoroa, Pistacia, Rhus, Schinus.*

Anacardium occidentale   Cashew Nut
Brazil, Caribbean   Mkanju (Swahili)

A spreading tree with large leathery leaves, growing under ideal conditions to 10 m., widely planted and now naturalised at the coast, where it was probably introduced by the Portuguese in the 16th century. Both the English and the Swahili names are derived from the South American Indian name 'Acaju'.

Bark: dark brown, very rough. **Leaves:** alternate, rather leathery, broadly oval, to 15 x 8 cm.; apex distinctly rounded, midrib and veins prominent pale green; margin wavy. **Flowers:** very small, star-shaped, creamy white, sometimes marked with red, in terminal clusters. Only a few of the flowers develop into fruit. **Fruit:** hard, kidney-shaped nuts, attached to the base of a shiny orange-yellow 'cashew apple' which is not a fruit but a swollen flower stalk. The true fruit are the nuts, which fall to the ground when ripe and are collected from under the trees.

The cashew apple is edible and slighly acid; the juice can be drunk fresh or fermented into liqueur wine, and the pulp can be used for making jam. Cashew nuts are low in calories and high in edible oil and protein, but the dark brown outer covering contains a different, poisonous oil which burns the skin and which must be roasted off before the kernel can be eaten. The nuts are today shelled and roasted by machine in a factory at Kilifi, and are a valuable export.

The cashew-shell oil, despite being poisonous, has medicinal properties and a surprising variety of other uses. It can be mixed with cement for weatherproofing and used as a wood preservative against termites, and the distilled oil is used in the manufacture of varnishes, inks, tiles and even brake-linings.

Practical notes: grown from seed or by grafting, best in warm, humid climates on well-drained, sandy soil, where it will bear fruit in 3 years or less and continue in production for 20 years. The tree will also grow on poorer soils in lower rainfall areas, but not in saline soil.

1

Anacardium occidentale

ANACARDIACEAE

Mangifera indica
Northern India, Burma

Mango
Mwembe (Swahili)

    A densely foliaged evergreen tree with a sturdy trunk and rounded crown, usually 10 to 15 m. in height but occasionally growing to 30 m., planted from sea-level to 2,000 m. and now naturalised at the coast. These shady trees were so popular as meeting places and the fruit so widely traded that the main market in Mombasa is named Mwembe Tayari, and mango trees throughout East Africa mark the routes of the early Arab traders and the Indian railway workers.

    Bark: light grey, becoming dark brown and fissured with age. **Leaves:** dark green, alternate, somewhat crowded at the ends of branches; younger leaves limp, mature leaves leathery, narrowly lance-shaped, up to 30 cm. long, smelling of turpentine when crushed; midrib pale, prominent below. Young leaves are often bright pink or copper-coloured. **Flowers:** numerous, very small, cream-coloured to pinkish brown, in large terminal pyramids to 60 cm. in height. Pollination is by flies and insects rather than bees, but as only one of the 5 stamens is fertile, relatively few fruits develop. **Fruit:** large and heavy, up to 15 cm. in length, almost round to irregularly ovoid, ripening from green to yellow, red or orange-pink, depending on the variety. The large seed is surrounded by delicious juicy golden flesh, very rich in vitamins A and C. The fruit hang on long stalks and fall easily, resulting in considerable wastage.

    Practical notes: a dark, handsome ornamental tree for parks and large gardens, preferring good deep soil in hot, wet climates but also succeeding in much drier, less favourable conditions. Trees for fruit production are usually selected by grafting, the best varieties of fruit being free from fibre and from the taint of turpentine from the skin.

Ozoroa insignis ssp. reticulata *(Heeria reticulata)*
indigenous

Tropical Resin tree
Mwaalika (Swahili)

    A much-branched shrub or tree with milky, resinous latex, 3 to 15 m. in height, widely distributed in wooded savannah, rocky hillsides and forest margins from the coast to 2,200 m.

    Bark: grey, corky, much fissured. **Leaves:** lance-shaped, usually in whorls of 3; very variable, 5 to 17 cm. in length, smooth dull green above, with conspicuous parallel veins; apex tapering to rounded, often with a bristle-like tip, base tapering to a 3 cm. stalk; margin inrolled, midrib prominent below. The lower leaf surface and young branchlets are densely covered with velvety whitish hairs. **Flowers:** small, white to yellowish, in erect terminal or axillary sprays. **Fruit:** small, red, kidney-shaped, black and shiny when ripe, drying to resemble currants.

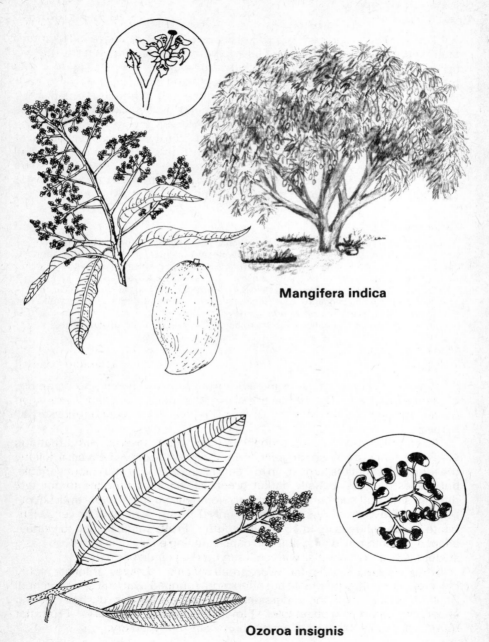

Mangifera indica

Ozoroa insignis

ANACARDIACEAE

Pistacia aethiopica
indigenous   Muheheti (Kikuyu)

A spreading evergreen tree or shrub, 3 to 15 m. in height, often multi-stemmed, occurring in dry upland forest and wooded savannah from 1,500 to 2,500 m., often in association with *Juniperus procera;* now also fairly widely planted for agroforestry as it tolerates drought and poor soil.

Bark: brown-black, resinous; twigs and leaves turpentine-scented when crushed. **Leaves:** compound, to 10 cm. long; leaf stalk winged; leaflets usually 3 to 4 pairs, broadly oval, about 4 cm. long, with no stalk and no terminal leaflet; apex rounded, often notched. **Flowers:** small, yellowish or purplish, in compact axillary spikes up to 5 cm. long. **Fruit:** small, rounded, red on one side, to 5 mm. in diameter, with a mango-like smell when crushed.

The commercial Pistachio nut comes from the tropical species *Pistacia vera,* but this has never been successfully introduced into Kenya.

Rhus spp.

In Africa this is a widespread, somewhat shrubby genus of trees with trifoliate leaves, flowers in branching heads with the sexes usually separate and small, thinly fleshy red fruit. In North America, an outstanding ornamental is *Rhus typhina,* known as the Sumac tree, with brilliant red autumn leaves and red fruit. The botanical name *Rhus* is the Greek word for red.

The two most common indigenous species of *Rhus* are described below. The leaves of both species are much eaten by goats and also by giraffe. *Rhus* is quick-growing and drought-resistant, widely used for charcoal and slow-burning firewood. The twigs are used as toothbrushes, and various infusions used in traditional medicine to treat coughs, colds and stomach pains.

Rhus natalensis
indigenous   Muthigiu (Kikuyu)

Usually a bushy, many-branched shrub with a tendency to scramble, occasionally a tree to 8 m., widespread in grassland and wooded savannah in all regions other than very dry areas. This species is very variable in all respects.

Bark: grey-brown, young branchlets paler, often covered with breathing pores. Branches are mostly angular, forming elbow shapes. **Leaves:** trifoliate, the terminal leaflet the largest, up to 9 cm. in length; shape and colour variable, but leaves hairless, usually darker green above; apex rounded to pointed, margin smooth, sometimes obscurely toothed; young leaves and shoots reddish. **Flowers:** very small, petals only 1.5 mm., greenish or yellowish-white, in loose heads up to 15 cm. in length. **Fruit:** small, oblong to kidney-shaped, smooth red, drying dull and papery, falling easily. The thin flesh has a sweet taste, and is popular with children herding cattle or goats.

Rhus vulgaris is a similar, widespread species. **Leaves:** trifoliate, softly hairy, dull green, very variable but often more rounded, with the apex notched. Stalks, branchlets and the undersides of the leaflets are densely hairy; young shoots are eaten as a vegetable. **Flowers:** head densely hairy. **Fruit:** flat round discs, only 3 to 5 mm. across, brownish-red when dry.

5

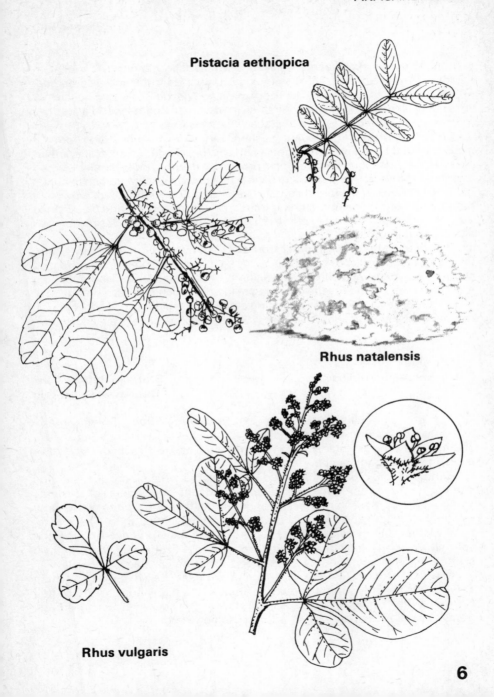

Pistacia aethiopica

Rhus natalensis

Rhus vulgaris

6

ANACARDIACEAE

Schinus molle
Peru, Andes

Pepper Tree

A light green evergreen tree with characteristic hanging or 'weeping' foliage, growing to 10 or 15 m. with a short, gnarled trunk and a spreading, rounded crown. Also known as the American Mastic Tree, this species is commonly planted in dry, warm climates in many parts of the world as well as most districts of Kenya, where in places it has become naturalised.

Bark: dark brown, rugged and peeling: very sticky resinous latex forms if the bark is cut. **Leaves:** compound, to 30 cm. long; leaflets numerous, linear, resinous, to 7 cm. long with no stalk, producing a strong peppery smell when crushed. **Flowers:** very small, greenish to yellowish white, in conspicuous hanging clusters. **Fruit:** on female trees only, small rounded berries in prominent dangling chains, turning from green to red, purple and black. Dried berries can be ground into a coarse brown pepper, and both leaves and berries can be used in curries.

Practical notes: fast-growing from seed and very tolerant of most soils, including both black cotton and dry sandy soil: widely planted as an attractive shade tree, extremely drought-resistant once established and reaching maturity in less than 20 years. Pruning of lower branches is recommended to help grass grow underneath, and siting away from buildings will avoid the fall of heavy branches as the tree ages. Seedlings are widely available from nurseries.

Schinus terebinthifolius *(Schinus terebranthi)*
Brazil

**Brazilian Pepper Tree,
Christmas Berry Tree**

A shorter, rather less graceful species than *Schinus molle,* growing to 7 m. in height with a somewhat twisted appearance, but in Kenya often pruned to an attractive semi-circular shape or grown into a hedge. Crushed leaves have an identical pungent, peppery smell.

Bark: dark grey, deeply furrowed with age; branchlets crowded, stiff and angular, in contrast with the pliable, pendant branchlets of *Schinus molle*. **Leaves:** dark shiny green, compound, leaflets 3 to 6 pairs with a large terminal leaflet; shape narrowly oval, the terminal leaflet up to 10 cm. long; margin often slightly serrated; leaf stalks reddish, usually winged. **Flowers:** very small, white, bell-shaped, in erect spikes. **Fruit:** deep pink to vivid scarlet, slightly larger than the preceding species, in conspicuous clusters.

Practical notes: fast-growing, preferring less harsh conditions than *Schinus molle:* fairly common in urban areas in the highlands as a shade tree or ornamental. However, in Florida and Hawaii this species has invaded vast tracts of land and is regarded as a troublesome weed.

7

Schinus molle

Schinus terebinthifolius

APOCYNACEAE   Oleander family

A large family of mainly tropical trees, shrubs and lianes, most producing a white latex and almost all with funnel-shaped blossoms. The twisted appearance of the flower buds is characteristic. Members of this family have simple, usually glossy leaves with entire margins.

Many species are exceptionally poisonous, and contain cardiac glycosides or potent alkaloids. In Kenya arrow poisons have been made for centuries from the *Acokanthera* tree and from the fleshy, pink-flowered Desert Rose *Adenium obesum*, both members of the Oleander family. However, recent research has also yielded valuable drugs for the treatment of arthritis, high blood pressure and cancer

Members of this family in Kenya include *Acokanthera, Adenium, Carissa, Nerium, Plumeria, Rauvolfia, Tabernaemontana, Thevetia.*

Acokanthera oppositifolia *(Acokanthera longiflora)*   Mururu (Kikuyu)
indigenous

An attractive small tree or multi-stemmed shrub, rather less compact than *A. schimperi* but common around Nairobi and often planted in gardens.

Leaves: tough and glossy, larger and more elliptic, up to 10 cm. in length, sharply pointed at the apex.   **Flowers:** longer, up to 3 cm., fragrant.   **Fruit:** larger, up to 5 cm. long, plum-like and purple when ripe, said to be edible.

A useful dark green tree or shrub which will survive periods of drought. Seedlings are sometimes available in nurseries.

Acokanthera schimperi
indigenous

Poison Arrow Tree
Murichu (Kikuyu)

A dense, dark evergreen tree with a sturdy trunk and rounded crown, sometimes multi-stemmed, usually to 5 m. in height, sometimes to 10 m.; occurring in thickets and grasslands from 1,100 to 2,300 m., often at the margins of dry forest or forest remnants.

Bark: dark brown, fissured with age.   **Leaves:** opposite, dark glossy green above, paler and duller below; young leaves reddish; texture stiff, size and shape variable, 3 to 6 cm. in length, broadly rounded; apex often tipped with a sharp point; margin entire.   **Flowers:** tubular, about 1.5 cm. long, white or flushed with pink, in dense, fragrant axillary clusters.   **Fruit:** oval berries, up to 1.5 cm. long, turning from green to yellow, red, purple and black. The ripe fruit are eaten by birds and monkeys.

Practical notes: from the gardener's point of view, well worth planting as a forest margin tree of great character. Seeds are plentiful but rather difficult to germinate, and so far seedlings are difficult to obtain. Prefers rich, well-drained forest soil, but capable of growing in black cotton soil and other dry sites. Trees are slow-growing, but are reputed to live to a considerable age.

(continued)

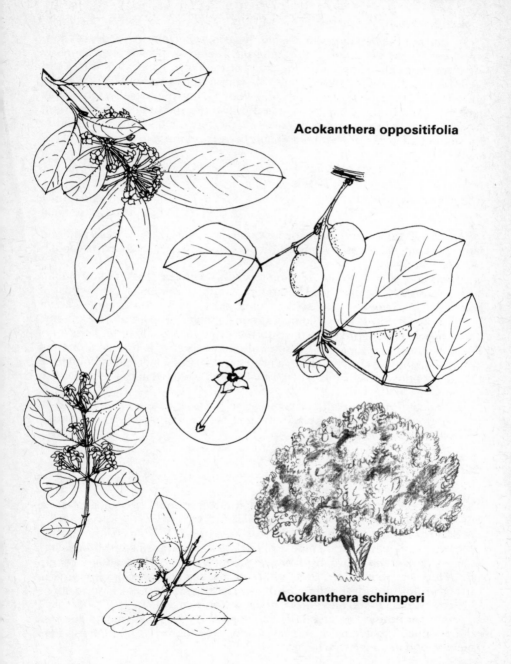

Acokanthera oppositifolia

Acokanthera schimperi

10

Acokanthera spp. (continued)

All parts of the *Acokanthera* are highly toxic, especially in the dry season, with the possible exception of the ripe fruit. The arrow poison used by many African tribes was made by boiling chips of the bark or the roots into a tar, which was often mixed with fig latex. A wound from an arrow dipped in the poison would lead to paralysis and death within a few minutes. Poisoning has been recorded from eating meat grilled over a fire made from *Acokanthera* sticks, and stock browsing on young leaves die very rapidly from heart failure. Fortunately such cases are rare, probably because of the very bitter taste of the sap.

There is no known antidote.

Adenium obesum   Desert Rose
indigenous   Mdiga, Mdagu (Swahili)

A thickset succulent shrub, occasionally a tree to 6 m., widespread and familiar in hot, dry areas of Kenya from the coast to 1,500 m. All parts contain copious watery sap.

Bark: grey-green, smooth; stems swollen. **Leaves:** thick, fleshy bluish-green, narrowly elliptic, to 15 cm. in length, crowded at the ends of branches. **Flowers:** showy bright pink to deep rose, funnel-shaped, about 5 cm. across. **Fruit:** long thin pink-green capsules, in pairs, to 24 x 2 cm., drying brown and splitting to release narrow cylindrical seeds about 1 cm. long. These bear tufts of long silky white hairs at each end, and bowl along the ground looking like cartwheels on a fixed axle. Arrow poison is obtained from the seeds, and the branches and the main roots are used at the coast for fish poison.

Practical notes: a useful ornamental in rocky or arid areas, producing a thick underground stem; grown from seed or from cuttings, in pure sand or very well-drained soil.

Carissa edulis   Carissa
indigenous   Mukawa (Kikuyu)

A spiny evergreen found as a shrub, scrambler or small tree, widespread in bush and dry forest margins from the coast to 2,000 m.

Bark: grey, smooth, with straight woody spines up to 5 cm. in length, often in pairs, sometimes branching; milky latex present. **Leaves:** opposite, leathery dark green above, broadly oval, about 5 cm. long, often with a sharp tip. **Flowers:** about 2 cm. long, white inside, red outside, very fragrant, in attractive pink terminal heads. **Fruit:** oval berries, about 1 cm. long, in dense clusters, turning to red and purple; edible when ripe.

Practical notes: tolerates dry conditions and most soils, including black cotton; difficult to establish, but capable of growing from seed into an eye-catching and impenetrable hedge.

11

Adenium obesum

Carissa edulis

APOCYNACEAE

Nerium oleander   Oleander
Mediterranean, Asia minor

An attractive ornamental shrub 2 to 5 m. in height, often multi-stemmed, flowering freely for many months of the year. Native from the Mediterranean region to Japan and cultivated throughout East Africa up to 2,200 m., thriving in dry, sunny localities; common as a standard in the streets of Nairobi.

Bark: pale grey, smooth.   **Leaves:** opposite or in threes, stiff dull greyish-green, narrowly lance-shaped, up to 20 x 3 cm.; side veins markedly parallel.   **Flowers:** funnel-shaped, up to 5 cm. across with 5 petals and a fringe of scales in the throat; flowers single or double, in loose terminal groups. Colours range from white to cream, pink, orange and crimson.   **Fruit:** long thin double capsules, about 12 cm. long, splitting to release seeds bearing tufts of hairs.

All parts of the Oleander are highly poisonous, the leaves and flowers containing cardiac glycosides. Fortunately the sap is so bitter that few animals will be tempted to browse, but 20 gm. of leaves will kill a horse or a cow, and only 1 to 5 gm. is needed to kill a sheep.

Nevertheless, this plant was highly esteemed in ancient Arab medicine for heart and circulation problems, and the roots were used as a cure for ringworm. The flowers produce good honey.

Practical notes: not to be exposed to browsing animals or curious children, but in other respects a remarkably tolerant evergreen shrub or attractive hedge. Easily grown from cuttings rooted in sand or water, and can be heavily pruned.

Plumeria rubra   Frangipani
Central America

A familiar flowering shrub or small tree to 5 m. with thick, forking, semi-succulent branches which produce quantities of poisonous milky latex if they are damaged. Widely cultivated throughout the tropics, and in Kenya grown from the coast to 2,000 m.

Bark: grey, smooth, with leaf scars prominent on the branches.   **Leaves:** large, leathery, dark green, crowded at the ends of branches; leaves lance-shaped, tapering to base and apex, usually about 20 cm. long but in some forms up to twice that length; veins regular and prominent. Leaves are usually shed during the dry season, after which the flowers appear.   **Flowers:** 5 waxy, rounded petals forming a broad funnel, 6 cm. across, the lobes pink and the throat yellow, in heavily scented terminal groups.   **Fruit:** paired capsules up to 25 cm. in length.

Practical notes: readily grown from large cuttings, which must be left to dry out for a day or two before planting in well-drained soil. Fairly slow growing, but tolerant of drought and adaptable to most soils.

(continued)

Nerium oleander

Plumeria rubra

APOCYNACEAE

Plumeria rubra (continued)

Many forms and hybrids have been developed, with innumerable variations of colour and leaf shape. Modern study indicates that they all belong to the one species described above, despite the existence of other names such as *Plumeria alba*.

The white and yellow-flowered forms are common in the East from India to Singapore, and have been widely planted in Kenya. A fine evergreen form at the coast has darker, glossier leaves with a rounded apex, with larger white flowers on long stalks.

In India, Sri Lanka and S.E. Asia the flowers are widely used in religious ceremonies. In East Africa the tree is often planted in cemeteries.

Rauvolfia caffra *(Rauvolfia natalensis)*
indigenous   Mwerere (Kikuyu)

An evergreen tree 6 to 20 m. in height with a dense, rounded crown, common in Meru district and the Kedong valley, often along streams or watercourses.

Bark: grey, smooth, cracking with age into rough, regular blocks.   **Leaves:** in whorls of 3 to 5, each lance-shaped, up to 25 cm. long, tapering to the base; thin dark glossy green above; midrib characteristically impressed, leaf stalk thin, grooved, very short, to 3 cm. long.   **Flowers:** white, very small, in large spreading heads on secondary branches.   **Fruit:** on branched stems, fruits in pairs, often only one developing, rounded, fleshy, up to 1.5 cm. long, shiny green, turning black and eaten by birds.

All parts contain latex, once thought to be a cure for malaria but now known to be ineffective. An alkaloid called reserpine, used as a tranquilliser in the treatment of high blood pressure, is obtained commercially from the root bark of related species.

Tabernaemontana stapfiana *(Conopharyngia spp.)*   **Wild Magnolia**
indigenous   Mwerere (Kikuyu)

A heavily-leaved evergreen tree to 10 m. in height, found in wet upland forests; common at Limuru, Kericho and around Mt. Kenya. All parts produce copious milky latex.

Bark: grey-brown, rough.   **Leaves:** large, glossy dark green above, up to 30 x 10 cm.   **Flowers:** creamy white, fragrant, up to 6 cm. across, very like those of the exotic *Frangipani*.   **Fruit:** in large rounded pairs, up to 20 cm. across, dark green mottled with white. When ripe the skin splits open, revealing a sticky orange pulp around the seeds. Fruit rotting on the ground has an unpleasant smell, but the tree in full flower is very ornamental.

15

Rauvolfia caffra

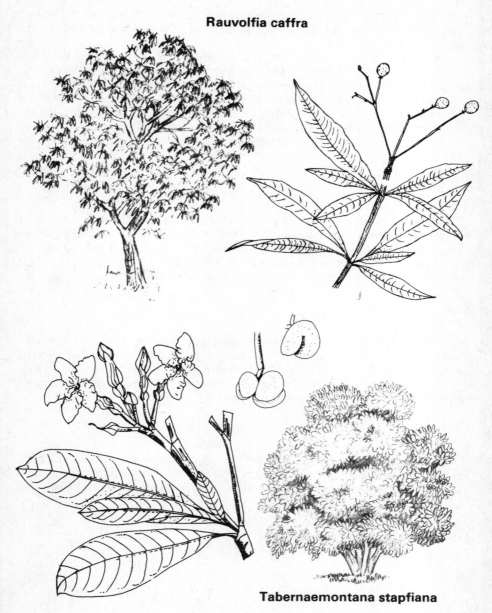

Tabernaemontana stapfiana

APOCYNACEAE

Thevetia thevetioides   **Thevetia, Yellow Oleander**
Honduras, Tropical America, Mexico

A striking evergreen ornamental tree to 8 m., with an open, upright shape, cultivated in warmer districts from the coast to 2,000 m. and widely planted in and around Nairobi.
Bark: grey, smooth, rough with age.   **Leaves:** narrow, linear, up to 15 cm. in length, dark glossy green and quilted above, in dense spirals towards the ends of the branches.   **Flowers:** bright satiny yellow, trumpet-shaped, up to 12 cm. across, heavily scented, in terminal clusters. The unopened buds are twisted, always to the right.   **Fruit:** large, green, rounded, up to 6 cm. across, on a long stalk. The fruit contains two large dark seeds, which are the source of a powerful heart drug, and in Hawaii the fruit are cultivated and exported for this purpose.

Thevetia peruviana is a slighly smaller species, often a multi-stemmed shrub.   **Leaves:** shorter, about 10 cm. in length.   **Flowers:** yellow, trumpet-shaped, slightly smaller, with the green base extending along the margins of the 5 petals.   **Fruit:** smaller, about 3.5 cm. across.
There are other varieties with white or salmon-orange flowers.

Again all parts of the *Thevetia* are actively poisonous, although elephants have been known to eat the fruit of a tree planted outside the warden's house at Voi. The milky latex is especially poisonous, and a drop on the skin raises a fierce blister. They must not be planted where stock have access to them, or where dried leaves can be swept up with hay.

Practical notes: a tough, drought-resistant ornamental, grown in sandy soil from seed or cuttings, which needs little attention once established; useful as a hedge. Flowering is encouraged by pruning about a month before the rains.

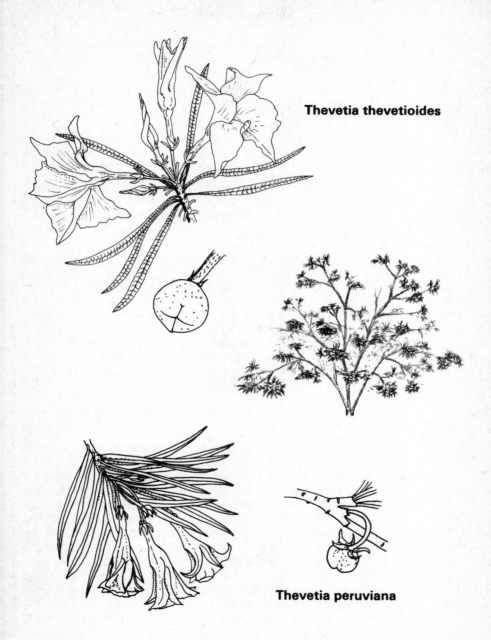

Thevetia thevetioides

Thevetia peruviana

18

ARALIACEAE   Ivy family

A medium-sized family with both tropical and temperate members, the best-known being Ivy *Hedera spp.* and Ginseng *Panax quinquefolia,* whose roots are widely used in China as a stimulant with supposed aphrodisiac properties.

The Kenya representatives of this family are mostly trees of a palm-like appearance, with large compound leaves massed at the ends of branches and soft, generally useless wood. The genus *Cussonia* is endemic to Africa; 4 out of the 19 species occur here, and are the trees that are popularly known as Cabbage Trees.

Members of the family in Kenya include *Cussonia, Polyscias, Schefflera.*

Cussonia holstii   Cabbage Tree
indigenous   Muroha (Kikuyu)

A large, rounded tree to 15 m. in height, widely distributed in highland forest or forest margins from 1,500 to 2,500 m.; common in areas such as Nanyuki and surprisingly also found on rocky sites at lower altitudes in areas such as Moyale and Kibwezi. A few remnant trees grow on the Limuru and Kikuyu sides of Nairobi.

Bark: dark brown, rough, thick and corky.   **Leaves:** compound, crowded at the ends of branches in large, rounded clusters, each up to 70 cm. in diameter; leaflets usually 5, on stalks up to 6 cm. in length radiating from the ends of the main leaf stalks, which are about 30 cm. long; leaflets dark shiny green, unequal-sided, up to 10 cm. long; apex distinctively pointed, margin corrugated and roughly toothed; veins conspicuous above.   **Flowers:** greenish yellow, inconspicuous, packed along thick flower spikes up to 30 cm. in length, the spikes crowded and prominently erect from the tips of branchlets.   **Fruit:** small, fleshy, closely crowded along the flower spikes.

The wood is soft and of little value.

Cussonia spicata   Cabbage Tree, Elephant's Toothbrush
indigenous   Mwenyiere (Kikuyu)

A curious-looking deciduous tree with a paw-paw like appearance, to 12 m. in height, scattered in forest margin areas or in the open from 1,200 to 2,200 m.

Bark: pale grey, rough, thick and corky.   **Leaves:** compound, crowded at the ends of branches in large clusters, each up to 70 cm. in diameter; leaflets usually 1 to 3 pairs plus a larger terminal leaflet, on stalks radiating from the ends of the main leaf stalks, which are up to 40 cm. long; leaflets dark bluish-green, unequal-sided, 10 cm. or more in length; apex and base tapering, margin jaggedly toothed. The leaflet stalks bear unusual wings, which resemble inverted wedges.   **Flowers:** greenish-yellow, closely packed along erect terminal flower spikes up to 15 cm. in length, the spikes forming conspicuous heads above the leaves.   **Fruit:** small, angular, soft and purple when ripe, packed along the spikes like cells of a honeycomb.

The roots are succulent and edible, mashed roots being used at one time in parts of Africa to treat malaria.

19

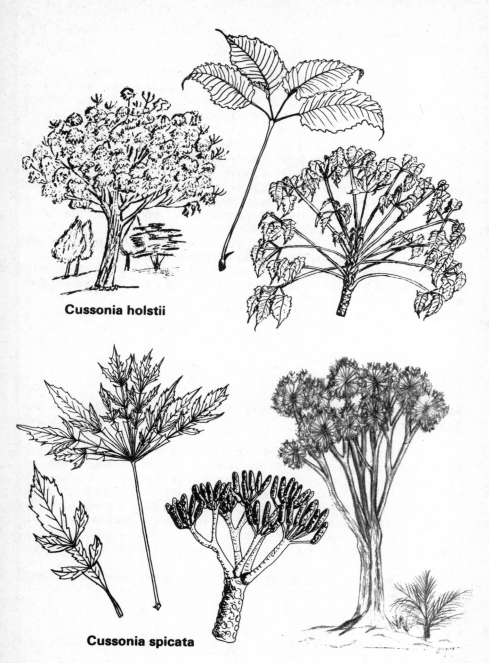

Cussonia holstii

Cussonia spicata

Polyscias kikuyuensis
indigenous

Parasol tree
Mutati (Kikuyu)

A tall forest tree to 25 m. in height with a long, straight, slender trunk and high whorls of branches resembling the spokes of a parasol or umbrella, widely distributed from 1,500 to 2,500 m. in wetter highland forests like the Kakamega forest; often occurring in tea-growing districts. A few remnant trees can be found in the Nairobi area.

Bark: grey, smooth.   **Leaves:** compound, pinnate, very large, up to 1 m. or more in length; leaflets opposite, usually 8 to 14 pairs plus a terminal leaflet, dark green above, about 14 x 8 cm., apex tapering, base rounded, underside coated with soft golden hairs. The bole, branches and young stems are marked with prominent leaf scars.   **Flowers:** cream-coloured, in small groups, on axillary spikes over 30 cm. in length; calyx densely hairy.   **Fruit:** small, more or less oval, often ribbed, closely clustered.

The wood is white, soft and entirely odourless, and is used for food containers, tea-chests and plywood. It makes poor fuel.

Practical notes: a decorative species, fast-growing and potentially useful in agroforestry as the high crown lets in sunlight and the leaves produce good mulch.

Schefflera actinophylla *(Brassaia actinophylla)*
Queensland, Australia

Queensland Umbrella Tree
Octopus Tree.

A handsome evergreen tree with unusual flower heads, up to 10 m. in height, increasingly planted in Nairobi as an ornamental and also often found as a pot plant. A specimen can be seen in the grounds of the National Museum.   **Leaves:** compound, on long stalks, with 7 to 16 stalked leaflets radiating to form parasol-like rosettes; leaflets glossy dark green, narrowly elliptic, up to 25 cm. long, tapering to base and apex.   **Flowers:** small, dark red, crowded along spectacular spikes a metre or more in length, radiating from upper branches like the tentacles of an octopus.   **Fruit:** small, rounded, purplish-red when ripe.

There are three indigenous species of *Schefflera*, but these are confined to limited areas of highland forest.

Polyscias kikuyuensis

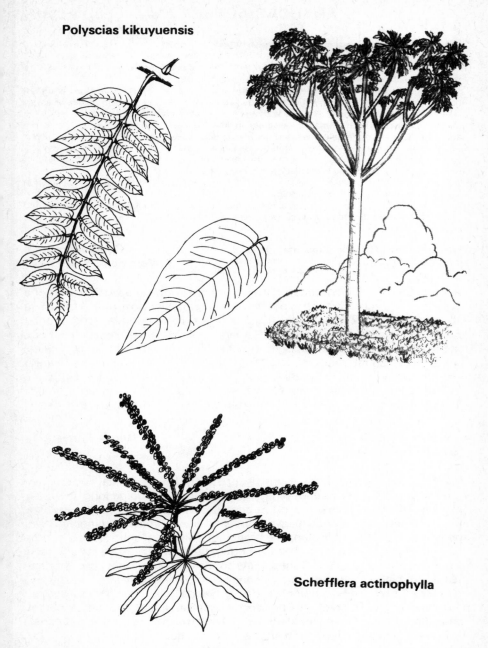

Schefflera actinophylla

ARAUCARIACEAE   Monkey-puzzle family

A family of tall, imposing conifers with layered branches, named after the Araucarian Indians of the southern Andes but found on both sides of the Pacific from South America to Australia. A number have long been established in Nairobi and the highlands as unusual ornamentals, and are also occasionally interplanted in plantations.

Although they bear some resemblance to and are often called Pines, Araucarias are in an entirely distinct family. The whorls of branches bear branchlets covered with spirals of small, overlapping leaves which vary in shape with age and on different parts of the tree as well as in different species. Male and female cones grow on different trees or on separate branches of the same tree. The woody female cones are large and distinctive, resembling green pineapples; mature cones disintegrate on the ground to release large seeds, often winged, which develop beneath each cone. The male pollen-producing cones are either solitary, narrow and upright, or are clusters of loose hanging branchlets, resembling fat catkins.

The wood of all Araucarias is resinous and straight-grained, resembling pinewood, used in South America for timber and paper pulp.

The first two species described belong to the group with broad, flat leaves and large cones, and the others to the group with narrow, curved leaves and small cones.

Araucaria angustifolia *(Araucaria brasiliana)*   **Candelabra tree,**
S. Brazil, Argentina   **Parana Pine, Brazil Pine.**

A tree to 35 m. with a rather flattened crown and well-spaced whorls of a few heavy, horizontal branches bearing green branchlets in terminal tufts. The tall, massive trunk resembles coils of thick rope between the branch scars.   **Leaves:** mature leaves stiff, sharp-pointed, lance-shaped, to 6 cm. long.   **Cones:** male cones upright, to 10 x 2.5 cm., with tight brown scales; female cones squat, rounded, to 17 x 12 cm., the dark brown scales bearing sharp, recurved points.   **Seeds:** wingless, to 5 x 2 cm., nearly 1 cm. thick.

This is a tree of cooler climates, well suited to the Kenya highlands. Seeds may germinate below parent trees, seedlings showing the juvenile foliage.

Araucaria bidwillii   **Bunya Bunya Pine**
Coastal Queensland

A fast growing tree to 50 m. with a spreading crown, conical and shapely when young but a tall column when fully mature, developing long, drooping branches. The trunk may be up to 1 m. across, covered with rough, bumpy bark and prominent leaf scars.   **Leaves:** juvenile leaves most commonly seen, apparently in double rows along the branchlets; each leaf shiny, tough, sharp-tipped, 2 to 6 cm. long. At the ends of branchlets the leaves are smaller and form tight, prickly spirals.   **Cones:** male cones up to 18 x 1 cm., upright near the ends of higher branches; female cones erect, remarkably large and heavy, up to 30 x 23 cm. and weighing up to 5 kg. **Seeds:** joined to the cone scales, pear-shaped, up to 6.5 x 3 cm. The seeds are still an important item of diet for some aborigines in Queensland, with the result that felling there is restricted.

This species does well at lower altitudes with good rainfall.

23

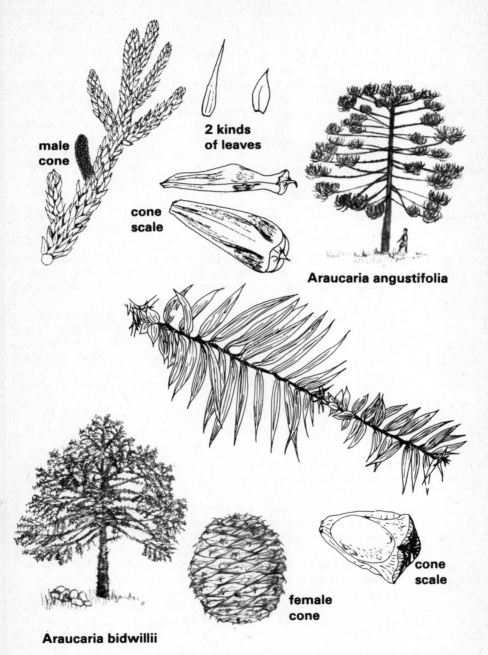

male cone

2 kinds of leaves

cone scale

Araucaria angustifolia

Araucaria bidwillii

female cone

cone scale

24

ARAUCARIACEAE

Araucaria columnaris *(Araucaria cookii)*   **Cook's Araucaria,**
New Caledonia, Polynesia   **Cook's Island Pine.**

A narrow, towering tree to 70 m., with short horizontal branches covered with slender branchlets, giving the appearance of a dense green column. **Leaves:** in tight rows, the mature branchlets resembling shiny, plaited cords; mature leaves rigid, curved inwards, only 5 mm. long; juvenile leaves larger and softer.   **Cones:** male cones to 6 x 1.5 cm.; female cones egg-shaped, to 15 cm. high, covered with bristle-like appendages from each cone scale.   **Seeds:** to 3 cm. across, with well-developed membranous wings.

A row of these huge trees can be seen in the Nairobi Arboretum and others are popular in gardens, probably because they take up less space than other Araucarias.

Araucaria cunninghamiana   **Hoop Pine,**
Queensland, New South Wales,   **Moreton Bay Pine.**

A less regular tree to 50 m. or ocasionally to 70 m., with long, upcurved branches bearing dense tufts of branchlets. The trunk may reach a massive 3 m. in diameter, and the rough, shiny brown bark is often in horizontal hoops, peeling in thin layers.   **Leaves:** juvenile leaves rather triangular, sharp-pointed, spreading, to 2 cm. long; mature leaves softer, curved inwards, overlapping, crowded along the branchlets.   **Cones:** male cones to 7 cm. long, in pendulous clusters, turning orange-red with pollen; female cones green, about 8 cm. high, covered with stiff recurved points from each scale.   **Seeds:** small, with membranous wings.

In Queensland this is the principal softwood timber used for indoor carpentry, veneers and plywood.

Older branches are brittle and may fall unexpectedly. This species is sometimes used as an indoor ornamental.

Araucaria heterophylla *(Araucaria excelsa)*   **Norfolk Island Pine,**
Norfolk Island, South Pacific   **Star Pine.**

A majestic tree to 70 m., maintaining a fine pyramidal shape as it matures, with regular whorls of spreading branches, the lowest sweeping the ground.   **Leaves:** mature leaves most commonly seen, covering the branchlets like soft green fingers; each leaf shiny, soft, curving inwards, up to 1.5 cm. long.   **Cones:** female cones squat, rounded, about 10 cm. high, often broader than long.   **Seeds:** to 3 cm. long, with well-developed wings about 1 cm wide.

This species is a favourite ornamental in seaside resorts from the Pacific to the Mediterranean, as the waxy coating on the leaves makes the tree completely salt-resistant. There are several cultivated varieties, some of which are used as pot plants.

25

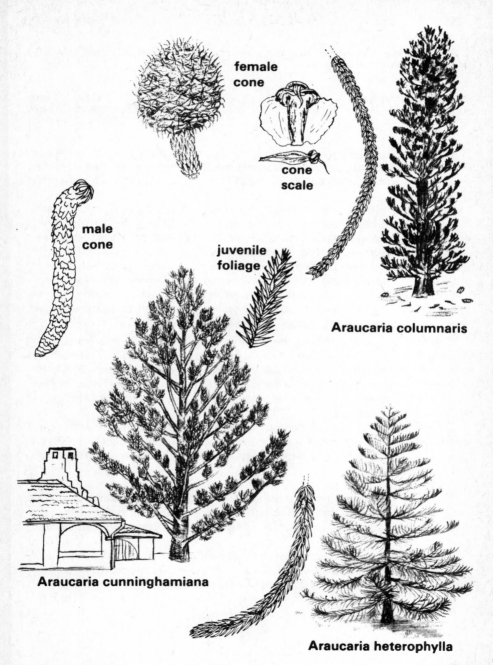

female
cone

cone
scale

male
cone

juvenile
foliage

Araucaria columnaris

Araucaria cunninghamiana

Araucaria heterophylla

26

BALANITACEAE   Desert Date family

A small tropical family with only one genus, Balanites, of which there are several indigenous species. All species have strong spines.

Balanites aegyptiaca
indigenous

Desert Date
Ol-ngoswa (Masai)
Mjunju (Swahili)

A slow-growing evergreen tree to 6 m. or occasionally to 10 m. in height, the crown often rounded into a tangled mass of thorny branches; found in savannah grassland from sea-level to 2,000 m., often in sandy or black-cotton soils.

Bark: grey to dark brown, deeply fissured and scaling into ragged, corky squares; young branchlets green and smooth, with soft, forward-pointing spines to 8 cm. long; older branches dry and brittle, with sharp, woody spines which are sometimes absent.   **Leaves:** grey-green, leathery when mature; leaves unusual, compound with only 2 leaflets, each more or less oval, to 5 cm. but often smaller, tapering to the base; stalk short.   **Flowers:** yellowish-green, to 1.5 cm. across, in small fragrant clusters in the leaf axils.   **Fruit:** date-like, about 5 cm. long, rounded at both ends, yellow when ripe, containing a hard, pointed seed surrounded by sticky, yellow-brown edible flesh.

The fruit are produced even in very dry years. This tree is greatly valued in the driest areas of Kenya both for its fruit and its uses for stock. The fruit and foliage are browsed by goats and camels and also by game, especially giraffe, and trees neatly pruned by giraffe are conspicuous in the Nairobi National Park. The wood is heavy, durable and termite resistant, and is used for carving and farm tools as well as for fuel.

The bark is used as a fish poison, and the fruit, although harmless to man and warm-blooded mammals, produces a potent emulsion which kills both the freshwater snails that carry bilharzia and the water-fleas that carry guinea-worm disease.

Balanites glabra is a similar, very spiny species, found on alkaline clay soils in the Nairobi National Park and in Turkana District, mostly in river beds. The leaves have no stalk, and the fruit are green-striped, turning pink, also edible.

Balanites wilsoniana is the common species found in coastal forests, also in Machakos district and the Chyulu hills. The stems are deeply fluted and the spines usually forked. The fruit are eaten by elephant.

Balanites aegyptiaca

BIGNONIACEAE   Jacaranda family

A tropical family of trees and shrubs with showy flowers, which includes many climbers grown as garden ornamentals such as the Golden Shower *Pyrostegia venusta* and the Zimbabwe Creeper *Podranea brycei*. The family is represented in Kenya by a number of outstanding flowering trees, some indigenous like the Nandi Flame *Spathodea campanulata* and some exotic, like the superb Brazilian *Jacaranda mimosifolia*. The indigenous Sausage Tree *Kigelia africana* also attracts attention for its unusual fruit.

Members of this family in Kenya include *Jacaranda, Kigelia, Markhamia, Spathodea, Tecoma, Tecomaria*.

Jacaranda mimosifolia *(Jacaranda acutifolia)*

Brazil

COLOUR PLATE VIII

Jacaranda, Brazilian Rosewood

A handsome deciduous tree, spectacular in full flower, usually growing to 15 m. but occasionally to 30 m., introduced to Kenya early in the century by the fathers of the St. Austin's Mission. The Jacaranda is now familiar and widely grown throughout the tropics, and has been planted all over East Africa up to 2,200 m., in places becoming naturalised.

Bark: pale grey, smooth, becoming browner, corrugated and peeling with age.   **Leaves:** fern-like, feathery, twice-compound or bi-pinnate, up to 40 cm. in length, crowded in terminal whorls; leaflets numerous, very small, each with a pointed apex, borne on up to 20 pairs of side ribs or pinnae; leaflets bright green when young, darker with age.   **Flowers:** striking mauve-blue, in profuse terminal clusters, each flower bell-shaped, about 4 cm. long, with 5 lobes, the throat and stigma creamy white. Mature trees are often covered with flowers before any leaves appear, and the flowers form a conspicuous carpet on the ground after falling. **Fruit:** flattened rounded woody capsules with a wavy edge, up to 7 cm. in diameter, brown to almost black when mature, splitting on the tree to release numerous seeds with transparent wings.

Flowering is erratic, and flowering times vary in different places across the highlands. In Nairobi the main season is between September and November, but a tree in flower can be found somewhere in Nairobi all the year round. A white-flowered variety exists, and a few have been planted in Nairobi gardens.

There are over 40 species of Jacaranda, and in South America, where this tree is called Brazilian Rosewood and is used for cabinet-making, several species are used for timber or wood-carving.

Practical notes: fast-growing, easy to establish from seed or cuttings, and widely obtainable from nurseries. Prefers good red soil, but remarkably tolerant of less favourable conditions. A credit to any garden or avenue, but best planted away from flower beds as leaf-fall is considerable and roots can be troublesome. Young trees may need pruning to stop them becoming lanky and bent.

29

Jacaranda mimosifolia
(also COLOUR PLATE VIII)

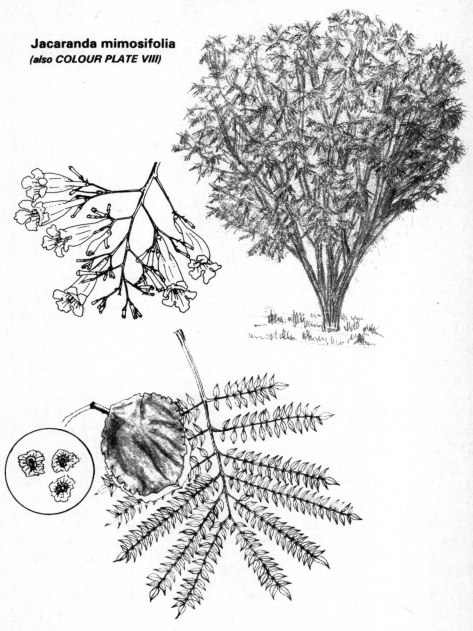

BIGNONIACEAE

Kigelia africana *(Kigelia aethiopum)*   **Sausage Tree**
indigenous   *COLOUR PLATE I*   Muratina (Kikuyu)

 A savannah tree with a rounded crown and low-hanging branches, growing to 9 m. in open woodland but twice that height in riverine fringes, widely distributed from the coast to 1,850 m. A few grow in the Nairobi area.

 Bark: grey to pale brown, smooth, finely fissured and flaking thinly with age. **Leaves:** compound, arising in threes, crowded at the ends of branches; leaflets usually 3 to 5 pairs plus a terminal leaflet, each broadly elliptic, up to 10 cm. in length; apex rounded or tapering, often sharply tipped; margin wavy, veins prominent below; rather yellowish-green above and exceedingly harsh and rough to the touch, especially on the upper surface. **Flowers:** on long, rope-like stalks usually 2 to 3 m. but up to 7 m. in length. The flowering spray at the base can be a metre long, consisting of up to 12 dark maroon flowers, each shaped like an upturned trumpet, to 15 cm. across; petals convoluted and crumpled, with heavy yellow veins on the outer surface. The smell is unpleasant and attracts bats, which pollinate the flowers at night. **Fruit:** very unusual, like grey sausages up to a metre in length hanging from the long, distinctive stalks and weighing up to 10 kilos. The seeds embedded in the fibrous pulp are released only when the fruit rots, and the hanging stalks often remain prominent after the flowers and fruit have fallen.

 The unripe fruits are poisonous, but the ripe fruits, although inedible, are baked and sliced to help the fermentation of local beer. Extracts of the fruit have medicinal properties and may be useful in treating skin conditions.

 An unusual traditional belief had it that a fruit hung in a hut would protect the hut from whirlwinds.

Markhamia lutea *(Markhamia hildebrantii,* *COLOUR*   **Markhamia**
indigenous   *Markhamia platycalyx)* *PLATE IV* Muu, Muho (Kikuyu)

 An upright evergreen flowering tree with a tall trunk and a high, sometimes irregular crown, usually 10 to 15 m. in height, occurring from 1,500 to 2,000 m around Nairobi and Nyeri and in Nyanza Province; also widely planted in other good rainfall areas.

 Bark: light brown, with fine vertical fissures. **Leaves:** compound, up to 30 cm. in length, often in terminal groups; leaflets dark green above, with a wavy, corrugated appearance, 3 to 5 pairs plus a terminal leaflet, each up to 10 cm. long, wider towards the apex and narrowing towards the base; veins prominent below, side veins looping before the margin. A pair of round, leafy stipules appear at the base of the leaf stalk. **Flowers:** bright yellow, in showy terminal clusters, each flower trumpet-shaped, to 6 cm. long, with 5 frilly lobes, the throat striped with orange-red. The buds are yellow-green and furry, and split down one side as the flower emerges. **Fruit:** very long, thin brown capsules, to 75 cm. in length, hanging in clusters and tending to spiral, splitting on the tree to release abundant seed with transparent wings, 2.5 cm. long.

(continued)

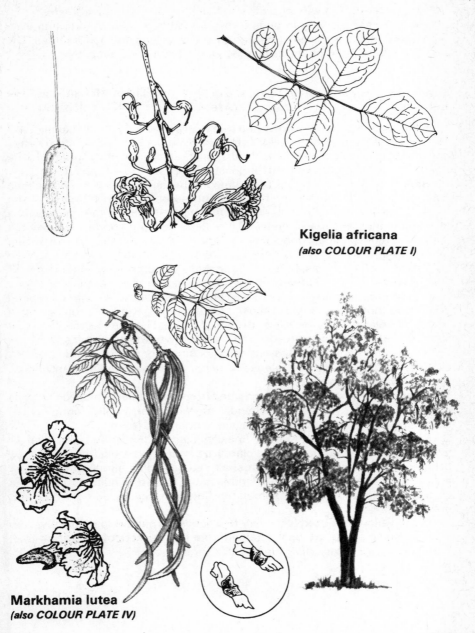

Kigelia africana
(also COLOUR PLATE I)

Markhamia lutea
(also COLOUR PLATE IV)

32

Markhamia lutea (continued)

Practical notes: a very attractive indigenous species, flowering for much of the year, fast-growing in good forest soil and resistant to drought. Well worth planting as a screen or background for gardens and golf-courses. The tree has a long tap-root and should be planted in a good deep hole.

Spathodea campanulata *(Spathodea nilotica)*　　**Nandi Flame, African Tulip Tree**
indigenous　　　　　　　*COLOUR PLATE V*　　　　　　Kibobakasi (Swahili)

A handsome deciduous flowering tree with a rounded crown, usually 10 to 15 m. in height, native to the Lake Victoria basin in Uganda and Western Kenya and also to West Africa; now widely planted as an ornamental throughout the tropics and in Kenya grown from the coast to 2,000 m.
Bark: pale greyish-brown, fairly smooth, becoming rougher and scaling with age. Older trees develop rounded buttresses towards the base of the trunk.　**Leaves:** compound, to 40 cm. in length; leaflets 3 to 6 pairs plus a terminal leaflet, each oval, up to 12 cm. long, tapering sharply to a pointed apex; veins conspicuous, underside softly furry; leaves yellow-green maturing to dark green, with a wavy, rather puckered appearance; leaf blister often noticeable. Young shoots, buds and branchlets are densely covered with soft yellow-brown hairs.　**Flowers:** fiery orange-red, in vivid terminal clusters each flower irregularly trumpet-shaped, about 12 cm. long, with the frilly petal edges and throat tinged with yellow. Flowers emerge in turn from rounded whorls of enlarged, spathe-like buds, which contain copious watery fluid that squirts out if the buds are pierced.　**Fruit:** dark brown woody capsules, to 25 cm. in length, often seen in pairs, sometimes single or more, standing erect, splitting on the ground to release abundant flat seeds with transparent, rounded wings, to 3.5 cm. across.

A yellow-flowered variety, propagated from trees that developed naturally in the indigenous forests of Uganda, is also occasionally found as an ornamental. There are several large specimens around Nairobi.
Practical notes: one of Kenya's finest indigenous flowering trees, ideal for gardens, parks or avenues. Young plants are widely available from nurseries; best planted in red or forest soil in sheltered positions, although capable of succeeding in black cotton soil. Under moist, warm conditions growth is moderately fast and trees will sometimes flower in 3 years; drought-resistant once established.

In the yellow-flowered form very few seeds germinate to produce yellow trees again so plants are best obtained from root suckers of the parent tree. Young trees are occasionally found in nurseries.

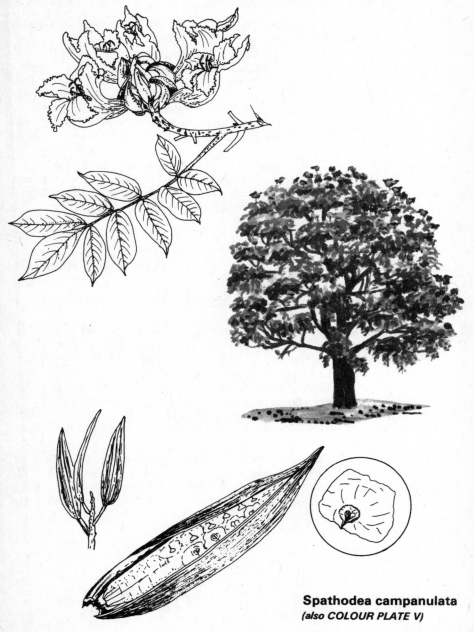

Spathodea campanulata
(also COLOUR PLATE V)

34

BIGNONIACEAE

Tecoma stans   **Tecoma, Yellow Elder,**
Mexico, Tropical America .   *COLOUR PLATE II*   **Yellow Trumpet-tree**

An ornamental shrub or small tree, erect but somewhat straggling, usually to 5 m. in height but occasionally larger.
Bark: grey-brown, rougher with age.   **Leaves:** compound, leaflets 2 to 5 pairs plus a larger terminal leaflet, each lance-shaped, up to 10 cm. long, tapering to the apex; margin serrated; mid-green above and soft to the touch.   **Flowers:** pale to bright yellow, in terminal clusters, each flower trumpet-shaped, up to 6 cm. long, with 5 rounded lobes, marked with fine reddish lines.   **Fruit:** narrow green capsules up to 18 cm. long, drying pale brown and remaining on the tree in untidy clusters for many months; seeds winged and prolific.
Practical notes: fairly widely planted in Kenya; fast-growing, drought resistant and easily reproduced, but said to be slow to flower over 2,000 m. Some nurseries now recommend instead of this *Tabebuia serratifolia* from the West Indies and Venezuela, which has profuse, clear yellow flowers.

Tecomaria capensis   **Tecomaria, Cape Honeysuckle**
South Africa

A multi-stemmed evergreen shrub, climber or small tree to 5 m., widely grown as an ornamental hedge.
Bark: pale brown, heavily dotted with breathing pores or lenticels.   **Leaves:** opposite, compound, leaflets 2 to 5 pairs plus a larger terminal leaflet, shiny dark green above, broadly oval, 1 to 3 cm. long; apex tapering, margin shallowly toothed. Small pockets of hairs in the axils of the veins are just visible on the underside.   **Flowers:** showy orange to scarlet, occasionally yellow, in profuse, erect terminal sprays, each flower funnel-shaped, up to 4 cm. long, with 4 long protruding stamens, upper petals slightly hooded, lower lobes reflexed.   **Fruit:** dry capsules, to 10 cm. long, in upright clusters, drying brown and falling early; seeds with transparent wings, to 2.5 cm.
Practical notes: widely cultivated and easily grown, even in full sun and dry conditions. Suckers freely and roots wherever the suckers touch the ground, requiring ruthless pruning to keep it in place when used as a flowering hedge. Best suited to larger gardens or compounds.

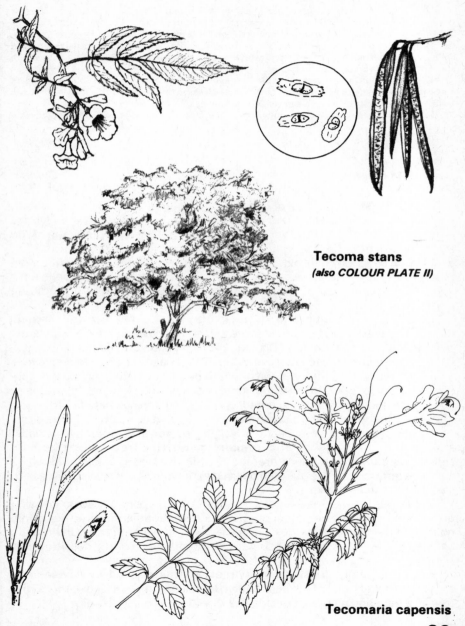

Tecoma stans
(also COLOUR PLATE II)

Tecomaria capensis

BOMBACACEAE   Baobab family

A small family of tropical flowering trees, the most familiar exotic being the spectacular Brazilian *Chorisia speciosa,* known in Kenya for many years under the name 'Bombax'. Other important exotic species in this family are the Kapok Tree *Ceiba pentandra* from tropical America, which grows at the coast, the Balsa Wood Tree *Ochroma pyramidalis,* with its remarkable lightweight timber, and the Durian, *Durio zebenthinus* from Malaysia and South East Asia, which bears the highly prized durian fruit.

In Kenya the outstanding species is the indigenous Baobab Tree *Adansonia digitata*, with its massive, bottle-shaped trunk. In common with many trees in this family, the swollen trunk stores water, allowing the tree to survive in very dry conditions.

Members of the family in Kenya include *Adansonia, Ceiba, Bombax, Chorisia, Rhodognaphalon.*

Adansonia digitata   **Baobab**
indigenous   Mbuyu (Swahili)

A striking deciduous tree of immense girth, up to 25m. in height, bare of leaves for as much as 9 months of the year; common at the coast and in dry savannah inland up to 1,250m. Despite its soft pithy wood this is one of the longest-lived trees in the world; carbon dating has shown trees 5m. in diameter to be 1,000 years old and the very largest specimens to be as much as 3,000 years old. Portuguese cannon balls from nearly four centuries ago have been found embedded in living trees that line the approach to Mombasa harbour.

Bark: grey, smooth and fibrous, often pock-marked and heavily folded. **Leaves:** dark green, soft and rather shiny; leaves compound, 'digitate' or finger-like, leaf stalk about 10cm long; leaflets usually 5, sometimes 3 to 9, each broadly elliptic, up to 15cm. long, tapering to base and apex; lower leaflets smaller. **Flowers:** solitary, 5 waxy white petals surrounding a ball of fine stamens; up to 20cm across, upside down on long, hanging stalks; very short-lived and unpleasantly scented, opening at night, pollinated by fruit bats and flies. Bushbabies are also attracted by the sweet nectar. **Fruit:** large, hard-shelled capsules up to 24cm. in length, covered in greyish, velvety hairs, hanging on long stalks and remaining on the tree after ripening. Numerous dark brown seeds are enclosed in a whitish, edible pulp which contains tartaric acid; the pulp can be used for flavouring, or soaked in water to make a refreshing drink.

The leaves are used as a vegetable, and the fibrous bark is used for weaving and making rope. The wood is spongy and holds quantities of water; elephants gouge out the trunks with their tusks to reach the water in times of drought, causing many trees to collapse. Others continue growing despite being hollowed out, and show remarkable powers of regeneration.

Not surprisingly, these strange trees are surrounded by a wealth of traditional beliefs, one of the best-known legends being that God uprooted the tree in a rage and planted it upside down, with its roots in the air.

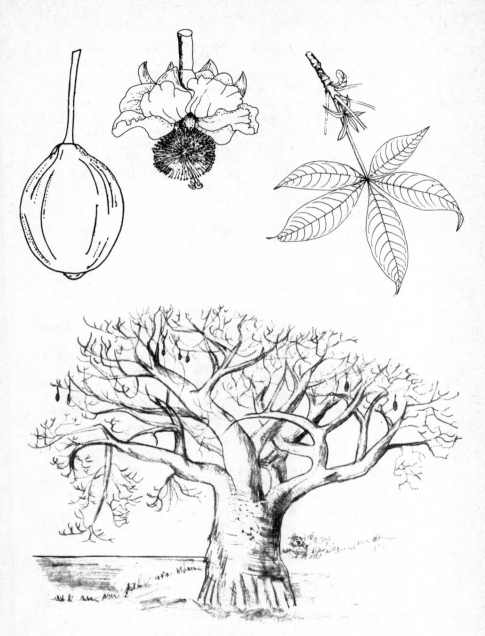

Adansonia digitata

BOMBACACEAE

Ceiba pentandra (*Bombax ceiba*)   **Kapok Tree**
South and Central America   Msufi (Swahili)

A tall deciduous tree with conspicuous horizontal, layered branches, up to 30m in height, with the trunk covered with sharp conical spines when young and often heavily buttressed with age; commonly cultivated at the coast.

Bark: grey; greenish on branches.   **Leaves:** compound, digitate, 5 to 15 leaflets radiating from a long stalk; each narrowly elliptic, up to 20cm long.   **Flowers:** small, to 3cm. across, white to pinkish, in axillary clusters; outer surface of the petals woolly; smell not unlike sour milk; pollinated by bats. **Fruit:** large woody capsules, to 30 cm. long, conspicuous when the tree is bare. The seeds are encased in long, silky white fibres known as kapok.

The fibre is remarkable, water-repellant and eight times as light as cotton, each fibre consisting of a single air-filled cell. Kapok is used for life-jackets, mattresses, protective clothing and insulation, but with a high cellulose content it burns easily.

Bombax malabaricum, the Red Silk Cotton Tree from S.E. Asia, has large, bright red flowers; the fibre is widely used in India, but is not of high quality.

Chorisia speciosa   **Chorisia, 'Bombax'**
Brazil   *COLOUR PLATE VI*

A spectacular deciduous tree with a swollen, spiny trunk, growing to 25m. with a high, rounded crown; widely planted from the coast to 2,000m. and common around Nairobi, often flowering when the tree is bare of leaves.

Bark: grey and smooth, the spiny bosses disappearing with age; bark greenish on younger branches.   **Leaves:** compound, digitate, 5 to 7 leaflets radiating from a long stalk; each up to 15cm. long but often smaller; apex tapering, midrib prominent below; margin serrated.   **Flowers:** large, striking, to 15cm. across, 5 mauve-pink petals, edge crinkly, yellowish-white streaked with pink towards the centre; central thick column of joined stamens, with protruding style and stigma.   **Fruit:** oval woody capsules, to 15cm. long, smooth pale brown, thickly fibrous, splitting open on the tree. The seeds are embedded in masses of fine white fibres, which are a useful kapok.

Practical notes: fairly fast-growing from seed or large cuttings; widely available from nurseries. Best in good red soil, but will succeed in black cotton soil if the site is well-drained. A show-piece for parks, avenues or golf courses, but needs siting with care because of its extensive root system and the fall of leaves and fluffy fibre.

Rhodognaphalon schumannianum (*Bombax rhodognaphalon*)   **Wild Kapok**
indigenous
A tree of the coastal forest, from 15 to 35m. in height.

Bark: smooth, greenish-yellow with high buttresses.   **Leaves:** palmate, dark green and shiny.   **Flowers:** large, greenish-white or apricot yellow, with red stamens. The silky fibre surrounding the seeds is brownish and is used locally for stuffing cushions and mattresses.

39

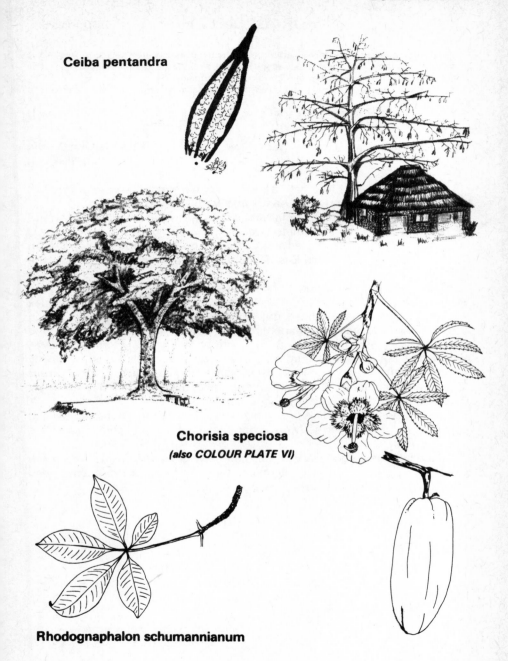

Ceiba pentandra

Chorisia speciosa
(also COLOUR PLATE VI)

Rhodognaphalon schumannianum

BORAGINACEAE   Cordia family

A relatively large family, mainly of herbs from the Mediterranean region but including a largely tropical group of trees and shrubs. Nearly all species have alternate, roughly hairy leaves, the name of the family being derived from the Latin 'burra', a hairy garment.

The genus Cordia contains trees and shrubs from tropical and warmer regions of Asia, Africa and America.

Members of this family in Kenya include *Cordia, Ehretia*.

Cordia africana *(Cordia abyssinica, Cordia holstii)*   **Large-leaved Cordia**
indigenous   Muringa (Kikuyu)

A deciduous forest tree with a rounded crown and often rather crooked trunk, eye-catching and very handsome in flower, growing to 10 m. or occasionally to 25 m. in high rainfall areas such as the Kakamega forest, where the bolé may reach 1 m. in diameter. Occurs in forest and savannah from 1,200 to 2,000 m., sparsely distributed around Nairobi but common in pastureland in Central Province and Meru District, often with beehives hanging in the branches.

Bark: pale brown, smooth, finely fissured, darker and rougher with age.   **Leaves:** large, broadly oval to almost rounded, to 16 cm. in length; apex tapering abruptly, base rounded; dull dark green above, paler beneath, drying crisp; midrib and veins prominent below; young shoots, leaf stalks and undersides of leaves covered with soft, light brown hairs.   **Flowers:** showy, pure white, funnel-shaped, up to 2.5 cm. across, petals crinkly, sweetly scented, in dense terminal masses. The nectar is very attractive to bees.   **Fruit:** round, yellowish, about 1 cm. in diameter, held in a hairy, cup-shaped calyx. The seeds are enclosed in sweet, sticky flesh.

The heartwood is reddish-brown, light and fairly durable but often twisted and difficult to saw, formerly used for making furniture and mortars for crushing grain.

Practical notes: a good shade tree, fairly slow-growing but flowering in 3 to 5 years. Will grow in drier conditions, but best in forest soil in good rainfall areas. Leaf-fall in the dry season is heavy, but makes good mulch.

Cordia africana

42

BORAGINACEAE

Cordia ovalis
indigenous

Sandpaper Cordia
Mukuu (Kikuyu)

A multi-stemmed shrub or rounded tree to 6 m., occasionally to 12 m., widespread in dry areas from sea level to 1,800 m.; easily recognised once identified.
Bark: blue-grey, thin and fibrous, peeling in strips, resembling the bark of a *Eucalyptus* or gum tree.   **Leaves:** broadly oval to almost round, 5 to 8 cm. long, margin lightly scalloped; texture like sandpaper above, softly hairy below, with 3 prominent veins rising from the leaf base; branchlets, leaf and flower stalks densely covered with rusty hairs.   **Flowers:** pale yellow, to 1 cm. long, sharply fragrant, in terminal clusters.   **Fruit:** oval, pointed, yellow to orange, about 2 cm. long, held in a hairy, cup-shaped calyx.

Cordia sebestena
West Indies

Geiger Tree

An evergreen shrub or small tree to 10 m. with brilliant orange-red flowers, widely planted along the streets of Mombasa and elsewhere at the coast.   **Leaves:** large, broadly oval, to 20 cm. long; texture thick, rough and hairy.   **Flowers:** showy, orange-red, funnel-shaped, up to 3.5 cm. across with 6 rounded petals, in terminal clusters.   **Fruit:** small white berries with sweet, sticky flesh, used as cough sweets.
This species grows easily from seed or cuttings, and will reach full height in a few years.

Cordia subcordata
indigenous

Mbongolo (Swahili)

A leafy shrub or small tree to 8 m., common on coastal sand just above the high water mark; also found along the shoreline throughout the Indian and Pacific oceans.   **Leaves:** smooth, wavy, strong bright green, broadly oval, to 15 cm. long; stalks up to 5 cm.   **Flowers:** pale orange to pink, funnel-shaped, up to 3 cm. across, with 5 or 7 crinkly petals.   **Fruit:** grape-sized, up to 2 cm. long, red when ripe, almost completely enclosed in a persistent calyx.
This is a sacred tree in Polynesia.

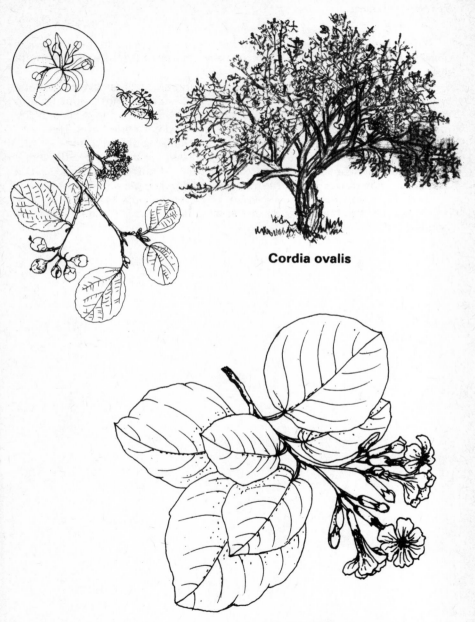

Cordia ovalis

Cordia sebestena

44

BORAGINACEAE

Ehretia cymosa *(Ehretia sylvatica)*
indigenous   Murembu (Kikuyu)

An untidy shrub or many-branched tree to 15 m. in height, widely distributed from 1,200 to 1,850 m., usually at forest margins in better rainfall districts.

Bark: grey to dark grey, rather rough; young branchlets covered in dense white hairs.   **Leaves:** broadly elliptic, 7.5 to 20 cm. in length; apex tapering rather abruptly; texture roughish, glossy or matt dark green above, paler below; midrib and veins prominent beneath and covered with fine hairs. The leaves are often eaten away by insects.   **Flowers:** small, about 6 mm. across; petals white and reflexed; stamens protruding, brown and hair-like; flowers in crowded terminal heads, often covering the tree.   **Fruit:** almost round, to 1 cm. across, in wide heads, hard green turning bright orange, edible but very acid.

The roots and leaves are known to be poisonous, but with apparent inconsistency they have a reputation as an aphrodisiac. The leaf juice is styptic and is used for healing wounds.

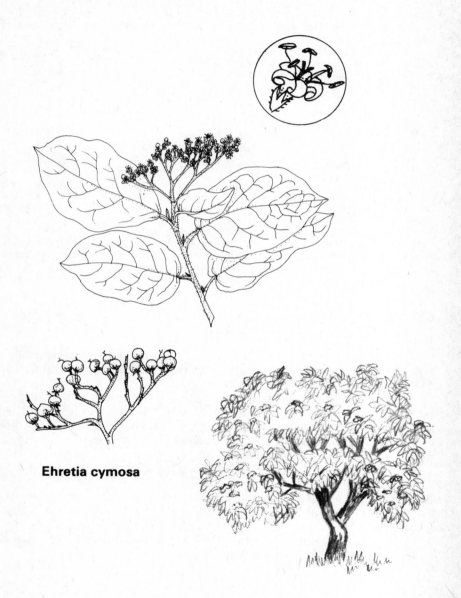

Ehretia cymosa

BURSERACEAE   Myrrh family

A tropical family found in Africa, Malaysia and Central America, characterised by aromatic resins used even in Biblical times for incense and perfumes. The genus *Bursera* in Central America includes species called Turpentine Trees, and the resins are still used on a small scale for incense, soaps, lacquers and varnishes.

Frankincense comes from the resin of *Boswellia carteri* and other species found in Somalia, whereas myrrh is extracted from *Commiphora abyssinica* and other species indigenous to Arabia and Ethiopia. Both genera occur in Kenya, but no plants in this family are yet of any commercial importance here.

Commiphora spp.

This is the largest indigenous genus in this family, with about 30 species. A forest tree, the ash-like *Commiphora zimmermannii* is found in Central Province where it is known by the Kikuyu name Mutunguka. *Commiphora baluensis*, Itula in Kamba, is common in the Kibwezi area and reaches 5 to 9 m. in height, the timber being used by Kamba woodcarvers. The rest are typical of the driest thornbush areas of Kenya like the Kora reserve, and are generally easy to recognise by their twisted branches and peeling, papery bark.

The genus has been described as 'frustrating', largely because the trees and shrubs are leafless for most of the year. The different species are distinguished by their resins and colours of bark as well as details of leaves and spines, but re-classification continues and only one species is described here.

Commiphora africana
indigenous

Iguu (Kamba)
Mbambara (Swahili)

A deciduous thorny shrub or small tree, usually to 5 m. but occasionally to 10 m. in height, widely distributed in all dry regions of the Coast, Northern and Southern Provinces and Thika district.

Bark: grey-green, peeling in papery scrolls; underbark green, yielding a pale sap; branchlets spine-tipped. **Leaves:** trifoliate, finely velvety, the terminal leaflet much the largest, up to 8 cm. long, tapering to the base; apex rounded, margin coarsely toothed. **Flowers:** small, to 5 mm., green turning red, in tight axillary clusters. **Fruit:** rounded and pointed, pinkish-red, about 1 cm. long, thinly fleshy, containing a single stony seed.

Various medicinal properties are attributed to the resin, bark and fruit; cuttings root easily, and the tree is widely used as a live fence. Young leaves sprout on the bare trees towards the end of the dry season, as a signal of the approaching rains. However, although the leaves look inviting they are not eaten by game, as they contain bitter tannins.

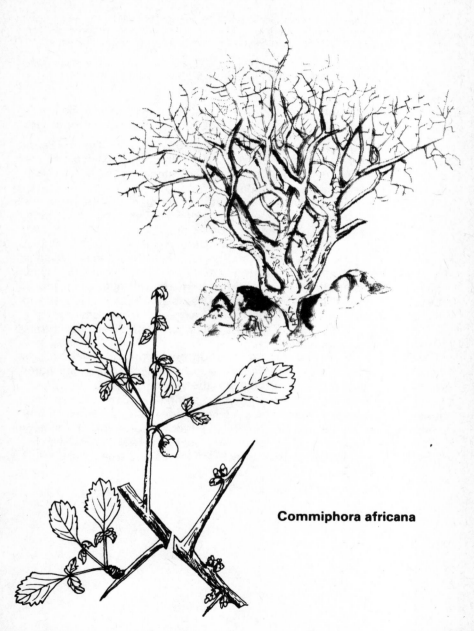

Commiphora africana

CAESALPINIOIDEAE   Cassia sub-family of Leguminosae

This sub-family includes some spectacular flowering trees of tropical forests as well as a number of climbers. The flowers are often large and showy, and may be somewhat irregular, with one of the five petals differing from the rest. Stamens are ten or less in number, and the leaves are usually compound.

Members of the sub-family in Kenya include *Acrocarpus, Afzelia, Bauhinia, Caesalpinia, Cassia, Delonix, Parkinsonia, Peltophorum, Pterolobium, Schizolobium, Tamarindus.*

Acrocarpus fraxinifolius
India, S.E. Asia

Indian Ash, Australian Ash, Shingle Tree

A very tall, fast-growing deciduous tree, up to 60 m. in height with a clean, straight trunk and bright red young foliage. Originally introduced in coffee and tea plantations as a shade tree and now widely planted around Nairobi and in better rainfall areas at medium altitudes.

Bark: pale grey, fairly smooth, often with horizontal markings. Branches bear conspicuous scars from detached leaf stalks.   **Leaves:** twice-compound, up to 1 m. in length, forming a regular, spreading pattern; leaflets opposite, usually 7 to 10 pairs; shape broadly elliptic, averaging 12 x 5 cm., tapering to the apex; texture thin, wavy, shiny mid-green.   **Flowers:** heads in dense clusters about 12 cm. in length, on long stalks from terminal branches; each flower with 5 orange-red stamens protruding from a cup of equal green petals. Flowers are short-lived, appearing when the tree is almost bare of leaves and attracting many sunbirds.   **Fruit:** thin, dark brown pods, up to 12 cm. in length, in persistent terminal bunches. The pods split down both sides on the tree, releasing numerous dark brown seeds.

The timber can be used for light construction, but is prone to attack by borer beetle; it is popular in Western Kenya for making beehives. The specific name 'fraxinifolius' means ash-like, and refers to the leaves.

Practical notes: extremely rapid growth, reaching over 3 m. in its first year and quick to regenerate after pruning. Widely available from nurseries: prefers red soil and good rainfall, but will tolerate periods of drought. Deservedly popular for avenues, parks and open spaces, but requires siting with care in gardens or golf courses due to the heavy fall of leaves and small branches.

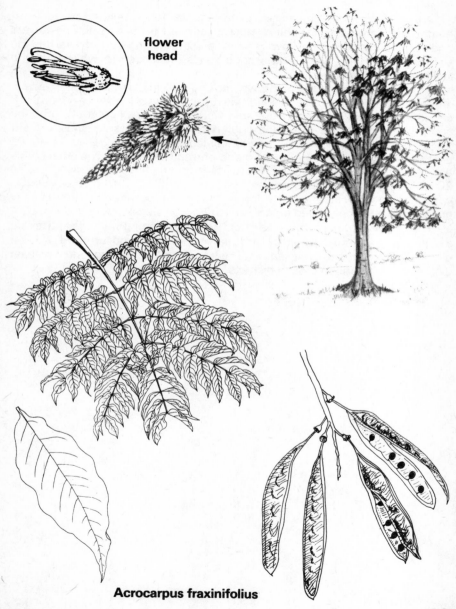

flower
head

Acrocarpus fraxinifolius

CAESALPINIOIDEAE

Afzelia quanzensis
indigenous

**Afzelia, Pod Mahogany,
Lucky Bean Tree**
Mbambakofi (Swahili)

A large deciduous timber tree of the coastal forest belt, up to 35 m. in height, with spreading branches almost as thick as the main trunk. The flowers and fruit are distinctive, the flowers bearing one large orange-red petal and the fruit pod containing black and orange seeds embedded in white pith and looking like a jewel case.

Bark: grey-green to pale brown, flaking in circular patches. **Leaves:** alternate, compound, to 30 cm. long, with up to 6 pairs of leaflets, each up to 10 cm. in length; leaflets broadly oval and shiny above; apex generally rounded and slightly notched; leaflet stalks often twisted. **Flowers:** in small fragrant groups, each flower with one prominent bi-lobed petal up to 2.5 cm. in length, orange-red with yellow veining; stamens long and protruding. The other petals are reduced to small scales. **Fruit:** dark brown flat woody pods, up to 20 x 10 cm., splitting open on the tree to reveal 6 to 10 shiny black seeds, which are eaten by elephant. The lower third of the seed is covered by a fleshy orange-red envelope called an aril, which hornbills seek out as a delicacy.

The timber is hard and durable in salt water, darkening with age and taking a high polish, still much prized by Lamu carvers for doors and furniture and also used for dhows and dugout canoes. The tree is now sadly rare, and deserves extensive replanting in coastal districts.

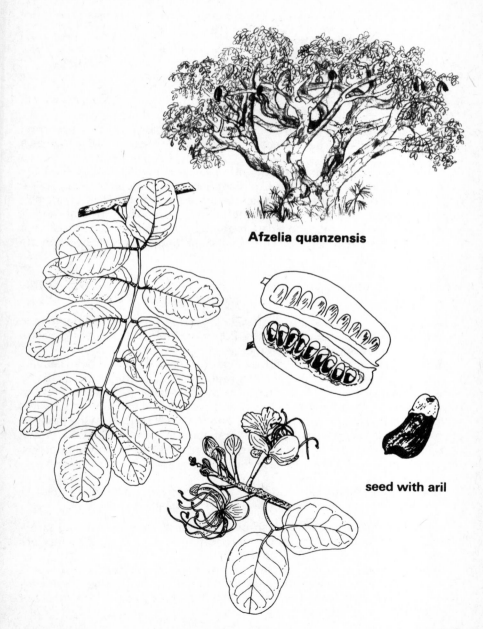

Afzelia quanzensis

seed with aril

CAESALPINIOIDEAE

Bauhinia   Bauhinia, Camel's Foot

Over 300 species of this genus of attractive flowering trees occur throughout the tropics, and most can readily be grown from cuttings or seed in almost any warm climate.

There are three indigenous species in Kenya, although the exotic species planted here are generally the more prominent. The genus was named after the twin brothers John and Caspar Bauhin, famous Dutch botanists of the 16th century, who are associated with the twin lobes of the distinctive 'camel's foot' leaves.

Bauhinia tomentosa   Msaponi (Swahili)
indigenous

A low shrub or small tree to 8 m., often with drooping branches, occurring in bush and woodland from the coast to 1,850 m. and sometimes grown as a hedge.
Bark: pale grey brown, fairly smooth.   **Leaves:** light green, about 7 cm. across, deeply lobed with a hair-like point between the lobes. Young stalks, buds, pods and often the undersides of leaves are covered in short, soft hairs.   **Flowers:** bright yellow, drooping and not opening fully; 5 petals up to 7 cm. long, one sometimes with a dark maroon spot near the base.   **Fruit:** flat pods, to 10 cm. in length, turning brown and splitting open explosively on the tree.

Bauhinia variegata var. variegata   Orchid Tree
India, Tropical Asia, China   *COLOUR PLATE III*

A small semi-deciduous tree, usually growing to 6 m. but sometimes to more than twice that, cultivated up to 2,200m. and in Nairobi flowering twice a year. This is the species most commonly planted in Kenya.
Bark: grey and smooth, furrowing and flaking with age.   **Leaves:** alternate, blue-green in colour, the two rounded lobes averaging 10 to 15 cm. across; veins prominent, radiating from the leaf base.   **Flowers:** in short terminal sprays, each head up to 12 cm. across, with 5 deep pink petals marked with rose, crimson or yellowish-green, and 5 arched stamens. One petal on each flower is different from the other 4 in shape and colour.   **Fruit:** flat brown pods, 20 cm. or more in length, in persistent and rather untidy bunches, twisting open on the tree to release round, flat seeds about 1 cm. across.

Bauhinia variegata var. candida *(var. alba)* has stiff, pure white flowers, sometimes with yellow markings, and is often available in nurseries.

Bauhinia purpurea has pinkish-purple flowers with overlapping strap-shaped petals, and differs in having only 3 fertile stamens and buds which are winged or ridged.
Bauhinia galpinii *(B. punctata)* is a shrub, often a vigorous climber, introduced from Southern Africa and sometimes seen in Nairobi as a hedge. The leaves are smaller and less deeply divided, and the flowers 6 to 8 cm. across, bright orange to brick-red in colour

53

Bauhinia tomentosa

Bauhinia variegata
(also COLOUR PLATE III)

54

CAESALPINIOIDEAE

Caesalpinia

A genus of tropical trees, grown for their colourful flowers. The stems are often covered with prickles, and the leaves twice-compound and feathery. Some species produce dyes or tannins, and one is a valuable commercial timber.

Caesalpinia decapetala
Tropical Asia, Mauritius

Mauritius Thorn
Mubage (Kikuyu)

A scrambling woody climber, shrub or tree to 7 m., armed throughout with sharp recurved prickles; widely naturalised and spread over much of Kenya up to 2,000 m., often found in disturbed ground.

Leaves: dark green above, paler below, twice-compound, with up to 10 pairs of side ribs; leaflets elliptic, 8 to 12 pairs, up to 2 cm in length; apex rounded. **Flowers:** pale yellow, in attractive terminal spikes up to 30 cm. long, each flower about 2 cm. across, with protruding orange stamens in a distinctive hanging group. **Fruit:** clusters of pointed pods, standing stiffly erect and turning dark brown, persisting for many months and scattering seeds as they open.

Makes an effective hedge, but soon becomes a troublesome weed.

Caesalpinia pulcherrima
Tropical America

Pride of Barbados,
Dwarf Poinciana
Mnyonyore (Swahili)

A shrub or small tree to 6 m., planted all over the tropics as an ornamental and common in gardens at the coast; naturalised both at the coast and in Machakos district.

Leaves: pale green, twice-compound, with up to 10 pairs of side ribs, stalks often armed with prickles; leaflets oblong, up to 12 pairs, to 2 cm. in length; apex rounded or notched. **Flowers:** brilliant scarlet-orange edged with yellow or occasionally entirely yellow, in terminal or axillary heads over 30 cm. long; each flower butterfly-shaped, about 3 cm. across, on a 6 cm. stalk, with frilly petals, one narrower than the other four; stamens long and protruding, with scarlet filaments. **Fruit:** flattened, hanging pods, irregularly oblong, to 12 cm. in length, turning dark brown, twisting open on the tree to set free small, flat seeds.

A decorative tree, sometimes grown as a fence, which at the coast is almost always in flower. Best at lower altitudes, readily grown from seed and drought-resistant even in poor soil.

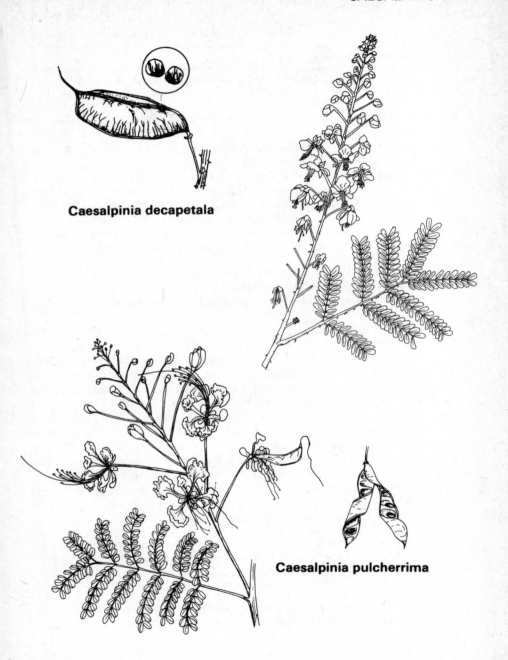

Caesalpinia decapetala

Caesalpinia pulcherrima

CAESALPINIOIDEAE

Cassia   Senna Trees

An easily recognised genus of over 500 species, most of which contain a laxative chemical in the leaves or fruit pulp. *Cassia senna,* a shrub found from Egypt to India, is the main source of the well-known medicine of that name.

A number of exotic and indigenous tree species are widespread in Kenya, preferring open, sunny positions and well-drained soil. All have cylindrical pods and flowers with 5 petals and 10 stamens, often unequal in size.

Cassia didymobotrya   Candle Bush, Peanut-butter Cassia
indigenous   Mwenu (Kikuyu)

A bushy shrub to 4 m., occasionally a tree to 6 m., common in damp hollows or well-watered sites from 900 to 2,200 m.

Leaves: compound, up to 45 cm. long; leaflets 10 to 20 pairs, each with a rounded apex bearing a conspicuous stiff, hair-like tip. Crushed leaflets smell of peanut butter. **Flowers:** bright yellow, the unopened dark brown buds crowning the flower spike. **Fruit:** flat dark pods, up to 10 cm. long.

The leaves, pods and roots are poisonous. For some reason the plant is objectionable to bees, which will vacate if leaves are brought into the house.

Cassia fistula or Indian Laburnum is widely planted at low altitudes, a striking tree with pale yellow hanging sprays of flowers. The large oval leaflets and the cylindrical black pods, to 50 cm. long, are characteristic.

Cassia spectabilis   Cassia
Tropical America

A rounded deciduous tree to 10 m., bearing showy clusters of yellow flowers, widely planted up to 2,000 m. and very common around Nairobi.

Bark: smooth, grey, with horizontal markings; rougher with age. **Leaves:** compound, up to 40 cm. in length, with 4 to 15 pairs of leaflets, each up to 7.5 cm.; leaflets narrowly elliptic, tapering to the apex, usually softly hairy below. Leaves are shed entirely, leaving the tree bare for many months. **Flowers:** bright golden yellow, in erect pyramid-shaped spikes 30 cm. or more in lenth. **Fruit:** up to 30 cm. long, cylindrical or flattened, honeycombed into horizontal seed chambers, persistent, turning from green to black.

Practical notes: quick-growing, flourishing even in poor or black-cotton soil, but not at its best if the site is too dry. Spectacular in flower and deservedly popular; widely obtainable from nurseries.

Cassia siamea from S.E. Asia has also been widely planted in lowland East Africa. The pale yellow flowers in drooping heads and the irregular shape of the tree distinguish it from **Cassia spectabilis.** This species is recommended for agroforestry, being fast-growing for shade, fodder, fuel and timber.

Cassia grandis, the Pink Shower from Central America may be found in gardens at lower altitudes. There are other pink-flowered species.

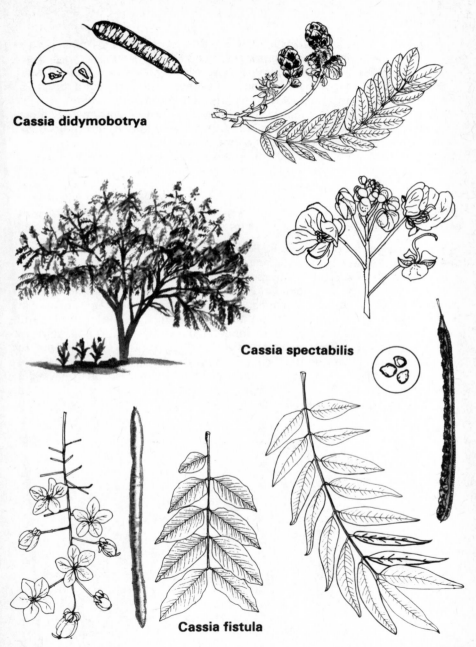

Cassia didymobotrya

Cassia spectabilis

Cassia fistula

Delonix elata
Mwangi (Kamba)
indigenous

A spreading deciduous tree, usually 5 to 8 m., sometimes to 15 m., with a rounded crown and drooping branches, occurring in hot, dry thorn-bush country from 100 to 1,000 m.; common towards Magadi and in Tsavo West.

Bark: smooth, shiny, greyish-white. **Leaves:** twice-compound, up to 15 cm. long, divided and subdivided; leaflets oblong, paired, about 1 cm. in length. **Flowers:** white, fading to creamy orange, with 4 wavy white petals and one smaller and yellow; stamens orange-brown, long and protruding. Only one flower in a group opens at a time. **Fruit:** thin reddish-brown pods, tapering at both ends, up to 20 cm. in length, persisting on the tree; seeds olive-brown, oblong, in horizontal seed chambers similar to **Delonix regia.**

Delonix regia *(Poinciana regia)*
Flamboyant
Madagascar   *COLOUR PLATE IX*   Mjohoro (Swahili)

A spreading decidous tree, in flower one of the world's most strikingly beautiful trees, growing to 10 m. but under ideal conditions to 15 m., with a flat or umbrella-shaped crown. Common at the coast, but at Nairobi's altitude flowering only erratically; now almost extinct in its native Madagascar.

Bark: grey and smooth. **Leaves:** light green and feathery, up to 60 cm. in length, twice-compound with up to 40 side ribs; leaflets small and oval-shaped, mostly less than 1 cm. long, folding with the dusk and falling in the dry season. **Flowers:** brilliant scarlet-red clusters, often appearing before the leaves, each flower up to 10 cm. across with 5 wavy petals, of which the uppermost is creamy white and splashed with scarlet. **Fruit:** heavy flat brown pods up to 75 cm. in length, honeycombed into horizontal seed chambers and remaining on the tree for many months. The tree is fast-growing from seed.

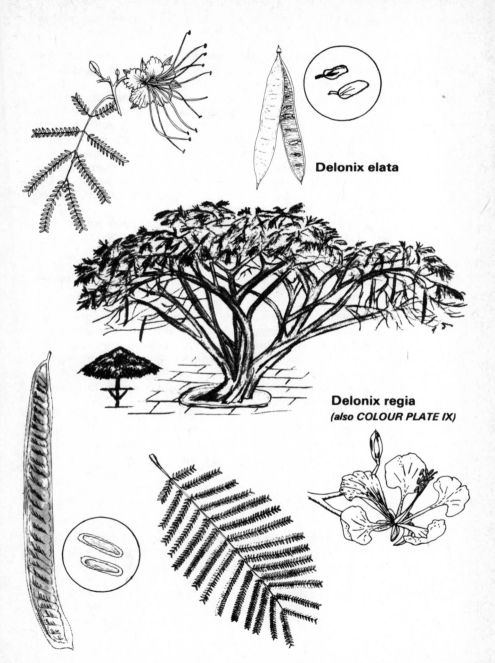

Delonix elata

Delonix regia
(also COLOUR PLATE IX)

CAESALPINIOIDEAE

Parkinsonia aculeata
Tropical America

Jerusalem Thorn

A spiny shrub or small tree to 6 m., with feathery foliage and angular, often drooping branches; widely planted in poor or sandy soils at lower altitudes for fuel and fodder, and showing signs of becoming naturalised.
Bark: smooth greenish-yellow on branches; branchlets armed with spines. **Leaves:** not obviously compound; leaf stalks in 1 to 3 pairs, each stalk flattened and winged, up to 30 cm. in length but less than 5 mm. in width; leaflets oblong, extremely small, in widely-spaced pairs; often completely absent during drought, when the tree appears almost bare. **Flowers:** very sweet scented, up to 1.3 cm. across, bright yellow with orange stamens, the 5 petals crinkly and more or less equal; flower spikes axillary, about 15 cm. long. **Fruit:** narrow woody pods, up to 12 cm. long, pale brown, stalked, tapering to a beak, constricted between the seeds.
Germinates readily from seed, fast-growing and drought resistant; browsed by game and stock. Often planted as a hedge in near-desert conditions.

Peltophorum africanum
Southern and Central Africa

African False Wattle

A spectacular flowering tree with a rounded, spreading crown, growing in Nairobi to 5 m. or so but in its native wooded grasslands to 10 m. or more.
Bark: brown, rough, with wide vertical fissures. **Leaves:** feathery, twice-compound, with numerous very small oval leaflets. **Flowers:** bright yellow, fragrant, in conspicuous erect spray about 10 cm. in length; leaf stalk, flower stalk and calyx covered with rusty brown hairs. **Fruit:** flat pods, to 10 cm. in length, tapering at both ends, in dense clusters.
This species is easily grown from seed and deserves wider planting.
Another exotic species with attractive yellow flowers, **Peltophorum pterocarpum** from tropical Asia and Australia, has been planted along Mama Ngina Drive on Mombasa Island and elsewhere at the coast.

Pterolobium stellatum
indigenous

Mutangaruri (Kikuyu)

A common woody climber with a thick, knotted stem and feathery leaves, densely covered throughout with recurved prickles; widespread in drier forest and bushland from 900 to 2,300 m. and conspicuous in season, when the creamy white flower spikes mature into bright red, winged seed pods. These cover the tops of many trees in the highlands and are easily mistaken for red blossoms.

61

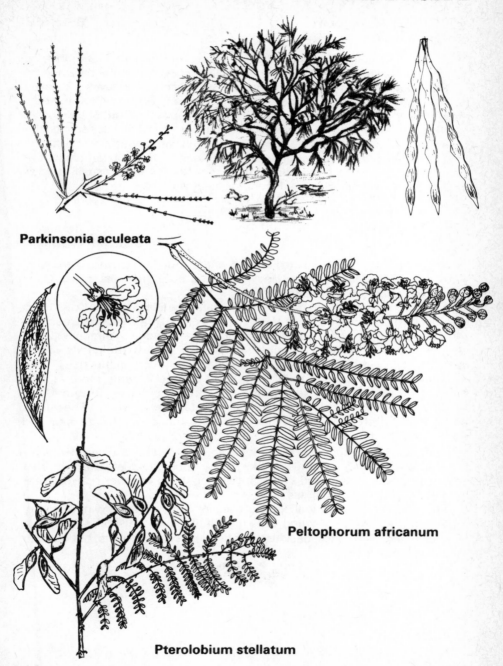

Parkinsonia aculeata

Peltophorum africanum

Pterolobium stellatum

62

CAESALPINIOIDEAE

Schizolobium parahybum   Guapiruvu
Brazil, Tropical America

A sparse, deciduous tree to 10 m. or more, with an unusual branching system resembling the spokes of an umbrella, noticeable on the bare tree.
Bark: greenish, with clear horizontal scars from detached leaves.   **Leaves:** twice-compound, very large and feathery.   **Flowers:** bright yellow, in erect, dense heads covering the tree before the leaves appear.   **Fruit:** unusual, thin and flat, up to 12 cm. long, shaped like a giant tear-drop. The pods split on the ground; each contains a single tightly-fitting seed with a wafer-thin wing.

This species is fairly fast-growing from seed, and has been planted in gardens and golf courses in the highlands. In the Nairobi area it usually flowers in October, but remains bare of leaves for many months.

Tamarindus indica   Tamarind
indigenous   Mkwaju, Msisi (Swahili)

A dense, shady evergreen tree to 25 m. with a rounded crown and drooping branches, widely distributed in drier grassland from the coast to 1,500 m.; often associated with termite mounds.
Bark: pale grey, flaking into rounded scales. **Leaves:** alternate, up to 15 cm. in length; compound, with 10 to 15 pairs of dull green leaflets, each up to 3 cm. long; base rounded, asymmetric; apex rounded to almost square, slightly notched. **Flowers:** small, about 2.5 cm. across, the petals yellow with scarlet veins. **Fruit:** mature pods variable but distinctive, often sausage-shaped, about 10 cm. long, pale brown, velvety, more or less constricted between the seeds; dry pods brittle, cracking irregularly to reveal a sticky brown pulp surrounding hard, dark brown seeds. The pulp is edible and slightly sour, popular for flavouring curries and maize meal and long recognised as a laxative and a treatment for fevers.

The dark brown heartwood is tough and well-grained, useful for boat-building and furniture and also making very good charcoal. The fruit pulp makes excellent chutney and a pleasant cooling drink, and over-ripe fruits are used to clean copper and brass.
Practical notes: a very adaptable species, fairly slow-growing but very long-lived, well worth planting at lower altitudes as a useful shade tree. Develops long, deep roots; deciduous under very dry conditions, but quick to grow bright new leaves.

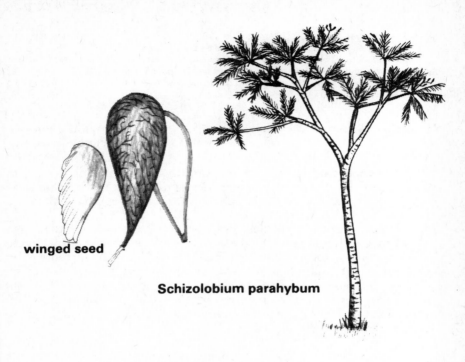

winged seed

Schizolobium parahybum

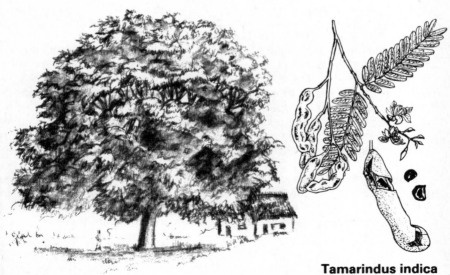

Tamarindus indica

64

CANELLACEAE   Warburgia family

A very small family of tropical trees with a restricted distribution, containing only about 16 species. All are aromatic, and most have medicinal properties.

The West Indian tree *Canella winterana* has aromatic inner bark which is used as a source of white cinnamon, although the true cinnamon trees belong to the Lauraceae family.

In Kenya the only genus is *Warburgia,* with two indigenous species. One of these, *Warburgia ugandensis,* is widely distributed in the East African highlands.

Warburgia ugandensis *(Warburgia salutaris)*
indigenous

Kenya Greenheart,
Pepper-bark tree
Muthiga (Kikuyu)

A large, handsome forest tree, growing to 25 m. but on river banks occasionally to 45 m., widely distributed in lower rain forest and drier highland forest areas from 1,000 to 2,000 m.; common around Nairobi, in the Mara and elsewhere.

Bark: rough, brown to black, cracked into rectangular scales; sap sticky.   **Leaves**: alternate, glossy dark green above, narrowly elliptic, up to 10 x 3 cm., tapering towards the base; margin wavy, with the extreme outer edge translucent; midrid prominent and raised below, often slightly off-centre.   **Flowers**: greenish-cream, inconspicuous, axillary, less than 1 cm. across.   **Fruit**: hard, rounded to egg-shaped, 3 to 5 cm. in length, on short stalks, turning from green to purple and black with a waxy bloom, containing several seeds.

After seasoning the heartwood develops a greenish tinge, although this fades with exposure to light. The wood is oily and very fragrant when freshly cut, not durable or resistant to termites, and burns with a strong smell of incense. The resin is used as a glue.

This tree has been used medicinally from early times; the former specific Latin name 'salutaris' means 'health-giving', and the Kikuyu name 'muthiga' is closely related to 'muthaiga', which is the general Kikuyu word for medicine. The bark is so much in demand that trees are often mutilated and even destroyed by greedy collectors. An infusion of the bark is taken as a cure for stomach-aches, diarrhoea, fever, toothache and general muscle pains, and powdered bark is taken as snuff to treat colds. The leaves, which are very hot to the taste, are sometimes used in curries as a chili substitute.

Practical notes: deserves wide planting as a shapely garden or golf-course tree, but young plants can be difficult to obtain from nurseries. Seedlings can sometimes be found in forest areas near older trees. Best planted in forest soil; growth is moderately slow, but the tree is hardy once established.

65

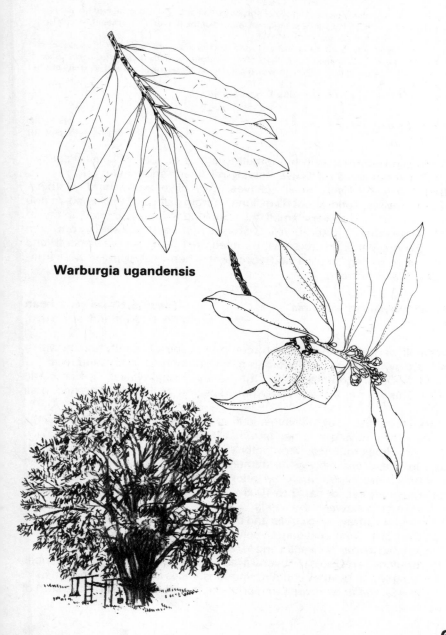

Warburgia ugandensis

CAPPARACEAE   Caper family

A medium-sized, mainly tropical family of shrubby trees and herbs, common in dry areas and easily recognised by the conspicuous spreading stamens of the flowers. A further characteristic is the stalked ovary, which becomes a stalked fruit.

The caper commonly used as a pickle is the bud of *Capparis spinosa*, a native of the Mediterranean region. In Kenya a substitute is obtained from the buds of *Capparis cartilaginea*, a fleshy shrub with large red fruit which grows on coral outcrops at the coast and on stony ground inland to 1,800m.

Members of this family in Kenya include *Boscia, Maerua.*

Boscia coriacea   **Boscia**
indigenous   Mnafisi (Swahili)

A tangled evergreen shrub or small tree to 3 m., one of several species common in the dry areas of Kenya, notably in Turkana and around Tsavo.

Bark: smooth, silvery grey. **Leaves:** grey olive-green, hard, leathery, usually narrowly elliptic, about 6 cm. long; margin paler and thickened; midrib prominent below. **Flowers:** small, to 3 cm. long, strongly scented, in dense heads; petals absent, 6 to 20 yellowish-green stamens spreading out from 4 pale green sepals. **Fruit:** small, rounded, to 1.5 cm. across, smooth and velvety when young, orange and succulent when ripe, popular with fruit-eating birds and baboons.

Maerua triphylla ssp. johannis   **Maerua, Small bead-bean**
indigenous   Mutumburu, Kathandika (Kikuyu)

A small, densely branched evergreen tree or shrub, usually to 4 m. with a rounded crown, widely distributed in grassland and dry woodland from the coast to 2,000 m.; common in the Rift Valley around Naivasha, Narok and Laikipia. This is one of many indigenous species, and is very variable in all respects.

Bark: brownish-grey. **Leaves:** dull green, both simple and trifoliate, trifoliate leaves having a larger terminal leaflet; shape narrowly oval, 2 to 10 cm. long; apex rounded, often notched. **Flowers:** small, whitish, several flowers in a head; greenish-white stamens prominent, spreading from 4 green sepals which are joined in a tube below the petals. **Fruit:** on long stalks, variable, usually cylindrical, 5 to 10 cm. long, pale creamy brown and furry, often constricted between the seeds.

The flowers attract many bees and butterflies, and the leaves are browsed by domestic stock and wild game, including elephants. An infusion from the roots was used to treat snakebite and as an aphrodisiac.

The branches and roots of several *Maerua* species are used by some tribes for clarifying water, but they contain toxic substances and may be a health risk.

White *Maerua* flowers are often prominent in dry bushland at the start of the rainy season.

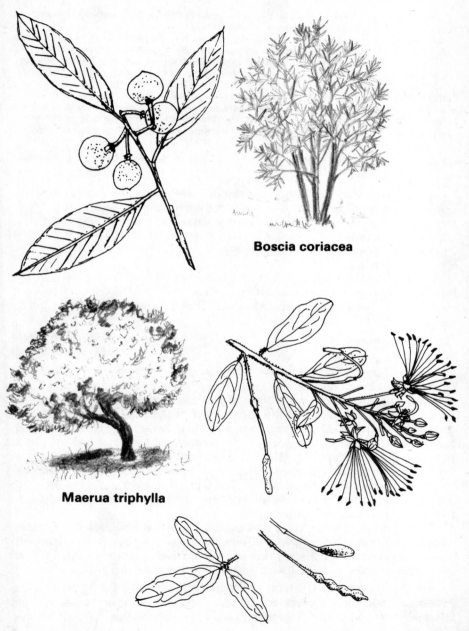

Boscia coriacea

Maerua triphylla

CASUARINACEAE   Casuarina family

A small, distinctive tropical family with only one genus but 65 species, botanically far removed from the pine family despite the common name Whistling Pine.

Casuarinas are specially adapted to hot, dry habitats and are widely used for windbreaks, timber and fuel. The function of leaves is taken over by slender grey-green branchlets which have armoured cells, making them much more drought-resistant than soft leaves. Extensive root systems enable them to grow in poor soils; they are nitrogen-fixing, and excellent sand stabilisers.

Casuarinas are common along coastlines from East Africa to Southern India, Malaysia and South Pacific, and are one of the characteristic trees of Australia. *Casuarina equisetifolia* is the only species indigenous to the Kenya coast or very long naturalised there, possibly coming from India or Australia many centuries ago. The specific name 'equisetifolia' refers to a primitive group of plants called Horsetails, a vivid description of the tufts of branchlets borne by both plants.

Casuarina cunninghamiana
Eastern Australia, Pacific Islands

Casuarina, Australian Beefwood.
River She Oak

A savannah tree to 23 m., more regular and shapely than the following species, widely planted in the highlands as a windbreak and as an ornamental. The trunk is often thickened at the base, and can become very large; the branchlets are noticeably shorter and thinner, 9 to 20 cm. in length, bearing 7 to 9 white-tipped leaf scales in each whorl, and the prickly fruits are smaller, about 1 cm. long.

In Australia the tree is known as Beefwood, because cattle will eat the branchlets when grazing is scarce. The name She Oak appears to be a misspelling of an aboriginal name Sheoke. The iron-hard timber was used by the aborigines for boomerangs.

Casuarina equisetifolia
indigenous

Casuarina, Whistling Pine
Mvinje (Swahili)

A coastal tree to 20 m. with 'weeping' foliage, sometimes stunted and bent by the wind, common in sand or coral just above the high water mark.

Bark: grey to blackish, much cracked with age, containing tannin.   **Leaves:** minute scales, just visible at the joints of the branchlets in whorls of 6 to 7; green branchlets, to 30 cm. long, hang down in crowded tufts along the woody branches.   **Flowers:** male flowers very small, seen as pollen-bearing tips at the ends of branchlets, 1 to 3 cm. long, usually uniformly greenish; female flowers in clusters on woody branches, each head stalked, about 5 mm. long, with prominent hairy red stigmas.   **Fruit:** prickly brown and cone-like, up to 2.5 cm. long, often in very dense clusters, drying and opening to release hundreds of very small, winged seeds.

The wood is reddish, hard and useful but prone to attack by termites, excellent for firewood and charcoal, used for building wharves or occasionally masts for dhows. This species has been extensively planted in the Bamburi quarry reclamation project. It also makes a good hedge.

Practical notes: fast-growing and very hardy once established, succeeding in exposed positions in black-cotton soil, sand or even murram, as well as tolerating salt and flooding. Seedlings are widely obtainable.

69

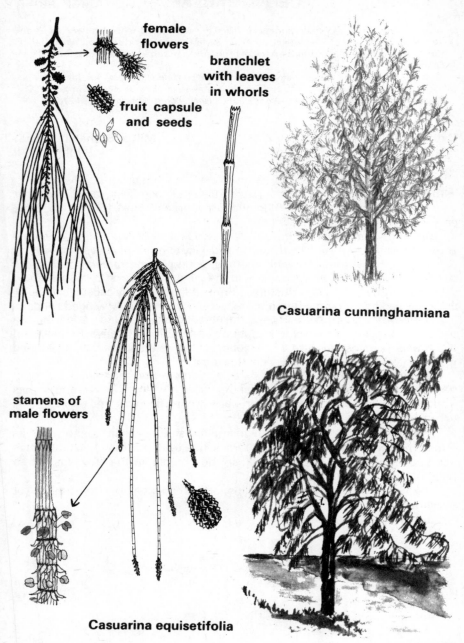

female flowers

branchlet with leaves in whorls

fruit capsule and seeds

stamens of male flowers

Casuarina cunninghamiana

Casuarina equisetifolia

CELASTRACEAE 'Miraa' family

A cosmopolitan family of trees, shrubs and climbers with simple, often leathery leaves and small, fairly inconspicuous flowers. Seeds often have a fleshy cap known as an aril, which may be brightly coloured. The family contains a number of ornamental shrubs with attractive leaves, such as *Euonymus*.

Several species in the family have leaves which are poisonous to stock, but the indigenous highland tree *Catha edulis* has leaves which are chewed as a stimulant, widely known as 'miraa'.

Members of this family in Kenya include *Catha, Elaeodendron, Mystroxylon, Maytenus*.

Catha edulis   **Miraa, Somali Tea, Khat**
indigenous   Muirungi (Kikuyu)

A much-branched shrub or tree, usually to 7 m. but occasionally to 25 m., with drooping, shimmering foliage, from a distance resembling a *Eucalyptus* or gum tree; occurring in wetter highland forest areas from 1,500 to 2,500 m., particularly around Meru and Kericho.

Bark: grey, smooth, becoming dark brown and rough with age. **Leaves:** opposite, broadly oval, to 11 cm. long, dull glossy mid-green above; net veining prominent below, margin evenly toothed, young stems reddish; leaf stalks flexible, allowing the leaves to shake in the wind. **Flowers:** very small, pale yellow, in branched axillary clusters. **Fruit:** 3-lobed woody capsules, about 1 cm. long, reddish-brown when mature, containing narrowly winged seeds.

The leaves and bark contain powerful narcotic alkaloids and the leaves, tied up in tight bundles, are very widely traded as a stimulant in Kenya, Somalia and the Arabian peninsular. Like all narcotics 'miraa' is addictive, and prolonged use can have dangerous and even fatal results.

Farmers who cultivate 'miraa' as a cash crop prune the trees for ease of harvesting and it becomes twisted and gnarled. Different leaves and shoots from different locations apparently produce varying flavours, and selling prices vary accordingly.

This species occurs in similar highland forest areas as far to the south as Cape Province in South Africa, but there is little evidence that the stimulant is used south of Kenya, possibly because the narcotic in the leaves is not so potent.

The tree is fast-growing and is usually propagated by root cuttings or suckers.

Catha edulis

CELASTRACEAE

Elaeodendron buchananii *(Cassine buchananii)*
indigenous

Elaeodendron
Mutanga (Kikuyu)

A dark green, densely foliaged tree with a sturdy trunk and rounded crown, to 10 m. or occasionally to 20 m. in height, occurring in dry upland forest and open woodland in Central, Rift Valley and Nyanza Provinces; common around Nairobi.

Bark: grey to grey-brown, becoming rough, darker and fissured with age. Globules of clear brown gum are often prominent. **Leaves:** young leaves bright green and stiffly erect, tapering to base and apex; older leaves leathery, darkly glossy above, broadly oval, to 10x6 cm.; apex blunt or notched, margin distantly or roundly toothed. Minute spines can be detected by running a finger along the leaf edge. **Flowers:** very small, yellowish, fragrant, in branched axillary heads to 10 cm. long, trees noticeable when in flower. **Fruit:** hard, oval, about 1 cm. long, single or in clusters, normally green, turning yellow to brown; much eaten by birds. The fruit are often enlarged and waxy yellow due to insect attack.

The leaves are extremely poisonous to livestock, but curiously not to giraffe. An infusion from the bark is widely used as a cure for diarrhoea, and the bark of many trees is mutilated by collectors as a result.

Practical notes: very slow-growing, but on forest soil developing from rather ill-proportioned young plants into dark, well-rounded background trees. Young seedlings bear very large, saw-toothed leaves. Trees are sometimes covered in webs made by small black-banded caterpillars, but these disappear in due course and spraying does not seem to be necessary.

Mystroxylon aethiopicum *(Cassine aethiopica, Elaeodendron aethiopicum)*
indigenous

Rurigi (Kikuyu)

A dense shrub or small tree with a short bole and pendulous, generally hairy branchlets, occasionally growing to 12 m., widely distributed in wetter savannah and woodland from the coast to 2,200 m., often near rivers or on termite mounds.

Bark: grey, smooth, becoming dark brown and rough with age. **Leaves:** alternate, on short stalks, glossy dark green above, variable in size but broadly oval, to 6 cm. long; apex rounded or notched, base distinctly rounded; margin shallowly toothed, veins and midrib petering out before the margin. **Flowers:** small, inconspicuous, yellowish-green, in small clusters of about 10 heads on slender axillary stalks. **Fruit:** oval, to 1 cm. long, often pointed at the tip, held in a distinctive hairy cup. The fruit turn bright red and are edible when ripe.

An infusion from the bark is used as a stomach medicine, and a brown dye is obtained from the resin.

73

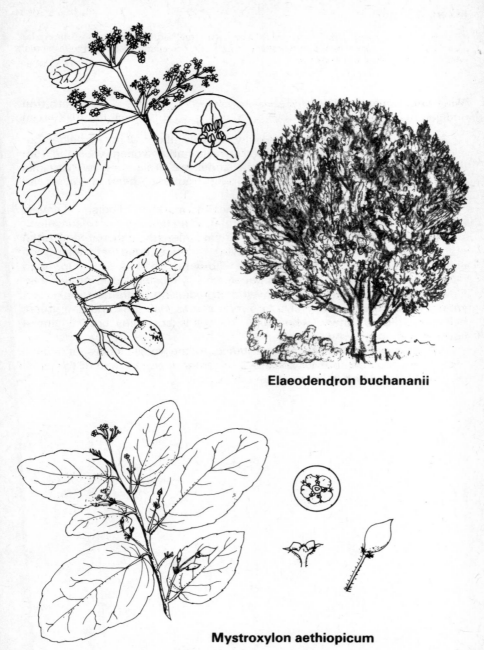

Elaeodendron buchananii

Mystroxylon aethiopicum

74

CELASTRACEAE

Maytenus spp.

A widespread tropical genus with over 200 species of small shrubs or trees, which often bear spines. All have simple leaves and rounded fruit capsules, containing seeds with a fleshy red, white or yellow cap known as an aril.

Maytenus senegalensis *(Gymnosporia senegalensis)*
indigenous

Confetti tree
Muthuthi (Kikuyu)

A shrub or small tree, often spiny, usually about 3 m. in height but occasionally to 8 m., widely distributed in savannah and open woodland from the coast to 2,200 m. When present the spines are straight but very variable, often white and slender, up to 7 cm. long, frequently bearing leaves and flowers.

Bark: light grey, smooth; young branchlets markedly reddish. **Leaves:** alternate or in small groups, pale blue-green, often thick and semi-succulent; shape and size very variable, from 2 to 12 cm. in length; apex rounded, often notched; base tapering; margin with shallow, rather rounded teeth, midrib and leaf stalk frequently tinged with pink. **Flowers:** small, 4 to 6 mm., with narrow yellowish-white petals, in dense axillary clusters covering the tree. Flowering is conspicuous but short-lived, and produces an extremely unpleasant smell. **Fruit:** 3-lobed capsules, to 6 mm. across, half pink and half green, becoming reddish-brown when dry. The seeds are shiny brown, almost covered with a soft white aril.

Various medicinal uses are attributed to the roots, leaves and bark, including a reputed cure for snakebite. Another species found at the coast contains a drug used in the treatment of cancer.

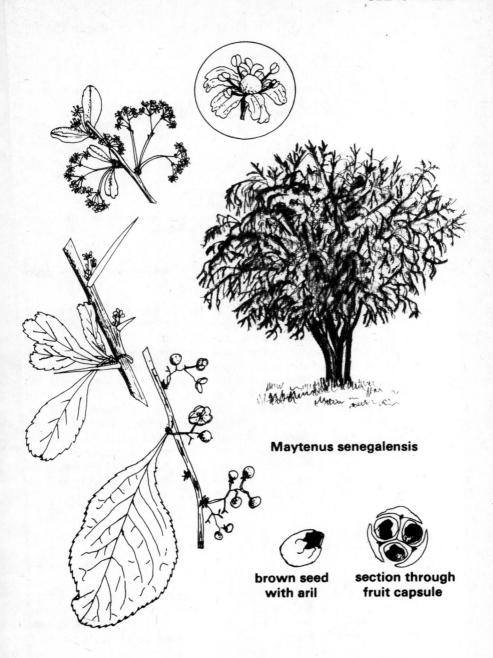

Maytenus senegalensis

brown seed
with aril

section through
fruit capsule

COMBRETACEAE Terminalia family

A mainly tropical family of trees, shrubs and climbers, all with simple leaves and flowers in clusters, often producing abundant nectar. The principal indigenous genus is *Combretum*, easily identified by woody fruit bearing four or five wings: by contrast, the related genus *Terminalia* has only two wings around the fruit, and even these are sometimes reduced to ridges. In this genus the flowers generally have no petals and it is the stamens which are conspicuous in both genera.

The popular ornamental Rangoon Creeper *Quisqualis indica* belongs to this family, as does the Somali riverine tree *Conocarpus lancifolius*, a fast-growing evergreen species introduced for agroforestry at the coast and prominent at the Bamburi quarry reclamation project.

Members of this family in Kenya include *Combretum, Terminalia*.

Combretum spp.

A diverse genus with over 30 indigenous species, many of them shrubs, several widely distributed. Others are climbers, the most ornamental being the widely distributed *Combretum paniculatum*, a scrambling species with clusters of bright orange-red flowers and typical pale brown, winged fruit which can be seen in the grounds of the National Museum in Nairobi.

Combretum molle *(Combretum splendens)*
indigenous

Velvet-leaved Combretum
Mukura, Murema (Kikuyu)

A spreading deciduous tree to 10 m. in height, the trunk crooked and branching early, widespread in dry wooded grassland from the coast to 2,200 m.; in Nairobi common at Muthaiga and towards Kiambu.

Bark: smooth grey-brown, with age becoming dark brown to almost black, deeply grooved and fissured into small, jagged sections.   **Leaves:** opposite but with one leaf frequently missing, broadly oval but very variable, from 11 to 17 cm. long; apex usually pointed, veins prominent, stalk very short; branchlets and leaves densely covered with velvety hairs.   **Flowers:** greenish-yellow, softly hairy, in dense axillary spikes up to 9 cm., heavily scented, attracting insects.   **Fruit:** 4-winged seeds to 2 cm., the wings broader than the seed, drying bright golden brown; persistent, resembling blossoms.

The wood is hard and yellow, used for implement handles and fence posts. In traditional medicine a decoction from the roots was used to induce abortion and to treat such widely varied complaints as leprosy, hookworm and snakebite.

Combretum schumannii
indigenous

Mgurure (Swahili)

A timber tree to 20 m., often crooked, from coastal forest and Kibwezi.   **Bark:** smooth, greenish-brown, flaking.   **Leaves:** opposite, oval to oblong, to 7 cm. long.   **Flowers:** very small, yellow, in crowded axillary spikes, conspicuous in blossom.   **Fruit:** to 2 cm. long; wings straw-coloured, over 1 cm. wide. The wood is very hard, dark purple to almost black.

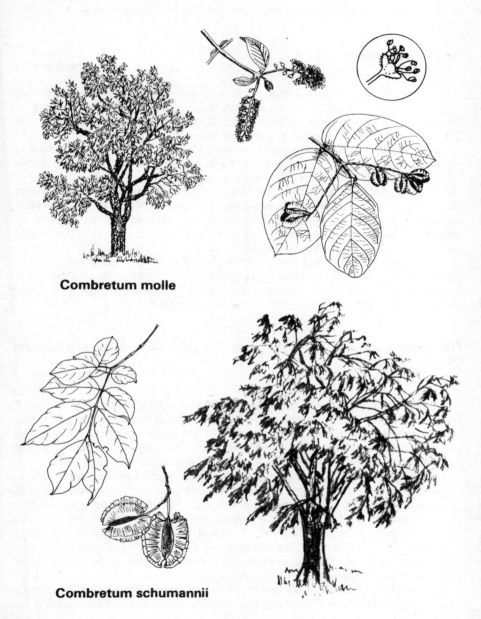

Combretum molle

Combretum schumannii

COMBRETACEAE

Terminalia spp.

A genus of very useful trees in dry areas, represented by twelve indigenous species and two well-known exotics.

Terminalia brownii
indigenous   Muhutu (Kamba)

A leafy, deciduous tree with an attractive, somewhat layered appearance, usually 4 to 5 m. in height but occasionally reaching 25 m., widely distributed in drier wooded savannah from 700 to 2,000 m., often near rivers in very dry areas; also planted in Nairobi city as a shade tree.

Bark: grey, vertically fissured; young shoots densely hairy. **Leaves:** spirally arranged, turning bright red before falling; broadly elliptic, wider towards the apex, length very variable, usually about 7 cm. but up to 16 cm.; apex usually pointed, sometimes notched; margin wavy, lateral veins prominent. The undersides of the leaves and the leaf stalks bear white hairs. **Flowers:** white to cream, unpleasantly scented, in axillary spikes to 12 cm. in length. **Fruit:** winged, smooth, rose-red to purple, to 5 cm. long, the length always less than three times the width.

This species is the most common *Terminalia* in Kenya, and is both drought and termite-resistant; leaf-fall is heavy, making excellent mulch, and the tree is widely recommended for agroforestry. Young plants are available in most nurseries, but are slow-growing unless well irrigated.

Terminalia catappa   **Indian Almond, Bastard Almond**
Andaman Islands,
India, Madagascar   Mkungu (Swahili)

A conspicuous, spreading shade-tree to 15 m. in height, common in coastal areas throughout the tropics and widely planted at the coast, where it has become naturalised; also in up-country districts such as Voi, Nairobi and Kisumu. Young trees have horizontal, layered branches, but the layers gradually disappear and mature trees have a broad, spreading crown.

Bark: greyish-brown, becoming rougher with age. **Leaves:** leathery, very large, clustered, turning bright red before falling; broadly elliptic, wider towards the apex, up to 30 x 15 cm.; apex pointed on young trees, otherwise rounded; base tapering, veins prominent. **Flowers:** individually small, with 5 greenish sepals, in spikes 7 to 20 cm. in length. **Fruit:** hard, about 7 cm. long, turning red, more or less rounded but blunt-tipped and slightly flattened, with two ridges but no wings. The fleshy shell is rich in tannin, and the kernel is edible, with an almond-like taste. The fruit floats in sea-water.

Practical notes: a handsome tree, fairly fast-growing from seed, preferring sandy soil and tolerating salt. The tree develops an extensive root system.

79

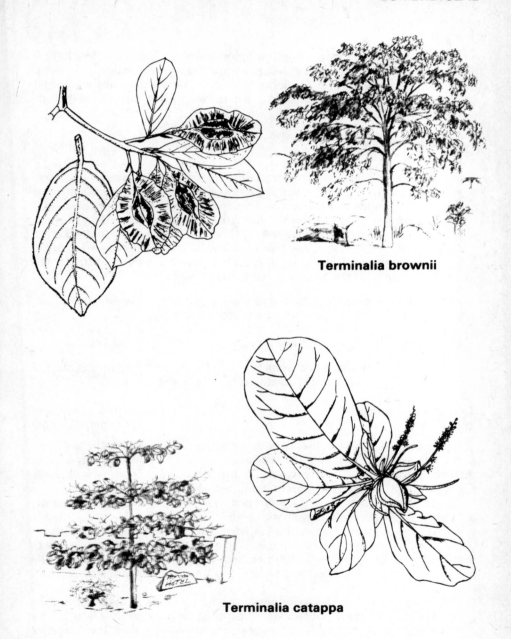

Terminalia brownii

Terminalia catappa

COMBRETACEAE

Terminalia kilimandscharica
indigenous   Muhuku (Kamba)

A dense, rounded tree to 10 m., common in dry areas such as Machakos, Thika, Kilifi and Lamu districts but also planted as far west as Kisumu. **Leaves:** mid-green, fairly large, to 9 cm. long, more hairy below than above; margin slightly inrolled, lateral veins prominent below. **Fruit:** purple, very conspicuous, about 8 cm. long.

Terminalia mantaly   Terminalia
Madagascar

An ornamental tree, usually evergreen at higher altitudes, growing to 10 m. with an erect stem and neat, conspicuously layered branches; widely planted as a street and shade tree around Nairobi and down as far as the coast.
Bark: pale grey, smooth, rather mottled. **Leaves:** smooth, bright green when young, in terminal rosettes of 4 to 9 unequal leaves on short, thickened stems; length up to 7 cm., apex broadly rounded, base very tapered, margin wavy. **Flowers:** small, greenish, in erect spikes to 5 cm. long. **Fruit:** small oval seeds, about 1.5 cm. long, with no obvious wings.

Practical notes: an excellent spreading shade tree, deservedly popular, fast-growing in better soils and drought-resistant once established. Young plants are widely available, but this species rarely flowers at higher altitudes and seeds are collected from trees planted in lower, hotter districts.

Terminalia orbicularis is a small tree in dry bushland with unmistakeable fruit, pink to bright red, almost round, up to 10 cm. in diameter.

Terminalia prunioides   Purple-pod Terminalia
indigenous   Mwangati (Swahili)

A shrubby, deciduous tree, usually about 3 m. but occasionally to 10 m., occurring in coastal forest and dry acacia bushland in the Taita, Tana and Lamu districts from 30 to 1,400 m., usually in drier areas than *Terminalia brownii;* conspicuous when covered with bright green young leaves.
Bark: grey, older bark grooved and ridged. **Leaves:** small, spirally arranged on spiky lateral twigs; shape variable, 4 to 7 cm. long, apex rounded or notched; 3 to 5 lateral nerves visible beneath. **Flowers:** white or cream, unpleasantly scented, in terminal spikes to 6 cm. long. **Fruit:** purple-red to brown, 3.5 x 2 cm., conspicuously notched, slightly smaller than *Terminalia brownii.* The fruit persist on the tree, and the leaves are browsed by game.

Terminalia spinosa is a spiny deciduous tree, occasionally to 15 m. with layered branches, found in coastal forest and in very dry parts of Kenya. The leaves are often red, and the flowers short pink and white spikes. The seeds are orange-brown, to 2 cm.; the wood is hard and durable.

81

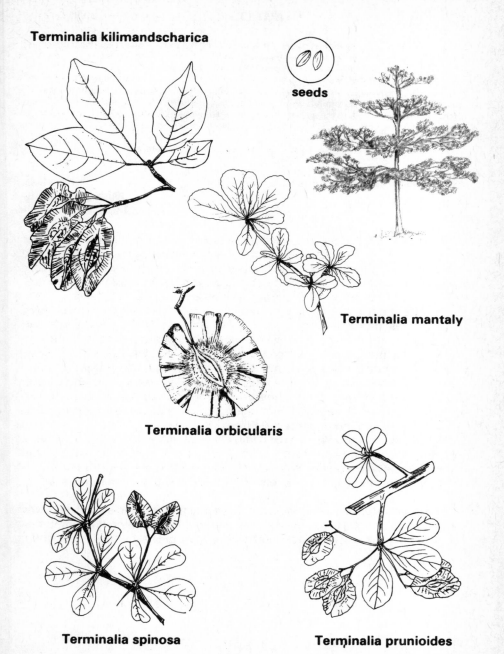

Terminalia kilimandscharica

seeds

Terminalia mantaly

Terminalia orbicularis

Terminalia spinosa

Terminalia prunioides

82

COMPOSITAE   Sunflower family

The sunflower or Daisy family is one of the largest and botanically one of the most advanced families in the world. It ranges from the tropics to the Arctic, and includes more than one-tenth of the world's flowers. Altogether there are some 25,000 species in 1,100 genera.

The family is generally easy to recognise, because the tiny flowers or florets are massed ('Compositae') into heads which themselves resemble single flowers. Most species are herbaceous, and a tall timber tree in this family like the indigenous *Brachylaena* is exceptional. However, a few other Kenya species grow to the size of small trees, among them the widespread Leleshwa bush *Tarchonanthus* and the Giant Groundsels *Senecio spp.*, which are confined to high mountain moorland.

Members of this family in Kenya include *Brachylaena, Tarchonanthus.*

Brachylaena huillensis *(Brachylaena hutchinsii)*
indigenous

Silver Oak
Muhugu (Kikuyu)
Muhuhu (Swahili)

A tall tree with grey-green foliage, steeply ascending branches and a narrow crown, the trunk often fluted and dividing close to the ground; to 15 m. in height, exceptionally to 30 m. with a bole up to 60 cm. in width. Occurs in dry forest and forest remnants at the coast, as well as in Nairobi and Central Provinces up to 2,000 m.; often prominent above the forest canopy.

Bark: pale to dark grey; vertically fissured and rather fibrous with age. **Leaves:** narrowly lance-shaped, to 10 cm. long, shiny mid-green above contrasting with velvety grey-white beneath; apex sharply pointed, base long and tapering; margin entire, often wavy, sometimes rolled under. Leaves on young plants and coppice shoots are much larger, with the margin coarsely toothed. **Flowers:** very small, white, in axillary clusters; male and female flowers on different trees; flower stalks covered with furry white hairs. **Fruit:** narrow seeds, to 5 mm. long, bearing thistle-like hairs, looking like fluff on the ground under female trees.

The wood is pale brown, hard and fairly heavy, with a fine, wavy grain; very durable in the ground and in salt water. This is one of the principal trees used by the Kamba woodcarvers, who are allowed to fell a limited number by the Forestry Department. Unfortunately, few really large trees can now be found.

Practical notes: slow-growing, but a fine indigenous species that deserves extensive planting. Requires red soil and moderate rainfall. Sometimes available in nurseries; needs attention when young, but hardy once established.

Brachylaena huillensis

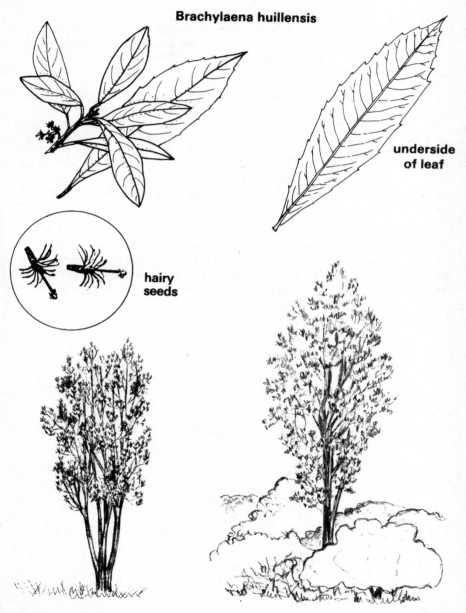

underside
of leaf

hairy
seeds

COMPOSITAE

Tarchonanthus camphoratus   Ol-leleshwa (Masai)
indigenous   Kileleshwa (Kikuyu)

A much-branched shrub or spreading tree, rarely more than 6 m. in height, occurring in a wide variety of habitats in drier areas from 1,400 to 2,200 m. and common over much of the floor of the Rift Valley and in Masai country, often on stony hills. This species gave its name to the Kileleshwa district of Nairobi, although few examples now survive there.

Bark: grey, rough, furrowed into peeling strips.   **Leaves:** narrowly lance-shaped, to 10 cm. long; apex bluntly pointed, margin entire, often wavy; texture soft, with a camphor-like smell when crushed. Young shoots and the undersides of leaves are densely covered with creamy-white hairs, giving the tree a silvery-grey appearance.   **Flowers:** male and female on different trees, massed into large terminal sprays; male flowers creamy brown, female flowers paler, developing into the woolly fruiting heads.   **Fruit:** minute seeds, each bearing dense white hairs so that the heads resemble small balls of cotton wool.

The wood is hard and heavy, making crooked but very durable fence posts. Splinters are poisonous, causing septic sores which are slow to heal.

The Masai favour the aromatic leaves as a deodorant, and often carry a few sprays; they use the branches for fuel and charcoal, and make 'rungus' or knobkerries from the rootstock. However, the species is regarded by farmers as a weed; it is extremely hardy, and regenerates remorselessly when cut down or burnt in bush fires.

85

Tarchonathus camphoratus

CONVOLVULACEAE   Morning Glory family

A medium-sized family of worldwide distribution, in which climbers with long trailing and twining stems often predominate. In dry or semidesert climates woody shrubs are more common. In Kenya there are both indigenous shrubs and woody climbers, and in dry areas white flowers of the genus Ipomoea may cover other vegetation, often in dense profusion.

Flowers are usually funnel-shaped, with five joined petals. Two of the best known flowering species are the blue-flowered climber Morning Glory *Ipomoea purpurea* from tropical America and the Beach Morning Glory *Ipomoea pes-caprae,* the mauve-flowered creeper which invades beaches and sand dunes throughout the tropics.

The most important crop plant is the Sweet Potato *Ipomoea batatas,* root tubers swollen with food store being fairly typical of the family.

A species reaching tree size such as the exotic *Ipomoea arborescens* is unusual, and indeed is the largest member of this family.

Ipomoea arborescens   Morning Glory Tree
Central America

A small deciduous tree with arching branches, usually 3 to 4 m. in height, often multi-stemmed, planted as an ornamental around Nairobi and at lower altitudes.

Bark: pale grey.   **Leaves:** up to 14 x 8 cm., heart-shaped, tapering to the apex and unfolding from the centre; texture soft, veins clearly marked, margin wavy; stalk to 6 cm.   **Flowers:** white, funnel-shaped, up to 10 cm. across, the throat streaked with purple, the flowers often covering the tree for several weeks before the leaves develop. The flowers emerge from the short, rounded calyx as pink-tipped buds, and close at night.   **Fruit:** dry oval capsules, about 2 cm. long, becoming dark brown and splitting into 4 parts on the tree; seeds black, over 1 cm. in length, bearing 2 rows of long white hairs.

Practical notes: grown from seed and thriving in hot, dry areas at most altitudes; an attractive ornamental when in flower, but remaining bare for some time after the leaves have fallen.

Ipomoea arborescens

CUPRESSACEAE   Cypress family

A family of evergreen conifers, whose distinctive feature is that the branchlets are tightly wrapped in very small, scale-like leaves, overlapping so that no wood is visible. These twigs branch in several planes to give dense sprays of foliage, and the shape of mature trees is often very different from that of younger trees.

The genus *Cupressus* consists of about 20 species native to the temperate regions of southern Europe, southern U.S.A., China and the Himalayas. None are indigenous to Kenya, but various exotic species have become important plantation trees in the highlands.

The genus *Juniperus*, widely distributed in the northern hemisphere, comprises over 50 species of trees and shrubs and a number of ornamental garden varieties. Unlike cypresses they do not have woody cones but fleshy, berry-like fruit. The common European juniper *Juniperus communis* has bluish berries which are used worldwide to flavour gin. The only indigenous representative of this genus is *Juniperus procera*, the African Pencil Cedar, which is the largest juniper tree in the world.

The popular name Cedar is the cause of some confusion, because it has been given to various trees in several families which have similar aromatic wood. True cedars such as the Cedar of Lebanon *Cedrus libani* have erect, barrel-shaped cones, and belong to the Pine family Pinaceae.

Members of this family in Kenya include *Cupressus, Juniperus*.

Cupressus lusitanica   Mexican Cypress
Mexico, Guatemala

A fast-growing cypress to 35 m. in height, with a straight trunk and generally conical but rather variable shape and widely spreading branches. The branchlet systems are irregular and pendulous, in many planes rather than flattened into one plane.

Bark: reddish-brown, with vertical fissures; grey with age.   **Leaves:** dull blue-green to dark grey-green, in 4 ranks, with spreading, pointed tips. **Cones:** male cones like fat tips on the ends of fertile branchlets, producing clouds of yellow pollen dust: female cones round, up to 1.5 cm. across, with a characteristic waxy grey bloom when young, ripening brown in 2 years and opening to release many small, narrowly winged seeds from beneath each cone scale. The scales bear projecting central bosses, slender and pointed on upper scales, spreading or reflexed on lower scales.

The timber is pale brown, seasoning well but not durable in the ground; knots are common, but otherwise this is a first-class lightweight wood, very widely used for furniture, joinery and tea-chests.

Practical notes: this species represents over 40% of all plantation trees in Kenya, reaching marketable size in 20 years with a trunk up to 50 cm. in diameter. Grows best above 1,500 m. with good soil and fair rainfall, and coppices well, making a good hedge; also sold as a Christmas tree.

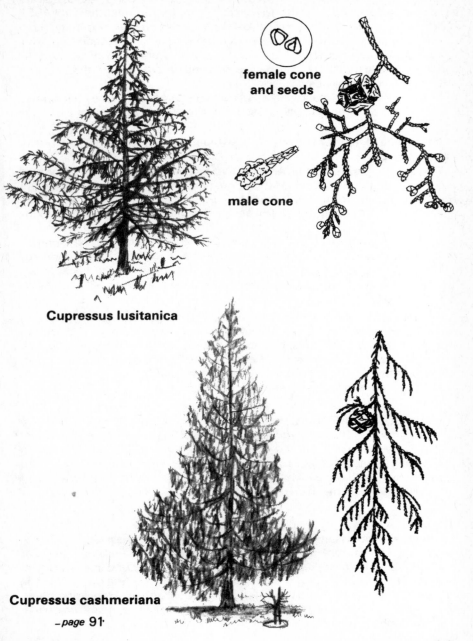

female cone
and seeds

male cone

Cupressus lusitanica

Cupressus cashmeriana

–page 91·

CUPRESSACEAE

Cupressus macrocarpa, the Monterey Cypress from California, once very popular in Kenya and widely used as a hedge, has not been planted since 1952 following heavy attack by cypress canker. This species is not easy to distinguish from *C. lusitanica* and hybrid varieties are fairly common. The conical crown may become more flat-topped, and the branchlets are erect or stiff, rather swollen towards the tips. The bark is brown and fibrous, grey with age, often scaling in large, flat pieces.

The specific name 'macrocarpa' refers to the large size of the cones, up to 3.5 x 2.5 cm., shiny brown with crescent-shaped ridges on the scales.

A few of the other ornamental cypresses planted in Kenya are briefly described below.

Cupressus arizonica, the Arizona Cypress, has a neat, rather rounded conical shape, generally smaller than *C. lusitanica.* The branchlets stand out strongly, and the foliage is a variable grey-green. The cones are shiny greenish-brown, knobbly, to 2.5 cm. across. The bark peels off in long, stringy strips.

Cupressus cashmeriana, the Kashmir Cypress, probably the most elegant of all the cypresses, has a narrow pyramidal shape with ascending branches and remarkably long, pendulous branchlets, which are conspicuously flattened. The small, dark brown cones closely resemble those of *C. torulosa.*

Cupressus funebris, the Mourning or Chinese Weeping Cypress, is surprisingly rounded and bushy when young or growing in the open. Branches are conspicuously pendulous, bearing flattened, grey-green branchlets with pointed leaves noticeable along the larger stems. The cones are about 1 cm. or less in diameter, on short, curved stalks, with 8 scales bearing very small bosses and only 3 to 5 seeds beneath each scale.

Cupressus sempervirens, the Mediterranean or Italian Cypress, has two distinct forms. The variety *sempervirens,* has stiff, erect branches almost· parallel to the stem, whereas the variety *horizontalis* has branches spreading out flat like a Cedar of Lebanon. In the Mediterranean region these trees reach immense size, up to 45 m. in height and 3 m. in girth, and are extremely long lived. The large oval cones, up to 3 cm. long, bear relatively few large, winged seeds.

Cupressus torulosa, the Himalayan or Bhutan Cypress, is a tall, handsome tree with a massive trunk. The variety *majestica* grown in Nairobi has a regular pyramidal shape and pendulous branches, reaching the ground unless pruned. The branchlets are often long and four-sided, flattened into one plane, with the ultimate divisions curved and whip-like. The cones are about 1 cm. in diameter, with 8 to 10 scales bearing small triangular bosses, often recurved, and 6 to 8 seeds beneath each scale.

91

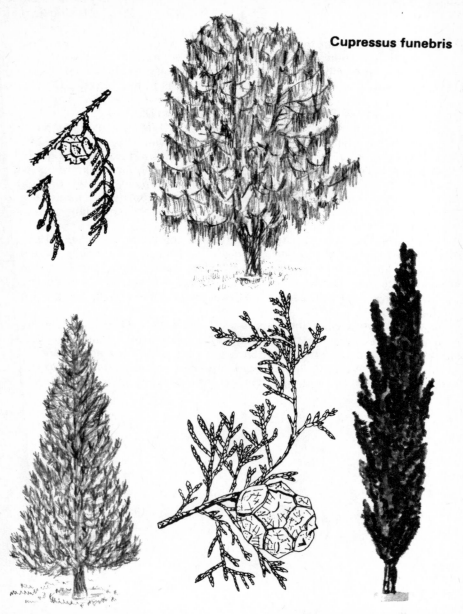

Cupressus funebris

Cupressus torulosa

Cupressus sempervirens

92

CUPRESSACEAE

Juniperus procera
indigenous

African Pencil Cedar
Mutarakwa (Kikuyu)

An evergreen timber tree to 40 m. in height, with a straight trunk and a pyramidal shape when young, spreading with age to form a high, irregular crown. The foliage is finer and more open than that of the common cypresses. Occurs in highland forest and forest remnant areas from 1,500 to 3,000 m., particularly on the lower slopes of Mt. Kenya, with many young trees prominent on the escarpments between Limuru and Naivasha.

Bark: thin, greyish-brown with shallow vertical fissures, darkening and often peeling in long strips with age. **Leaves:** juvenile leaves needle-like, prickly, to 1 cm. long, growing in threes, gradually giving way to dark green, scale-like mature leaves, which are triangular, sharply tipped and pressed close to the branchlets. **Cones:** male rounded, very small, yellowish, on short axillary branchlets; female soft, berry-like, rounded and fleshy, to 8mm. across, with a waxy bloom, purple-blue when mature, the greenish pulp containing 1 to 4 hard seeds.

The heartwood is reddish-brown and heavy, splintering easily but durable and highly resistant to termites, of major importance for building, joinery, roofing shingles and fence posts. The timber was formerly exported from Kenya for the manufacture of pencils, as the wood closely resembles that of *Juniperus virginiana,* the Eastern Red Cedar grown commercially in the U.S.A. for this purpose.

Practical notes: a fine indigenous tree, readily grown from seed, thriving best at higher altitude in better rainfall areas but surviving in surprisingly dry conditions once established; fairly slow-growing, more so in poorer soil, but long recognised as an excellent plantation species. Mature trees are now rare, and protection and re-planting of this species deserves high priority.

93

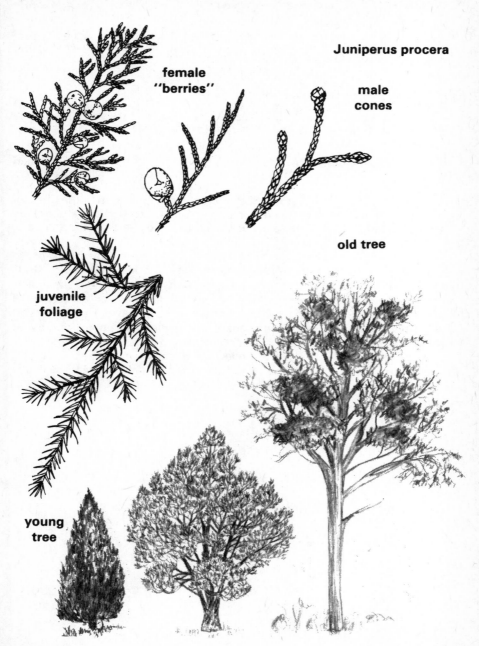

Juniperus procera

female
"berries"

male
cones

juvenile
foliage

old tree

young
tree

94

CYCADACEAE   Cycad family

A primitive group of woody plants which flourished over 200 million yeara ago, the survivors being widely scattered throughout the world, mostly in very dry areas. They are extremely slow-growing, and some of them are hundreds of years old.

Despite their appearance, these plants are neither ferns nor palms. This is an odd family, which lies between the conifers and true flowering plants. Male and female plants grow separately, and both generally produce cone-like structures between the leaves.

In Southern Africa, where there are over 20 species all cycads are protected. In East Africa there are two indigenous genera, *Cycas* and *Encephalartos,* but only the species described is at all common. Two exotic species of *Cycas* are also planted as ornamentals.

Encephalartos hildebrandtii   Cycad
indigenous   Mkwanga, Msapo (Swahili)

A palm-like tree with a stout, unbranched stem up to 6 m. in height, not uncommon in the Shimba HIlls and other drier forest and bushland areas of the coastal belt below 30 m.; also planted in Nairobi. The plant is often seen as a rosette of dark green, spiny leaves at ground level.

Leaves: compound, up to 2.5 m. in length, borne in whorls at the top of the stem; leaflets about 80 pairs, stiff and tough, often with spiny teeth about 20 cm. long, with many parallel veins — unlike the genus *Cycas,* where the leaves have a single midrib and the margin is always entire. **Cones:** female cones dull yellow, up to 50 cm. long, in the centre of the rosette of leaves, bearing fleshy, orange-red seeds up to 3 cm. long beneath each scale. Male cones, somewhat shorter and narrower, are borne on separate trees.

The hard, nut-like kernel can be boiled, dried and ground into a flour, and is still used to make a kind of bread by the Boni people of Lamu District. The fleshy seed covering and the starchy pith of the stem are also edible.

Encephalartos hildebrandtii

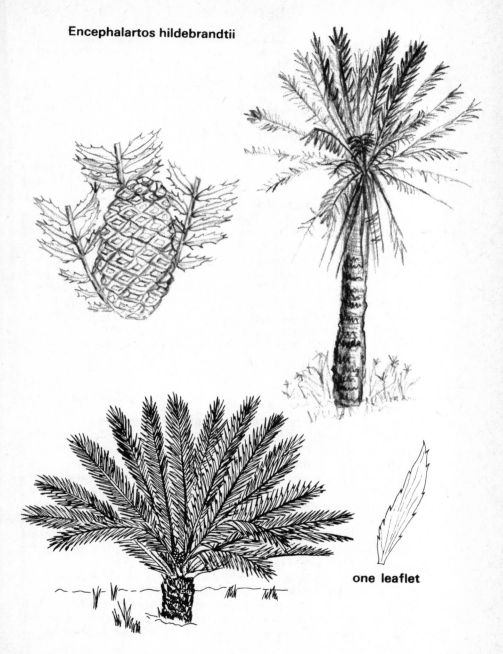

one leaflet

EBENACEAE Ebony family

A largely tropical and sub-tropical family named after the Ebony tree *Diospyros ebenum,* which is native to the rain forests of south-east Asia and Sri Lanka. There are over 400 species of *Diospyros,* mainly tropical, most of them producing hard, black heartwood. The genus includes *Diospyros virginiana,* the North American Persimmon, which has sweet, edible fruit.

The trade name African Ebony refers to both *Diospyros mespiliformis* and *Dalbergia melanoxylon.* The latter which is in the sub-family Papilionoideae is, however, also known as African Blackwood and was once called Zanzibar Ebony. It is commonly used in woodcarvings. *Diospyros mespiliformis* is indigenous to Kenya but now extremely rare.

Members of this family in Kenya include *Diospyros, Euclea.*

Diospyros abyssinica *(Maba abyssinica)* — Giant Diospyros
indigenous — Muiruthi (Kikuyu)

A tall forest tree reaching 30 or 40 m. in height, with a dark, slender trunk and a strangely small, mushroom-topped crown, occurring in coastal and highland forests up to 2,100 m.; fairly common around Nairobi and sometimes the dominant forest species, for instance in the Mara River region.

Bark: distinctive, very dark and rough, cracking into small purple-black squares. **Leaves:** lance-shaped, glossy dark green above, to 12 cm. long, tapering to the apex; margin wavy, midrib prominent below, leaf stalk short and grooved. **Flowers:** small, white, fragrant, in axillary clusters. **Fruit:** round, to 1.5 cm., red or yellow, black when ripe, held in a persistent cup-shaped calyx, sometimes in very dense clusters; much eaten by birds. Fallen fruit look like dried currants. The timber is white, hard and tough but difficult to plane smooth.

Euclea divinorum *(Euclea keniensis)* — Euclea
indigenous — Mukinyai (Kikuyu)

A much-branched evergreen tree to 10 m. but generally less in height, the crown often rounded but generally variable in shape; widespread in wooded grassland and scrub up to 2,100 m., quickly becoming the dominant species after bush-clearing, as on the Laikipia plateau.

Bark: grey, darker and cracking into squares with age. **Leaves:** mostly opposite, dull green and rather stiff, narrowly elliptic, young leaves up to 8 cm., mature leaves smaller; apex blunt, margin wavy; underside often bearing brownish powdery scales. **Flowers:** very small, creamy-white, in small sprays which persist after fading, giving the branchlets a spiky, ragged appearance. Flowering is fairly short-lived but sometimes conspicuous. **Fruit:** small, round, to 5 mm., purple-black when ripe.

Both the fruits and decoctions from the bark and roots are reputed to be purgatives, and the frayed ends of twigs are used as toothbrushes. The wood is hard and close-grained, widely used for hut construction and farm tools. Suckers grow from the roots up to a considerable distance from the main stem.

There are various other indigenous species of **Diospyros** and **Euclea.**

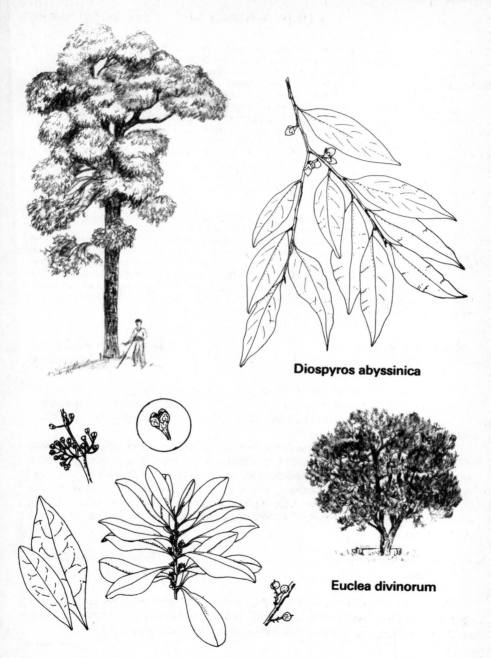

Diospyros abyssinica

Euclea divinorum

98

EUPHORBIACEAE Euphorbia family

A very large, cosmopolitan family of herbs, shrubs and trees, centred in the tropics and varying from tiny desert succulents to tall forest trees such as the Crotons of the Kenya highlands. One of the few features common to most members of the family is a 3-lobed fruit capsule: otherwise only fine details of the flower show the family relationship.

Economically important species include the Brazilian Rubber Tree *Hevea braziliensis,* the Cassava plant *Manihot esculenta* and plants producing castor oil, tung oil and candlenut oil. Many members of the family are ornamentals, and others produce timber and dyes.

There are over 5,000 species in 300 genera, grouped into 8 major botanical tribes or sub-groups, each of which is represented in Kenya. The family is named after the genus Euphorbia in the sub-group *Euphorbieae,* which although not typical in many respects is probably the most conspicuous.

Sub-group Crotoneae

The second most conspicuous sub-group of the Euphorbia family in Kenya includes the tree Crotons, of which three prominent indigenous species are described.

The sub-group *Crotoneae* covers over 700 species of tropical trees and shrubs, all with star-like hairs or silvery scales on the leaves. However, the ornamental shrubs known as Garden Crotons, although part of the Euphorbia family, are not classified as *Crotoneae* but belong instead to the sub-group *Jatropheae.* This includes exotics with stiff, shiny leaves such as the Variegated Laurel *Codiaeum variegatum* from S.E. Asia, planted in many gardens at the coast and at lower altitudes. The ornamental euphorbias *Acalypha spp.,* with thin, toothed leaves, are classified in the sub-group *Acalyphaeae.*

Croton dichogamus	**Orange-leaved Croton**
indigenous	**Kererwa (Kikuyu)**

A many-stemmed shrub or small tree to 3 m., occurring in dry bush and forest margin areas from the coast to 2,200 m., often around rocky outcrops. This species dominates parts of the Masai Mara and the Langata side of the Nairobi National Park.

Leaves: alternate, regularly spaced along slender branches, narrowly elliptic, up to 6 cm. in length, with the underside, young stems and fruit covered in dot-like silvery or sometimes golden-brown scales. Scattered leaves turn rusty orange on the upper surface, making this species eye-catching and easy to recognise. **Flowers:** few, inconspicuous, male and female separate, on short terminal spikes. **Fruit:** 3-lobed capsules up to 1 cm. across, in small terminal clusters.

Croton macrostachyus	**Broad-leaved Croton**
indigenous	**Mukindu-wa-njora (Kikuyu)**

A medium-sized deciduous tree, sometimes rather straggling, occasionally growing to 25 m. with large spreading branches; widely distributed in forest and forest margins in better rainfall districts from 600 to 2,000 m.

(continued)

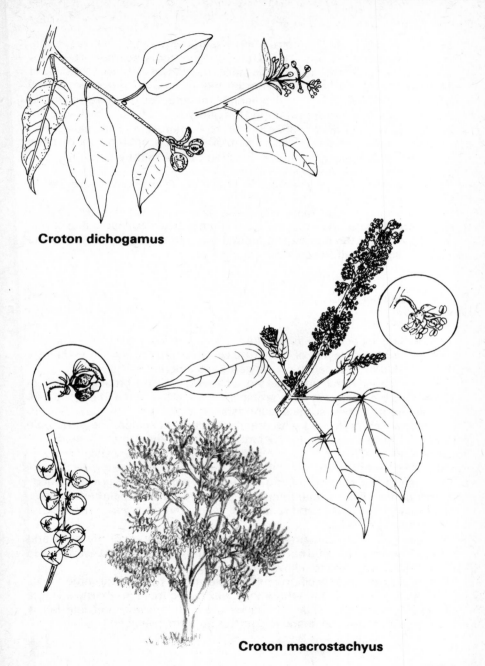

Croton dichogamus

Croton macrostachyus

100

EUPHORBIACEAE

Croton macrostachyus (continued)

Bark: pale, grey, fairly smooth, finely fissured with age.   **Leaves:** large, soft green, heart-shaped, up to 15 x 10 cm., on long stems crowded at the ends of branches; veins prominent, with two stalked glands just visible at the base of the leaf; texture more or less furry, margin slightly toothed. **Flowers:** creamy yellow, in erect spikes up to 25 cm. in length, on upturned branches, covering much of the tree. Flowers appear during the rains and are fairly short-lived, the flower spikes turning downwards as the fruits mature.   **Fruit:** pale green pea-sized capsules, on drooping spikes to 30 cm. long, splitting open on the tree to release 3 shiny grey seeds, covered at one end by a soft, creamy envelope called an aril, much sought after by birds.

The wood is soft and very perishable, with a rather unpleasant spicy odour when cut for firewood.

A decoction from the roots was used as a purgative and drunk as a treatment for malaria, and a curious superstition suggested that mumps could be cured by having the patient trot around the tree singing, after which the mumps would gradually disappear.

Croton megalocarpus
indigenous

Croton
Mukinduri (Kikuyu)

A spreading upper-storey forest tree to 35 m. or more, usually with a flattish crown and horizontal layers of branches; common around Nairobi and in dry upland forest, often planted in country areas as a boundary marker.

Bark: dark grey, rough and cracking.   **Leaves:** variable, broadly elliptic, up to 12 cm. long but often smaller; apex tapering, stalk thin, about 6 cm. long. The soft, dull green upper surface contrasts strongly with the pale, silvery underside, which is flecked with small, pale brown scales. **Flowers:** pale yellow, in hanging spikes to 25 cm. long, short-lived but conspicuous, appearing after heavy rain; flower buds small, pale brown, visible for many months. The flowers are mostly male, producing pollen, the few female flowers at the base of the stalk becoming the fruit.   **Fruit:** prolific greyish woody capsules, about 2.5 cm. in diameter, with compartments for 3 flattened seeds.

The wood is perishable and splits badly, and although a good firewood the smoke irritates the eyes.

The seeds or nuts contain oil and protein, and are eaten by birds and squirrels. The oil is a forceful purgative, and an infusion of the bark was used to kill intestinal worms and to relieve whooping cough.

Practical notes: the specific name 'megalocarpus' refers to the large seeds, which frequently germinate where they fall. Young trees are hardy and fast growing on forest soil. Older branches are rather brittle and leaf-fall is extensive, but its graceful shape makes this an attractive shade tree.

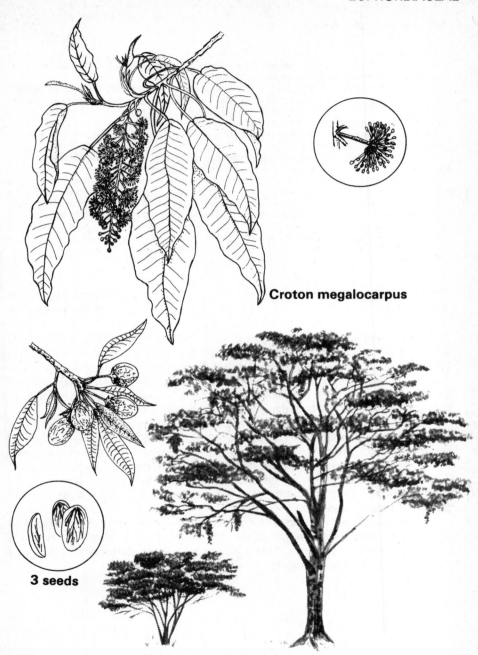

Croton megalocarpus

3 seeds

102

EUPHORBIACEAE

Sub-group Euphorbieae

The best-known tree in this sub-group in Kenya is the Candelabra Euphorbia, but there are altogether over 150 indigenous species of which about 20 are classified as trees or shrubs. In addition, a number of exotics are grown as ornamentals.

The feature distinguishing all plants in this sub-group from the rest of the family is the sticky white latex, which is almost always poisonous. Many are adapted to survive in hot, dry conditions, as green, succulent branches take over the leaf function, and many have thorns or spines. As a result, some spiny Euphorbia may at first be confused with the Cactus family *Cactaceae* which is native to the Americas, but cacti do not contain latex and have flowers of very different construction.

Euphorbieae flowers have several special features, and it is worth inspecting the flowers of the common Poinsettia *Euphorbia pulcherrima* to help to clarify them.

There are rarely any true petals. Male and female flowers are usually very small, developing separately although sometimes side by side, in a highly specialised cup-like structure called a cyathium. The cup contains only one female flower, on a stalk, and several male flowers, each with a stamen; the female flower develops into the 3-lobed capsule which contains the seeds.

The cup may display one to five variously shaped glands on the rim, which produce nectar. In addition, the cup may be surrounded by by 1 to 5 leaf-like bracts. Both glands and bracts may be brightly coloured, and both can be easily mistaken for the petals of an ordinary flower.

Members of this sub-group in Kenya include *Euphorbia, Synadenium.*

Euphorbia candelabrum
indigenous

Candelabra Euphorbia
Muthuri (Kikuyu)

A familiar savannah tree to 15 m. or more in height, with a short, thick trunk up to 90 cm. in diameter and a characteristic crown of massive ascending branches. This species is widely distributed in tropical Africa down to South Africa, frequently on rocky hills; in Kenya common in grassland and thornbush country from the coast to 1,850 m., often on termite mounds. There is an extensive forest on the hillsides above Lake Nakuru.

Stems: 4-winged, dark green and wavy when young, constricted at irregular intervals and bearing small paired spines, to 5 mm. in length, on small separated spine shields. The spines may be absent altogether on older trees.   **Flowers:** greenish-yellow, fleshy, with 5 glands, produced in groups of 3 to 6 on the stems above the pairs of spines. Abundant nectar attracts bees, but the honey cannot be eaten as it irritates and burns the mouth.   **Fruit:** green, pea-sized capsules.

The branches are soft and brittle, and produce copious very sticky latex. The latex is extremely toxic; a single drop in the eye may cause blindness, and will blister even the skin of a cow. Deaths have been recorded from attempts to use the latex in traditional medicine.

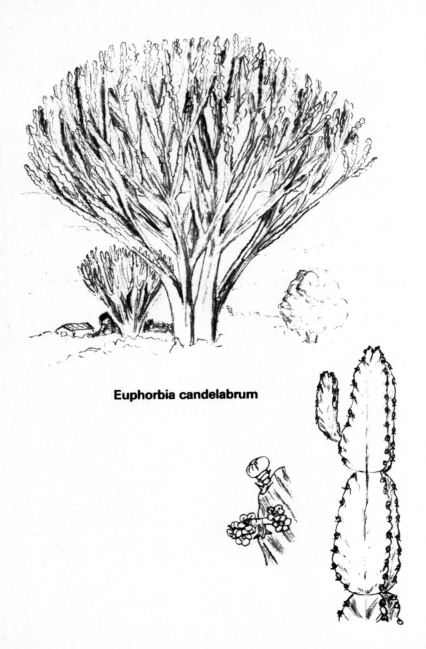

Euphorbia candelabrum

Other Tree-sized Euphorbias

There are a number of other large tree-sized Euphorbias in Kenya, but the species are distinguished by botanical details that give difficulty even to the experts.

Euphorbia obovalifolia is the common species on the Ngong Hills and other mountain forests, growing to 30 m. in height with a distinctive bare, cylindrical trunk and deciduous leves up to 12 cm. long on the spiny stem wings.

Euphorbia magnicapsular is common, often in sizeable forests, on the stony hillsides around Lake Naivasha.

Euphorbia robecchii is common in northern areas of Kenya, and a clump is conspicuous at Kenani, near Voi on the Mombasa Road.

A specimen of **Euphorbia bussei ssp. kibwezensis** can be seen in front of the National Museum in Nairobi.

These unusual trees are often planted in gardens as striking ornamentals. Any piece broken off will take root in well-drained soil.

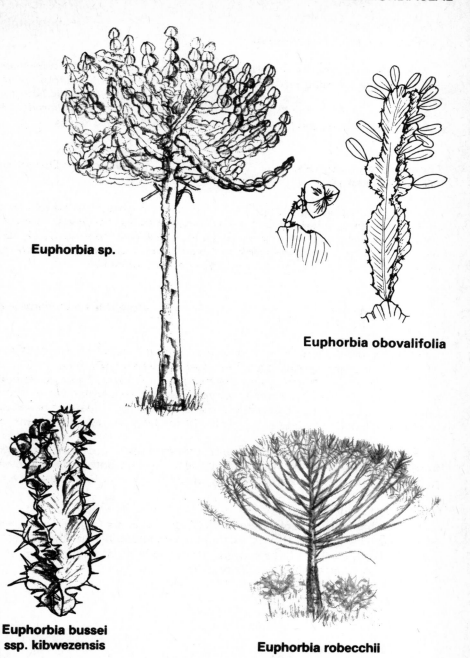

Euphorbia sp.

Euphorbia obovalifolia

**Euphorbia bussei
ssp. kibwezensis**

Euphorbia robecchii

106

EUPHORBIACEAE

Euphorbia cotinifolia
Mexico, South America, West Indies

Red Euphorbia

A fast-growing deciduous shrub or tree to 6 m., bearing coppery-red leaves and small cream-coloured flowers, widely planted around Nairobi as an ornamental. This species is fairly short-lived, and is conspicuously bare for several months of the year The sap is an irritant, and has been discovered to be carcinogenic. A dye used for wool can be extracted from the leaves.

Euphorbia leucocephala
Mexico, Guatemala

White lace Euphorbia

A deciduous shrub growing to 4 m., common in gardens in Nairobi. The **small leaves are in whorls, bright green with pink stalks. The flowers are very** small, surrounded by 5 white star-like glands which resemble thin petals and white leafy bracts, tinged with pink, to 1.5 cm. long. The flowers are borne in large heads and give an attractive effect of delicate white lace.

Euphorbia pulcherrima
Mexico, Central America

Poinsettia, Mexican Flameleaf

A widely-planted ornamental, growing to about 4 m. with a woody brown trunk and rather angular branches. The leaves are prominently veined, to 20 cm. long, with the apex tapering and the margin often lobed. The true flowers are inconspicuous, held in a green cup with one large yellow gland at one side, but these are encircled by conspicuous rosettes of coloured, leaf-like bracts up to 18 cm. in length. The bracts may be bright scarlet, pink, yellow or creamy in colour.
Practical notes: easily grown from cuttings; best in good soil, although fairly adaptable. Flowering in Kenya is in the dry season, and can be improved by pruning. The latex is toxic, particularly on an open wound. Can be grown as a pot plant.

Euphorbia milii var. splendens from Madagascar is a familiar low hedge plant known as Crown of Thorns, a common name described as "theologically and botanically incorrect". The stems are fleshy, armed with sharp spines, and the flowers are surrounded by bright red bracts.

107

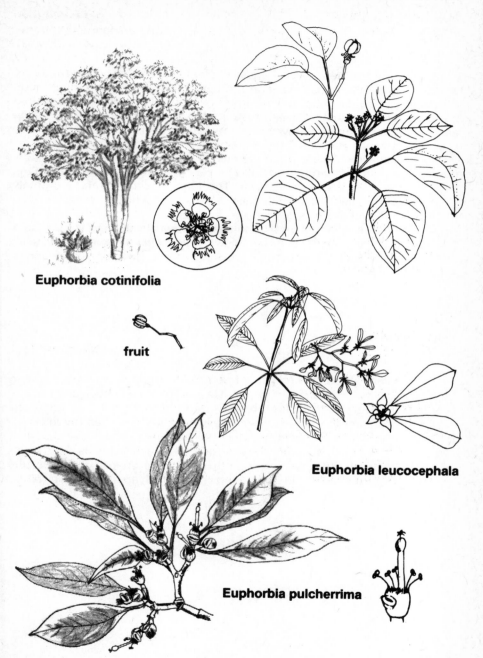

Euphorbia cotinifolia

fruit

Euphorbia leucocephala

Euphorbia pulcherrima

108

EUPHORBIACEAE

Euphorbia tirucalli
indigenous

Finger Euphorbia,
Rubber Hedge Euphorbia
Mtupa mwitu (Swahili)

A succulent, resilient shrub, frequently planted as a boma hedge in very dry areas but also occurring as a dense, straight-stemmed tree to 6 m. or more. Branchlets are smooth green and cylindrical, forming brush-like masses. **Leaves:** small leaves present only on very young stems, falling early. **Flowers:** small, yellow to creamy white, in dense clusters. **Fruit:** typical 3-part capsules, hard purple-green, less than 1 cm. across.

This species probably came from India in almost prehistoric times, but is now widespread and naturalised throughout Africa. The name 'tirucalli' is the native name from Malabar in India. The latex is copious and extremely poisonous to humans and animals alike, and alleged medicinal uses should be treated with the greatest care.

The plant is a well-known fish poison and insecticide, and is used as a mosquito repellent, but the latex contains too high a percentage of resin to be used for rubber. Sadly, a recent pilot project near Baringo for the extraction of hydrocarbons proved uneconomic.

Synadenium compactum
indigenous

Watha (Kikuyu)

A succulent shrub, sometimes a tree to 9 m. common in Nairobi and in Kiambu and Machakos districts, where it is used both as a hedge and to mark grave sites. **Leaves:** reddish purple or fleshy green, sometimes with both colours on the same leaf; leaves crowded at the ends of branches, broadly oval, to 10 cm. long, with a short, recurved tip. The midrib has a distinctive wing-like keel beneath the leaf. **Flowers:** small, in branched reddish heads about 6 cm. across, each group of flowers in the centre of a saucer-shaped gland. **Fruit:** typical dry 3-part capsules, on stalks, with seeds which are dispersed by birds.

Euphorbia tirucalli

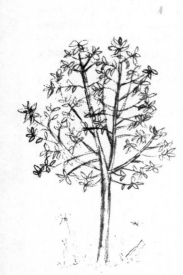

Synadenium compactum

110

EUPHORBIACEAE

Other members of the family *Euphorbiaceae* in Kenya include *Aleurites, Bridelia, Drypetes, Erythrococca, Manihot, Margaritaria, Ricinus.*

Aleurites moluccana — Candlenut Tree
South Pacific Islands, Malaya

A large, leafy tree with light greyish-green foliage, to 10 m. in height, planted around Nairobi and elsewhere as an ornamental.

Bark: grey brown, fairly smooth, finely fissured with wavy vertical lines. **Leaves:** large, spade-shaped, shiny, up to 20 cm. long, usually pointed, on long stalks in terminal whorls. The leaves are covered with powdery whitish hairs, more rust-coloured on the lower surface. **Flowers:** small, white, in large terminal clusters. **Fruit:** large, roundish, to 5 cm., with two black seeds.

The seeds are rich in oil, which is used for candles, soap, paint and varnish. Related species in the East produce the important tung oil.

Bridelia micrantha — Bridelia
indigenous — Mukoigo (Kikuyu)

A dense, spreading tree to 12 m., widely distributed in open woodland from the coast to 2,200 m., often near rivers.

Bark: grey; brown and flaking with age; young stems with a zig-zag appearance, dotted with conspicuous breathing pores or lenticels. **Leaves:** alternate, dark glossy green above, broadly elliptic, usually up to 12 cm. long; veins parallel, extending along the margin; margin wavy, slightly scalloped; leaf stalk short and slightly hairy. **Flowers:** very small, yellowish, in tight axillary clusters. **Fruit:** oval, axillary, about 8 mm. long, black and edible when ripe, used by the Masai to flavour milk.

The timber is dark brown and very durable, making excellent furniture. It also makes very good poles, firewood and charcoal, and is now unfortunately scarce as a result. The tree is fast-growing and easily raised from seed; well worth planting as an attractive shade tree.

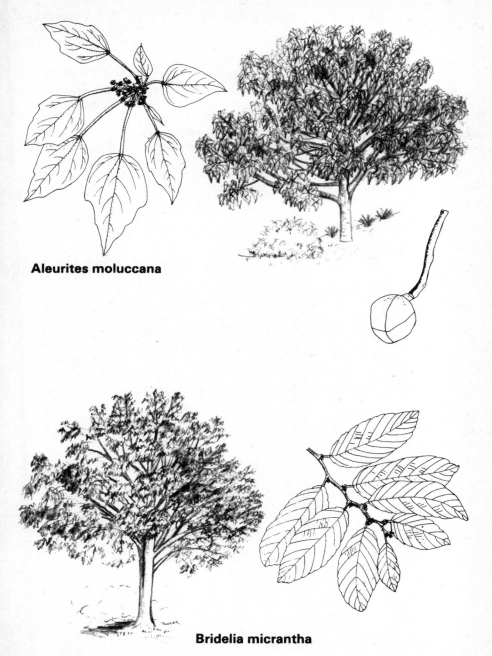

Aleurites moluccana

Bridelia micrantha

EUPHORBIACEAE

Drypetes gerrardii
indigenous

Drypetes
Munyenye (Kikuyu)

An evergreen forest or forest margin tree to 15 m., with dense, drooping foliage; common in the Nairobi area, also near Kericho and Kakamega.
Bark: smooth, grey or brownish, developing fine horizontal markings but not cracking or peeling. **Leaves:** alternate, arranged in one plane on thin, zig-zag branchlets; dark shiny green above, to 10 cm. long, apex pointed, base tapering, often asymmetric; midrib raised above and below; margin wavy, often with shallow, distant teeth. Leaf stalks and young stems bear sparse brownish hairs. **Flowers:** small, yellow, solitary or in clusters in the leaf axis. **Fruit:** small round berries, softly hairy, turning from yellow to orange-red, attracting birds and monkeys. The fallen fruits are black, resembling currants.

Erythrococca bongensis
indigenous

Muhara-ngware (Kikuyu)

A prickly shrub with slender branches, rarely a tree to 3 m., widespread at forest edges, often at the base of other trees; common around Nairobi. The prickles are in pairs, pale brown against the grey-green stems. **Leaves:** alternate, dark green, narrowly oval, to 7 cm. long but often smaller, tapering to base and apex; tip blunt or notched, margin scalloped or serrated, with small spines. **Flowers:** minute, greenish, on thread-like stalks in the leaf axils. **Fruit:** small berries, in threes, often not all developing, red when ripe.
The Kikuyu name, taken literally, means 'Guinea-fowl scratcher'.

113

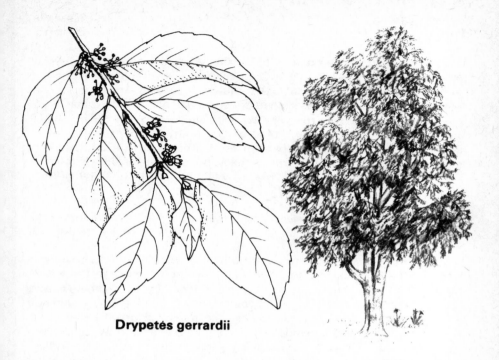

Drypetés gerrardii

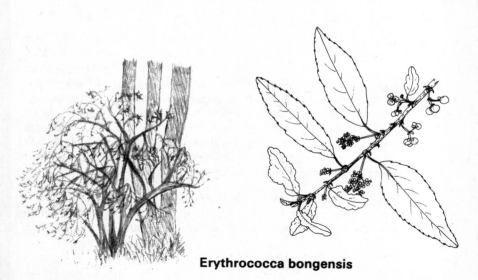

Erythrococca bongensis

114

EUPHORBIACEAE

Manihot glaziovii
Brazil

**Tree Cassava,
Ceara Rubber Tree**

A leafy deciduous tree related to the Cassava plant and bearing similar leaves, sometimes growing to 8 m. Originally introduced as a possible source of rubber but found to be difficult to tap regularly; now wild in parts of Uganda, sometimes planted against erosion in dry areas and also in the Nairobi area.

Bark: pale grey-brown, rough brown with age, with many horizontal leaf scars; producing copious latex.   **Leaves:** dark, shiny green, palmately lobed, with up to 7 very deep lobes, on crowded terminal stalks up to 40 cm. in length.
Flowers: small, yellowish. The tree is shady, but leafless for several months.
Cut branches root easily, and the tree is often grown as an ornamental.

Magaritaria discoidea *(Phyllanthus discoideus)*
indigenous

Margaritaria
Mukarara (Kikuyu)

An upright, deciduous, very variable tree, growing to 15 m. and occasionally more, occurring in thickets and forest margins over much of Kenya. Branchlets have a crowded, angular appearance, and are covered with breathing pores.

Bark: reddish and very stringy on young trees, becoming grey, rough and vertically fissured with age.   **Leaves:** alternate, thin bright green, broadly oval, up to 10 cm. long, often curving backwards; midrib and short leaf stalk often tinged with red.   **Flowers:** very small greenish yellow, in profuse axillary clusters. **Fruit:** green 3-lobed capsules, to 1 cm. across, splitting on the ground to release 3 shiny blue-black seeds.

Ricinus communis
indigenous to Africa

Castor Oil Plant
Mbono (Swahili)
Mwariki (kikuyu)

A widespread weedy shrub, often tree-sized, growing in dry country or disturbed ground from 600 to 2,000m ; first cultivated for castor oil in ancient Egypt and now widely naturalised through the tropics.   **Leaves:** large, palmately and deeply lobed, margin serrated, on long stalks.   **Flowers:** crowded on upright spikes; male flowers with creamy-yellow stamens; female flowers with a showy red stigma, borne on the upper part of the spike.   **Fruit:** round, deep red capsules, softly spiky, in dense clusters, with 3 large brownish seeds.

The seeds are poisonous, but the oil extract is heated and has been used for many centuries as a purgative. The leaves and residue from pressed seeds are poisonous to stock. There are some ornamental forms, but only one species.

115

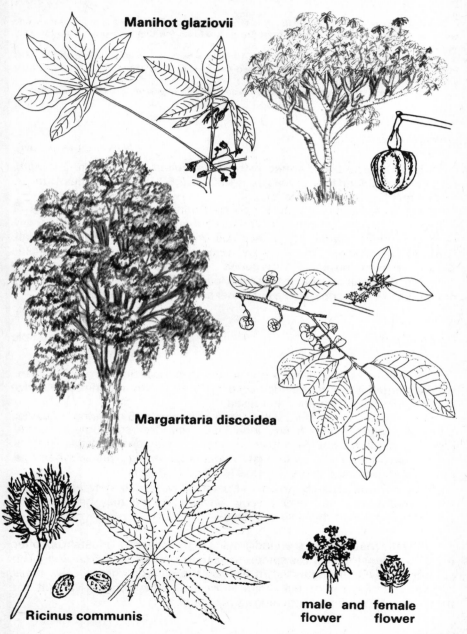

Manihot glaziovii

Margaritaria discoidea

Ricinus communis

male and female
flower

FLACOURTIACEAE   Kei-apple family

A large tropical and sub-tropical family of trees and shrubs. There are a few timber trees and some ornamentals, and one species from Burma produces the Chaulmoogra oil used to treat leprosy.

The family is widespread in Kenya, with 15 genera being represented, although the most familiar species is an exotic, the South African Kei-apple *Dovyalis caffra*. Several species bear woody spines and simple, alternate leaves.

Members of this family in Kenya include *Dovyalis, Oncoba, Rawsonia, Scolopia, Trimeria.*

Dovyalis abyssinica
indigenous   Mukambura (Kikuyu)

A small tree to 9 m., armed with robust spines up to 4 cm. in length, common in highland forest areas from 1,800 to 2,500 m., sometimes found as a remnant tree in coffee plantations.

Bark: grey, young bark thickly covered with brown breathing pores or lenticels.   **Leaves:** smooth, thin, shiny dark green, oval to oblong, to 5 cm. long; apex blunt, margin sometimes obscurely scalloped.   **Flowers:** small, with 5 to 8 green sepals, male flowers in clusters with many stamens, females solitary. There are no petals in this genus.   **Fruit:** round, on short stalks, about 1.5 cm. in diameter with persistent calyx lobes; green and velvety when young, orange-yellow when ripe, edible but rather acid, excellent for preserves.

Dovyalis caffra   Kei-apple
South Africa

A heavily armed evergreen shrub or small tree, occasionally reaching 8 m., widely planted in the highlands above 1,200 m. as an impenetrable hedge and in some areas becoming naturalised.

Bark: grey, fairly smooth, with strong spines up to 6 cm. long.   **Leaves:** thin, dark green, up to 5 cm. long; apex rounded, sometimes notched. **Flowers:** small, creamy yellow, with prominent stamens, in dense clusters. **Fruit:** round and fleshy, up to 4 cm. in diameter, orange-yellow when ripe, pleasantly flavoured and making excellent jelly and jam.

Practical notes: readily grown from seed, growth moderately fast; the plant is extremely hardy but very greedy. Severe pruning may be needed to encourage growth at the base of a hedge.

Dovyalis macrocalyx is an indigenous highland forest undershrub, often growing in dense shade. The spines are usually slender, up to 5 cm. long. This species is easily distinguished in fruit by the enlarged green calyx lobes, reflexed and fringed with sticky hairs, above the bright red, plum-like fruit. The fruit is sweet and edible, containing a single seed.

117

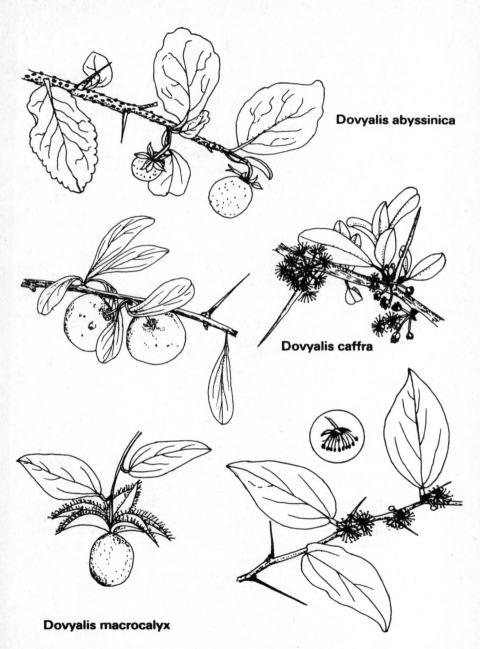

Dovyalis abyssinica

Dovyalis caffra

Dovyalis macrocalyx

118

FLACOURTIACEAE

Oncoba spinosa
indigenous

Fried egg Tree
Mwage (Kikuyu)

A spiny shrub or small tree to 6 m., widely distributed in both dry woodland and riverine forest from the coast to 1,800 m. This species is widespread from the Arabian peninsular to Southern Africa.

Bark: grey, fairly smooth, with straight axillary spines up to 5 cm. long; branchlets zig-zag, with many breathing pores. **Leaves:** alternate, strong shiny green, often recurved, broadly oval, about 8 cm. long but often smaller; margin with small teeth or scalloped, net veins noticeable; base tapering abruptly to a short stalk. Young leaves and stalks are often wine-red. **Flowers:** solitary, fragrant, up to 8 cm. across, resembling fried eggs, with many waxy white petals and a conspicuous central mass of orange-yellow stamens. The creamy central style is rounded, about 4 mm. across; division into lobes barely visible. **Fruit:** rounded, smooth and hard, about 5 cm. across, turning from yellow to brown, containing shiny brown seeds in a dry yellow pulp, which is sour and scarcely edible.

Oncoba routledgei *(Oncoba spinosa var. routledgei)* is a very similar species, occurring at higher altitudes from 900 to 2,500 m., typically in rain forest or river valleys in areas such as Limuru or Kericho. The leaves are tough, up to 16 cm. long, with the margin coarsely toothed, and the central style is clearly divided into several recurved branches.

The leaves and roots of both species were used for medicinal purposes, and the shells of the fruits can be made into snuff boxes, or rattles for children when the seeds inside are dry. The wood is hard and light brown.

Both species make attractive garden ornamentals and can be grown from cuttings into an effective hedge.

Rawsonia lucida *(Rawsonia usambarensis)*
indigenous

Rawsonia
Mutendera (Kikuyu)

A small timber tree, sometimes reaching 12 m. in height, scattered in forests in parts of the highlands including Nairobi, Meru and Kakamega.

Bark: brown, easily recognised, distinctively mottled and scaling to show pale grey or orange underbark. **Leaves:** alternate, stiffly leathery, vivid glossy green ('lucida') above, up to 15 cm. in length, tapering abruptly to the apex; net-veins prominent, margin sharply serrated, with the teeth pointing forwards. **Flowers:** creamy-white to pale yellow, to 2 cm. across, on shortly-branched axillary stalks. **Fruit:** rounded and fleshy, with a pointed tip, 1 to 4 cm. in diameter, drying yellow-brown and eventually splitting open.

The wood is hard, heavy, pinkish-red, and very resistant to termites.

119

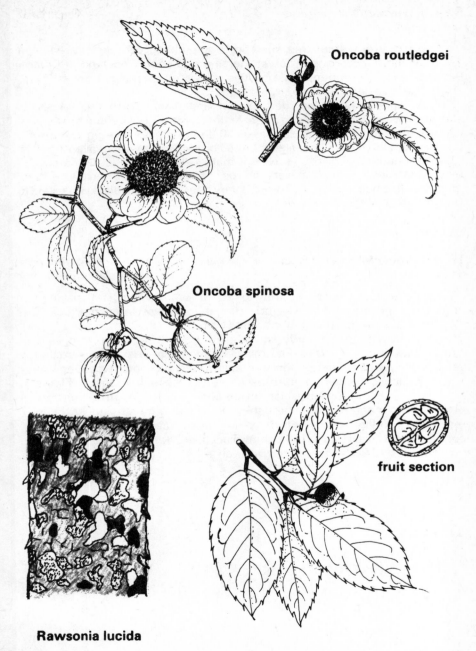

Oncoba routledgei

Oncoba spinosa

fruit section

Rawsonia lucida

120

FLACOURTIACEAE

Scolopia zeyheri *(Scolopia rigida)*   **Thorn pear**
indigenous

A spiny shrub or small tree, sometimes scrambling, occasionally reaching 15 m. or more, occurring at forest margins and open woodland in Central Province; common around Nairobi. The spines when present are stiff and sharp, usually axillary, 1.5 to 5 cm. in length.
Bark: light grey; rough, dark brown and flaking with age. **Leaves:** alternate, waxy dark green and stiffly leathery with age; size and shape very variable, oval to almost circular, up to 10 cm. in length; margin wavy, with unusual shallow serrations; apex blunted or notched; young leaves and leaf stalks sometimes reddish. **Flowers:** small, yellowish-white, with a central mass of stamens, in small axillary groups. **Fruit:** round red berries, to 1 cm. across, with a hair-like tip. The wood is very heavy and difficult to work, said to resemble that of the English pear.

Trimeria grandifolia ssp. tropica *(Trimeria tropica)*   **Wild mulberry**
indigenous   Muhindahindi (Kikuyu)

An understorey shrub or tree to 10 m. with twiggy, rather angular branchlets and large soft leaves, occurring in forest and forest margins from 1,800 to 2,300 m.; not uncommon around Nairobi.
Bark: greyish-brown, fairly smooth, flaking with age into thin vertical strips. **Leaves:** broadly oval to almost circular, up to 10 cm. in length, conspicuously veined from the base; margin serrated, apex rounded or notched; young leaves and stalks densely velvety, mature leaves more or less shiny above. **Flowers:** small, greenish, in crowded axillary spikes about 3 cm. in length which dry to a blackish colour and remain where they fall for many months under the tree, resembling mulberries. **Fruit:** dry yellow-brown capsules, to 5 mm. long, opening at the tip to release 1 to 2 shiny black seeds with a honeycomb pattern, half covered by a fleshy red cap known as an aril.

121

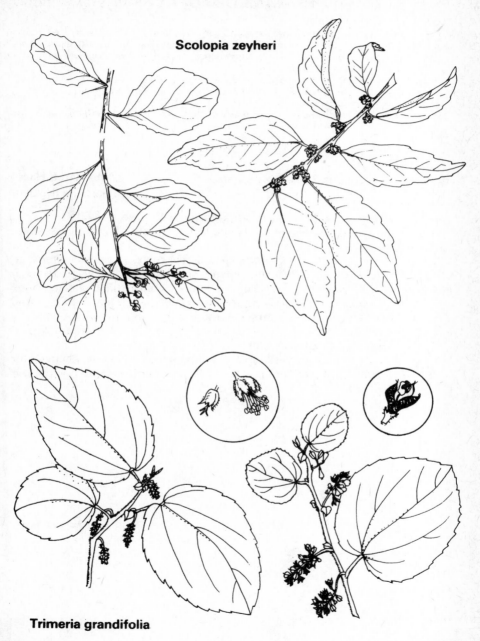

Scolopia zeyheri

Trimeria grandifolia

HAMAMELIDACEAE   Witch hazel family

A medium-sized family with about 100 species of deciduous trees and shrubs, centred in Asia but found in both hemispheres in temperate and sub-tropical climates. Several species yield fragrant resins used for gum, some like the North American Sweetgum *Liquidambar spp.* produce timber, and others have medicinal applications.

The North American Witch Hazel *Hamamelis virginiana,* with delicate yellow autumn leaves, produces the well-known soothing lotion. Witch hazel twigs have the unusual distinction of being favoured by water diviners for dowsing.

The genus *Trichocladus* is the only African genus in this family, and is distributed from East Africa through to Southern Africa.

Trichocladus ellipticus *(Trichocladus malosana)*   **White Witch Hazel**
 indigenous   Mubarakira (Kikuyu)

A scrambling shrub or thicket-forming evergreen tree growing to 10 m., often branching at ground level, occurring in forests from 1,200 to 2,800 m., often along streams.

Bark: grey, fairly smooth; branchlets softly rusty.   **Leaves:** alternate, glossy dark green above, contrasting silvery grey beneath, flecked with rusty dots; shape broadly elliptic, up to 15 cm. in length but usually shorter; apex tapering, base tapering to a 1 cm. stalk; midrib, veins and leaf stalk covered with rust-coloured hairs.   **Flowers:** yellow, strongly fragrant, in tight axillary or terminal heads to 2 cm. across, each flower with 5 strap-shaped petals.   **Fruit:** small round capsules.

The wood is hard and very tough, but bends easily and is widely used for poles for hut building. It was favoured by the Masai for the framework for their buffalo-hide shields.

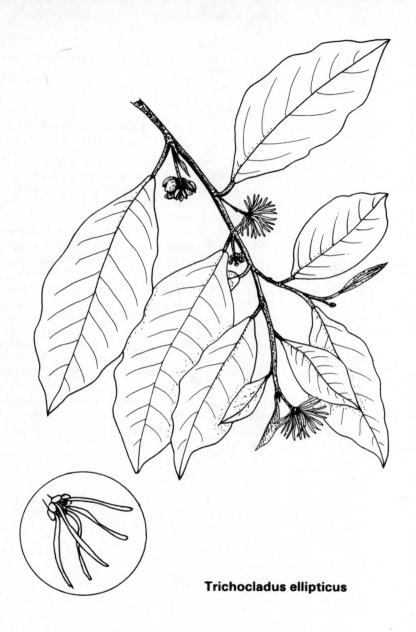

Trichocladus ellipticus

ICACINACEAE   Pear-wood family

A small family of trees, shrubs and climbers, almost all found in tropical rain-forest. A number of species produce valuable timber, and others have local uses for food, oils and medicine. All species have simple leaves and small, regular flowers.

Apodytes or Pear-wood is one of the few tall trees in the family, the genus being found also in Malaysia, N.E. Australia and Southern Africa.

Apodytes dimidiata
indigenous

Pear-wood, White Pear
Muganyoni (Kikuyu)

A tall forest tree, growing to 20 m. in high rainfall areas but elsewhere smaller and more rounded, often branching at the base. Widely distributed from the coast to 2,300 m., in forest ranging from the Shimba Hills to the Kakamega forest; common in the wet regions of southern and eastern Mt. Kenya, and occasionally found around Nairobi.

Bark: pale grey-brown, fairly smooth; darker, flaking and slightly fissured with age.   **Leaves:** alternate, shiny dark green above, drying black; shape variable, usually oval, up to 13 cm. long but often smaller; apex tapering, sometimes notched; margin very regularly wavy, sometimes slightly serrated; midrib paler, ridged only below, other veins inconspicuous, dividing irregularly. Young leaf stalks and part of the midrib are reddish, and the branchlets are generally thin and rather right-angled. **Flowers:** small, delicate white star-like with black anthers, fragrant, in striking terminal sprays over much of the tree. The flowering branchlets persist after the flowers fade, giving the tree a twiggy appearance. **Fruit:** small, 8 mm., flattened, black but not edible when ripe, with a fleshy scarlet appendage on one side giving the fruit a kidney shape.

The wood is light pink and very hard, much favoured in former times for making wagon wheels. Seedlings are said to be easy to raise, although they are slow-growing and need protection until they are established. This species makes an attractive, decorative garden tree.

125

Apodytes dimidiata

LAURACEAE Avocado family

A large tropical family of 2,500 species, centred in the rain forests of Southeast Asia and Brazil. The genus Ocotea, found in Africa from the Canary Islands to the Cape of Good Hope, contains several important timber trees such as the now rare South African Stinkwood *Ocotea bullata*.

Many species in this family contain aromatic oils used in drugs, soaps and perfumes. The Bay Laurel *Laurus nobilis* from the Mediterranean region is cultivated for the leaves used to flavour meat dishes, and the genus *Cinnamomum* provides both cinnamon and camphor. The Avocado *Persea americana* is widely planted in tropical and sub-tropical areas for its delicious fruit.

Members of this family in Kenya include *Ocotea, Persea.*

Ocotea usambarensis East African Camphor Wood
indigenous Muthaiti (Kikuyu)

A majestic evergreen timber tree with a massive trunk up to 3 m. across and a spreading crown, to 40 m. or more in height, the bole rarely straight, once a dominant tree in the wet forests of the eastern Aberdares and southern Mt. Kenya up to 2,600 m. and also in the Taita Hills, but now rare everywhere.

Bark: grey, granular, later reddish-brown, scaling in big rectangular flakes. **Leaves:** alternate, broadly oval to rounded, up to 8 cm. long; dark green above, whitish below, with strong brown veins; margin rolled under in mature leaves. **Flowers:** small, greenish-white, on short, branched stalks. **Fruit:** very small, hairy, 5 mm. long, held in a calyx cup.

Despite the common name and although the bark, leaves and wood are camphor-scented, they contain not camphor but a different oil. The timber is yellow-brown and hard, once much used for furniture and panelling.

Persea americana Avocado
Tropical America Mukorobea (Kikuyu)

A densely foliaged, evergreen tree to 10 m. or more, widely planted up to 2,200 m.; said to have been cultivated by the Aztecs 8,000 years ago.

Bark: grey to dark brown, rough and fissured with age. **Leaves:** large, alternate, to 20 x 10 cm., midrib and veins prominent; glossy dark green above, young leaves pinkish, turning lime-green. **Flowers:** small, abundant, pale yellow, in large terminal heads, only one in 5,000 flowers resulting in a fruit. **Fruit:** large, round to pear-shaped, the central seed surrounded by a thick layer of creamy, yellow-green flesh rich in fat, protein and vitamins.

There are some 300 cultivated varieties. Trees can be grown from seed, but may take 8 years to bear fruit and may not be true to type. Grafting is preferred, particularly for the variety 'Fuerte', of which Kenya exports large quantities to Europe. Trees reluctant to bear fruit apparently require shock treatment, such as cutting the roots in a trench, very narrow ring-barking or even beating the tree with a stick.

The bark, leaves and stones from the fruit are all toxic to browsing stock.

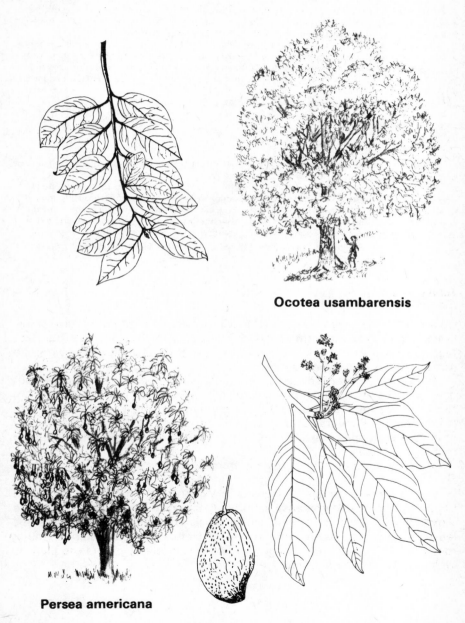

Ocotea usambarensis

Persea americana

LILIACEAE Lily family

The Lily family belongs amongst the Monocotyledons, the class of plants that includes the grass, banana, orchid, palm and sisal families. The Lily family is one of the largest of all families of flowering plants, and consists mainly of perennial herbs of worldwide distribution.

Tree-sized plants in this family are found in the genus *Aloe* as well as the genus *Dracaena*, although Dracaenas have only recently been moved back into the Lily family from their former classification amongst the *Agavaceae*. The stiff-leaved Agave family covers the commercial Sisal plant *Agave sisalana* as well as Yuccas, Furcraeas and similar plants grown in Kenya as garden ornamentals.

Members of the Lily family in Kenya include *Aloe, Dracaena*.

Aloe spp.

There are some 250 species of Aloe, all more or less succulent, the majority of them indigenous to the drier parts of Eastern, Central and Southern Africa.

The medicinal properties of some species were recognised in Europe as purgatives and tonics as much as four centuries ago, an outstanding example being *Aloe vera,* which probably originated in Southern Arabia or North Africa but which is now widely cultivated in tropical and sub-tropical regions. This plant has a long history in the treatment of burns and skin disorders, and today an extract from the pulp is much used in health preparations to soothe and heal the skin.

The collection of Aloes in Kenya is prohibited, but certain species are much eaten by elephants.

Aloe bainesii   Tree Aloe
South Africa

An unusual evergreen tree, 10 to 18 m. in height with a massive trunk, branching regularly to form a high, rounded crown. This species is native to high rainfall areas of South Africa, and has been planted in Kenya as an ornamental, especially in Nairobi.

Bark: grey-green, distinctively patterned, becoming smooth with age. **Leaves:** long and narrow, dull dark green, arching downwards in terminal rosettes; leaves up to 90 x 6 cm.; margins armed with small brown-tipped teeth. **Flowers:** orange to pinkish, tipped with green, in shortly branched, erect spikes up to 30 cm. long. **Fruit:** dry oval capsules, containing many small seeds.

This species is fairly fast growing, from cuttings or seed.

A common indigenous species in rocky bushland in the Mara, Narok and Kajiado areas is **Aloe volkensii,** commonly up to 4 m. but occasionally up to 7 m. in height. The thick stem is usually single and clothed with dead leaves; leaves are dull grey-green and spiny, up to 75 cm. long, in spreading terminal rosettes. The flowers are orange-red and very decorative, and the plant is widely grown as an ornamental in dry areas.

129

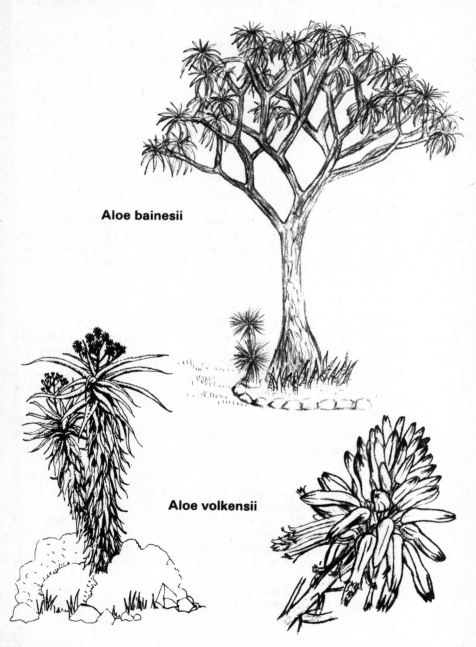

Aloe bainesii

Aloe volkensii

LILIACEAE

Dracaena spp. Dragon Trees

A palm-like genus with spine-free, straplike leaves in crowded terminal clusters, widely distributed in tropical Africa, Asia and Australia. The name of the genus comes from the Greek word for dragon, after a Mediterranean species with red resin in the trunk thought to resemble dragon's blood.

There are several indigenous species.

Dracaena ellenbeckiana *(Dracaena kedongensis)* Kedong Dracaena
indigenous

A spindly shrub or small tree with thin branches, usually about 4 m. but occasionally to 10 m. in height, found on dry slopes of the Rift Valley and in northern areas of Kenya.

Bark: dark grey, rather shiny, marked with leaf scars. **Leaves:** blue-green, in dense spreading terminal tufts; leaves very narrow, about 50 cm. in length, tapering gradually from a base only 2.5 cm. in width. **Flowers:** small, greenish, on terminal heads up to 75 cm. in length. **Fruit:** small berries, orange when ripe.

Dracaena steudneri Steudner's Dracaena
indigenous Muthare (Kikuyu)

A distinctive tree, growing to 12 m. or occasionally to 18 m., common in most high rainfall forest areas. Around Nairobi many are actual forest remnants, while others have been planted as ornamentals.

Bark: grey-brown, with horizontal markings from detached leaves. The trunk is often swollen at the base, and the few branches rise steeply from the woody stem. **Leaves:** dark shiny green, in large terminal rosettes; leaves over 1 m. in length, strongly fibrous, with no defined midrib or veins; centre thickened, margin crimped or partly wavy. **Flowers:** pale yellow-green, 6 narrow petals joined in a tube and 6 stamens; in tight terminal clusters on green branchlets forming a massive flowering head about a metre in height. The flowers open at night with a sharp sweet fragrance and fade next day. **Fruit:** small green berries, becoming red, later black and juicy, eaten by birds. The branchlets turn orange and are conspicuous and angular.

This species prefers moist forest soil, and is often planted as a boundary marker.

Both species of *Dracaena* are drought resistant and fast-growing from cuttings, and both are found in the grounds of the National Museum in Nairobi.

131

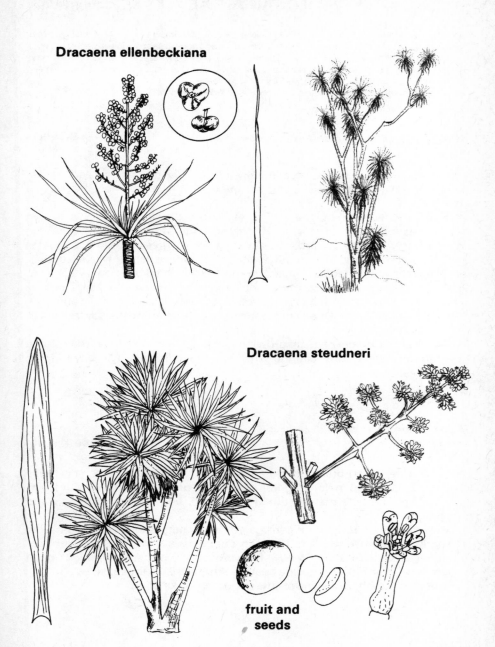

Dracaena ellenbeckiana

Dracaena steudneri

fruit and
seeds

LOGANIACEAE   Strychnos family

A diverse family of trees, shrubs and climbers with tubular flowers, often with a hairy throat. The family is found in both temperate and tropical areas, and some trees provide valuable timber.

The largest indigenous genus is *Strychnos,* and although very few local species have poisonous properties strychnine is extracted from the Indian species *Strychnos nux-vomica* and curare from the South American species *Strychnos toxifera.*

Members of this family in Kenya include *Buddleia, Nuxia, Strychnos.*

Buddleia polystachya *(includes Buddleia salvifolia)*   Buddleia
indigenous   Ruti (Kikuyu)

Commonly a tall shrub, occasionally a tree to 12 m., widespread in drier parts of the highlands above 2,000 m.; often seen as a high hedge in Kikuyu country.

Bark: reddish brown, the branchlets covered with dense, pale brown hairs.   **Leaves:** long, narrow, to 15 cm. in length; apex long and tapering, margin finely toothed towards the apex; light grey-green above, undersides and stems covered with dense, soft white hairs.   **Flowers:** very small, tubular, orange-yellow, hairy outside, in groups of 3 to 4 along flowering spikes up to 20 cm. in length; smell sharp, rather unpleasant.   **Fruit:** small dry capsules.

Branches are commonly used to wash cooking pots, as they are abrasive, making the water froth. Dried timber can be used for starting fires by friction, or used as kindling.

There are a number of quick-growing exotic species from Asia which make good ornamental shrubs, bearing white or mauve flowers, typically in long, thick spikes.

Nuxia congesta *(Lachnopylis congesta)*
indigenous   Muchorowe (Kikuyu)

A variable, much-branched tree, usually to 10 m. but occasionally twice that, locally common in drier high-altitude forest or forest margins from 1,500 to 2,800 m. The bole may be fluted or twisted, and the branches low and drooping.

Bark: blackish, rough and corrugated; branchlets 3 to 6-sided.   **Leaves:** dull dark green, broadly oval, to 12 cm. in length, usually in threes at the ends of branches; apex blunt or notched.   **Flowers:** small, white, sometimes tinged with mauve, in profuse congested heads.   **Fruit:** small hairy capsules.

The wood is soft, white and of little use except as kindling.

133

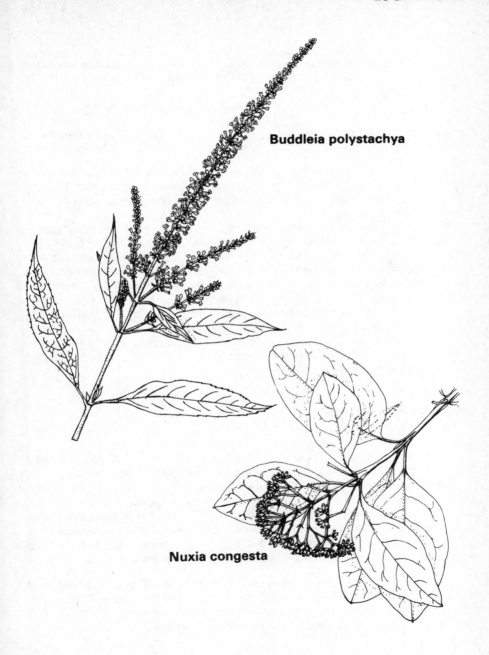

Buddleia polystachya

Nuxia congesta

LOGANIACEAE

Strychnos spp.

A genus of shrubs and trees, tending to scramble, with characteristic leaves borne in opposite pairs down the stem, each leaf with 3 to 5 veins radiating from the leaf base. Flowers are small and tubular, in groups, often with hairs inside the flower tube, and the fruit usually have seeds in a fleshy pulp. There are about ten indigenous species.

Strychnos henningsii *(Strychnos reticulata)*   Coffee-bean Strychnos
indigenous   Muteta (Kikuyu)

A very variable tree, usually dense and rounded, to 5 m. in height, occasionally growing to over 20 m., at first sight resembling an *Acokanthera;* occurring in drier localities from 500 to 1,850 m., common around Nairobi, often in remnant forest.
    Bark: pale grey-brown, darker with age.   **Leaves:** thick, leathery, glossy mid-green above, dull below; shape variable, broadly oval, to 6 cm. long but often smaller, with 3 strong veins from the base; apex sometimes rounded, sometimes tapering to a sharp tip; stalk very short, sometimes absent. Each pair of leaves is at right angles to the next pair along the stem.   **Flowers:** small, creamy-white fading to yellow, in dense axillary heads.   **Fruit:** small, rounded, fleshy, bright orange turning to dark purple, the thin pulp containing 1 or 2 white seeds which are grooved like a coffee-bean.
    The fruit and the bark contain toxic alkaloids and were used in traditional medicine as a purgative. A popular local soup, which is claimed to be an aphrodisiac, is made from the leaves.

Strychnos usambarensis
indigenous   Mutikani (Kikuyu)

A forest species growing to 10 m., not uncommon in mixed forest around Nairobi, also occurring in Central Province and in the Kakamega forest.
    Bark: dark grey, granulated; younger branches covered with breathing-pores.   **Leaves:** stiffy horizontal along the branchlets, smooth glossy dark green above, tapering to a long point, about 6 cm. long, often wider towards the base; veins from the base less prominent than *S. henningsii.*   **Flowers:** very small, greenish-white, in compact axillary heads; sweetly scented.   **Fruit:** small, about 1 cm. long, pointed, fleshy, waxy yellow when ripe.

The coastal savannah species known in Swahili as *Mtonga* is **Strychnos spinosa,** the branches bearing small thorns in scattered pairs. The fruit is unmistakeable, larger than a cricket ball, hard yellow-orange when ripe and edible, although the seeds within the pulp are poisonous.

135

Strychnos henningsii

Strychnos usambarensis

136

LYTHRACEAE   Pride of India family

A small tropical family centred in South-east Asia, containing some of the most ornamental of all flowering trees as well as some shrubs and many herbs. Petals are usually crumpled in the bud, unfolding to produce showy flowers; leaves are usually simple and opposite.

Several trees yield valuable timber, and some species produce dyes, henna dye being obtained from an indigenous Kenyan species *Lawsonia inermis,* also cultivated in other countries.

Members of this family in Kenya include *Lagerstroemia, Lawsonia.*

Lagerstroemia indica
Eastern Asia, Sri Lanka

**Pride of India,
Crepe Myrtle**

A shrubby, low-branching tree to 8 m. in height with stiff, erect branches, planted as an ornamental around Nairobi and elsewhere in the highlands.

Bark: grey, smooth; stems often square or ridged.   **Leaves:** dark green, often reddish, opposite, alternate or in whorls of 3 along the stems; leaves thick and fleshy, broadly oval, to 6 cm. long, often folded upwards from the midrib; apex pointed, veins hooped, tapering off before the margin.   **Flowers:** showy, about 3.5 cm. across, with 6 crinkly petals and golden-yellow stamens, in dense terminal heads; usually lilac-pink, sometimes white or crimson-purple.   **Fruit:** small woody capsules, dark brown when ripe.

Practical notes: a decorative ornamental with a fairly short flowering season, often seen pruned to medium height. Flowers only grow on the new season's wood. Can be grown from seed, but cuttings are more reliable.

An exotic species at the coast is **Lagerstroemia speciosa,** a much larger tree with leaves up to 30 cm. and crimson-purple flowers to 6 cm. across, in long-stemmed terminal heads.

Lawsonia inermis *(Lawsonia alba)*
indigenous

Henna, Zanzibar Bark
Mkokoa, Mhina (Swahili)

A shrub or small tree to 4 m., sometimes spiny, occurring in coastal districts and along river beds in northern areas; also widely distributed from North Africa and the Middle East to West and Central Africa.

Leaves: smooth, oval, about 2.5 cm. in length, often produced from short, spine-tipped branchlets; apex pointed, base tapering to a very short stalk; midrib depressed.   **Flowers:** small, sweet-scented, with 4 creamy-white petals crumpled in the bud, in long branching heads.   **Fruit:** small brown capsules, about 5 mm. in diameter, splitting into 4 sections.

The fruit and flowers are eaten by birds, and the foliage is eaten by game when grazing is scarce. The tree can be grown from seed or cuttings.

The orange-red dye known as henna is made by crushing dried leaves and shoots to a grey-green powder, soaking it in strong tea water and adding lemon juice. Henna has been used in Egypt, Arabia and the East from early times to stain fingers, toe nails, palms and soles with decorative patterns, particularly for Moslem weddings. It is used as a hair dye, a hair conditioner and as a fast colour for cloth and leather.

137

Lagerstroemia indica

Lawsonia inermis

MAGNOLIACEAE   Magnolia family

A medium-sized family of 12 genera, centred in South-east Asia and Japan and represented also in the warmer parts of North America. The family is notable for its large, showy flowers, and is thought by many botanists to be the most primitive family of flowering plants.

Magnolia itself is a genus of about 80 species of trees and shrubs, most of them producing beautiful white flowers. Magnolias prefer warm climates and rich, moist soil, and several species do well in gardens in the Kenya highlands.

Occasionally planted at high altitudes is the leafy North American hardwood *Liriodendron tulipifera*, the Tulip Tree or Yellow Poplar, a huge tree with truncated, maple-like leaves and striking orange and green tulip-like flowers.

There are no indigenous trees in this family, but one exotic species of the genus *Michelia* which has been widely planted in the tropics is fairly common around Nairobi and elsewhere in the highlands.

Michelia champaca
Himalayas, India, Java

**Fragrant Champaca,
Orange Champak.**

An evergreen tree with a rounded crown, usually to 10 m. but occasionally to 30m. in height, bearing some flowers for much of the year.

Bark: grey, smooth.   **Leaves:** large, oval, glossy mid-green above, paler and duller below; to 25 cm. in length, tapering to a pointed apex; side veins regular, tapering off before the margin; midrib prominent below.   **Flowers:** orange-yellow, turning brown, intensely fragrant, up to 7.5 cm. across, with 15 to 20 waxy, pointed sepals and petals in 3 whorls; stamens short, purple and white. The thick central greenish-white style persists after the petals have fallen.   **Fruit:** tight groups of green capsules, each 1 cm. long, covered in white wart-like dots, in crowded terminal clusters up to 15 cm. in length. The fruit turn from brown to black, splitting on the tree to release 2 to 5 tightly packed pink, angular seeds which produce a scented oil when crushed.

Champaca oil, distilled from the flowers, is used to make the finest French perfumes, and the tree is cultivated for this purpose in Madagascar and Reunion. This species originated in the Himalayas and is widely grown in India for timber and fuel. It also features frequently in Indian love poetry.

Michelia fuscata, an attractive evergreen shrub from China, has smaller, creamy-white flowers with a dark purple throat. The flowers are intensely fragrant, but only after four o'clock in the afternoon.

Practical notes: fairly fast-growing, preferring well-watered sites and good forest soil. In the highlands it makes a fine ornamental tree for gardens or avenues, and there seems to be no reason for it not to succeed at the coast. It can be grown from cuttings.

Michelia champaca

pink angular seeds

MALVACEAE   Hibiscus family

A cosmopolitan family with more shrubs or herbs than trees, centred in the tropics, particularly in South America, the most important economic plant being Cotton *Gossypium spp.,* with long hairs from the surface of the seeds which have been woven into cloth for thousands of years.

The largest genus in the family is *Hibiscus,* with some 300 species bearing well-known showy flowers, whose typical long central column is formed by the stalks of the stamens joined into a tube. The most familiar is *Hibiscus rosa-sinensis,* widely grown as an ornamental from the coast to the highlands and throughout the tropics; the many cultivated varieties range from pink to coral-red, yellow and orange, and many are trained as standards in the streets of Nairobi.

The bark and stems of many species yield tough fibres, and apart from experimental fibre crop species, two indigenous coastal trees in this family have bark which is used for cord. These are the Portia Tree *Thespesia populnea,* and the Tree Hibiscus *Hibiscus tiliaceus* near the mangrove belt. A striking tree in drier areas with yellow, Hibiscus-like flowers is *Azanza garckeana*.

Members of this family in Kenya include *Hibiscus, Lagunaria.*

Hibiscus schizopetalus   Coral Hibiscus,
indigenous   Fringed Hibiscus

A much-branched shrub or small tree to 5 m., sometimes stunted, occurring in coastal woodland, also widely planted at the coast as a garden ornamental; now common in many parts of the tropics.

Leaves: narrowly oval, to 10 cm. in length, tapering to the apex; base rounded, margin coarsely serrated.   **Flowers:** rose-pink to pale red with white markings, hanging from long, jointed stalks to 10 cm. in length, the 5 petals very deeply incised, twisted and curled back. The pink staminal tube hangs a further 8 cm. below the petals. Each flower lasts for only one day.   **Fruit:** dry, five-celled capsules, to 3 cm. long.

Like most Hibiscus, this species is grown from cuttings, but flowers only sparsely at higher altitudes. It has been widely used for cross-breeding.

Lagunaria patersonii   Pyramid Tree,
Queensland, Australia   Norfolk Island Hibiscus

An evergreen tree to 16 m. in height with upright branches; a species of coastal origin, but in Kenya also planted as a street tree in Nairobi.

Bark: grey, slightly rough, with narrow vertical fissures.   **Leaves:** alternate, oval, to 10 cm. in length, grey-green above, powdery pale grey to almost white beneath.   **Flowers:** rose-pink, to 6 cm. across, with 5 recurved petals and prominent yellow stamens on a short central column.   **Fruit:** dry, five-celled capsules, to 3 cm. long, drying light brown and splitting to reveal small, kidney-shaped seeds enclosed in barbed white hairs, which are so irritating to the skin that early Australian settlers called this the Cow Itch Tree.

Practical notes: fairly fast-growing from seed, tolerating sandy or black-cotton soil and salt-laden air; reasonably drought-resistant once established.

141

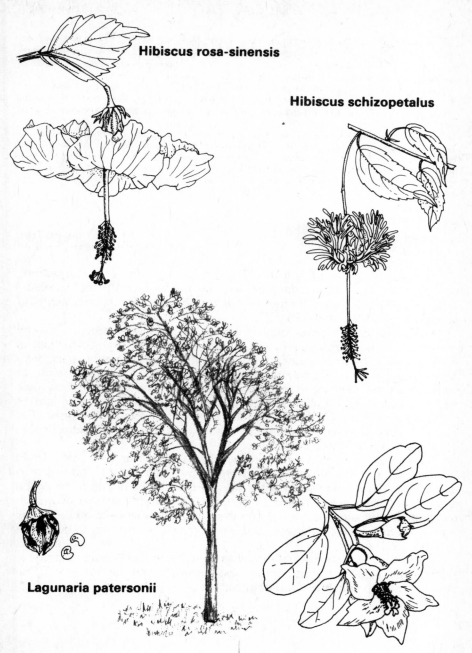

Hibiscus rosa-sinensis

Hibiscus schizopetalus

Lagunaria patersonii

MELIACEAE   Mahogany family

A family of trees and shrubs which includes several important timber trees, in particular the hardwood Mahogany from the rain forests of Africa and South America. The African Mahogany *Khaya anthotheca* is found only in Uganda, while in Kenya the indigenous *Trichilia emetica* or Cape Mahogany is now uncommon, although it is being replanted.

The tallest indigenous tree in Kenya is the stately Mukusu *Entandrophragma angolense,* up to 50 m. in height with the trunk clear up to 25 m. before branching steeply. In Kenya the tree is rare and confined to the Kakamega forest, but in Uganda it was an important timber and was exported as Budongo Mahogany.

The most noticeable trees in this family are three exotics, the ornamental Persian Lilac *Melia azedarach,* the coffee shade tree *Toona ciliata* and at the coast the well-known Neem Tree *Azadirachta indica.* Leaves are almost always compound, but the distinctive feature of the family is the ring of flower stamens, which are joined together to form a central tube.

Members of this family in Kenya include *Azadirachta, Ekebergia, Melia, Toona, Trichilia, Turraea.*

Azadirachta indica   **Neem Tree**
India, Sri Lanka   Mkilifi, Mwarubaini (Swahili)

A hardy, fast-growing tree to 18 m. in height with steeply ascending branches, deciduous only in drier areas; a valuable species with multiple uses, widely planted at the coast for fuel, timber and shade, and increasingly used in agroforestry in exhausted soils.

Bark: pale grey-brown, rough.   **Leaves:** fresh glossy green, crowded towards the ends of branches; leaves compound, with 5 to 8 pairs of leaflets up to 6 cm. long and a smaller terminal leaflet; apex pointed, base very asymmetric; margin coarsely toothed.   **Flowers:** small, fragrant, white or cream-coloured, hanging in long, few-flowered axillary sprays.   **Fruit:** oval greenish-yellow berries, about 2 cm. long, containing an aromatic oil which has medicinal properties and is used for treating skin diseases such as leprosy. The oil can be used as a paraffin substitute or to make soap, and the residue ('neem cake') is a good cattle feed and fertiliser.

The leaves contain azadirachtin, which is a powerful insecticide. Dried leaves placed amongst clothes will protect them from moths, and in stored grain will prevent insect attack without leaving any smell or aftertaste. At the coast green leaves are added to bonfires so that the smoke drives off mosquitoes and sandflies. A solution from the leaves sprayed on crops will protect them from locust attack, and attempts are being made to develop a commercial pesticide.

Tests of a drug from the leaf extract to treat chloroquin-resistant strains of malaria are at an advanced stage, and research also continues into the possible development of an oral contraceptive.

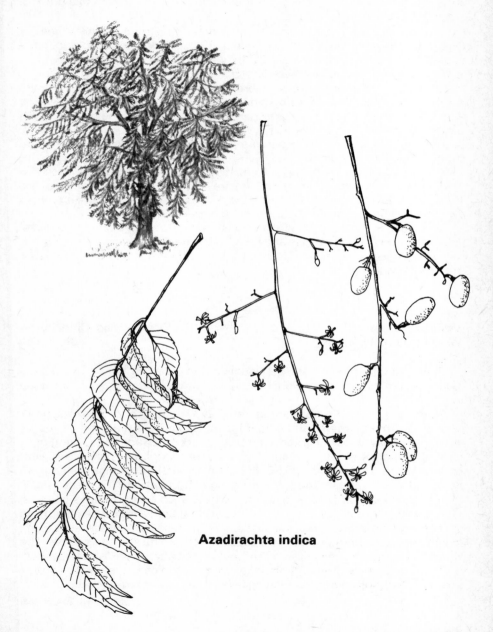

Azadirachta indica

MELIACEAE

Ekebergia capensis *(Ekebergia rueppeliana)*
indigenous

Cape Ash, Dogplum
Mununga (Kikuyu)

A large, ash-like deciduous tree with very wide distribution, sometimes in drier upland forest where it may reach 30 m., more commonly in open grassland near rivers, growing to 20 m. with a shady, spreading crown and making a popular venue for meetings or *barazas*.

Bark: grey, smooth, becoming brown and rough with age; branchlets conspicuously dotted with creamy-white breathing pores or lenticels. **Leaves:** compound, up to 30 cm. long, crowded at the ends of branches; leaflets thin glossy green, up to 5 pairs plus a terminal leaflet; leaflets up to 10 cm. long, tapering to base and apex; base asymmetric on lateral leaflets, with only the terminal leaflet having a stalk to 2 cm. **Flowers:** small, white tinged with pink, in loose axillary sprays up to 8 cm. long. The flowers are heavily scented and attract bees, so that beehives are commonly placed among the branches. **Fruit:** rounded, thin-skinned berries, up to 2.5 cm. in diameter, on long stalks in heavy bunches, yellow to red when mature.

The wood is tough and useful for household carpentry, but is not durable. Fresh seed germinates readily and the tree is fairly fast-growing, although so far young trees are difficult to find in nurseries. Well worth planting as an attractive shade tree.

Melia azedarach
Western Asia, Himalayas

**Persian Lilac, Chinaberry,
Bead Tree**

A deciduous ornamental tree, usually up to 10 m. in height with bushy foliage and trusses of lilac-coloured flowers; fairly widely planted in Kenya up to 2,000 m.

Bark: grey, smooth, becoming browner, rougher and furrowed with age; branchlets brown and knobbly, dotted with breathing pores or lenticels. **Leaves:** bright green at first, later dark green and shiny, hanging in terminal bunches; twice-compound, up to 40 cm. long, with 3 pairs of side ribs, each rib bearing 5 lance-shaped leaflets; leaflets to 8 cm. in length, tapering to base and apex; margin coarsely and irregularly toothed. **Flowers:** small, fragrant, pale lilac at first, later turning white, in profuse, rounded clusters; each flower to 1.5 cm. across, with a dark purple staminal tube protruding from the centre of 5 narrow, spreading petals. **Fruit:** fleshy yellow berries, 1.5 cm. in diameter, containing single hard seeds which can be strung as beads. The clusters of berries are conspicuous, and persist well after all the leaves are shed.

The berries are extremely poisonous, and human deaths as well as losses amongst stock and poultry from eating fallen fruit have been recorded.

(continued)

145

Ekebergia capensis

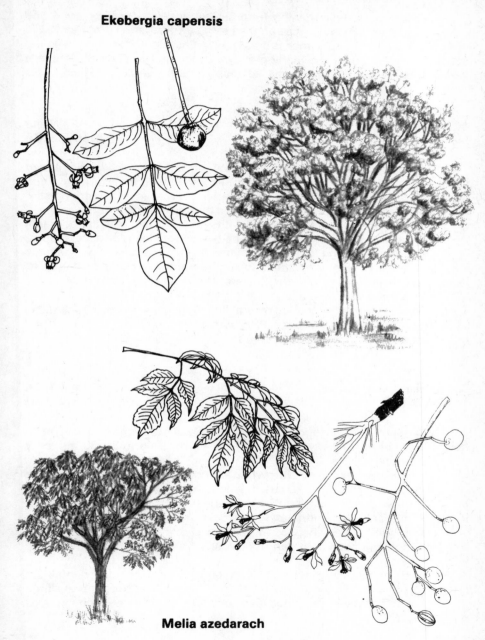

Melia azedarach

MELIACEAE

Melia azedarach (continued)

Practical notes: fast-growing from seed, but relatively short-lived and tending to rather unsightly shape after a few years. Flowering is attractive but in Nairobi fairly brief, and branches break easily. Best planted away from flower beds; the tree produces so many greedy suckers that in parts of Southern Africa where it has become naturalised this species is regarded as a pest.

Melia volkensii
indigenous

Melia
Mukau (Kikuyu)

A deciduous, open tree, sometimes growing to 15 m., widely distributed from sea-level to 1,200 m. in lower semi-arid savannah areas around Kitui, Machakos, Samburu, Taita and Voi. This species is also planted for agroforestry, as the fallen leaves provide a good mulch and the flowers encourage bees.

Bark: grey, fairly smooth, furrowed with age. **Leaves:** pale bright green, very noticeable in dry bush country; twice-compound, leaflets lance-shaped, up to 4 cm. long, tapering to the apex; margin slightly serrated. Young shoots are densely hairy. **Flowers:** small, white, fragrant, in loose sprays. **Fruit:** large, green, oval, to 4 cm. long, the clusters often conspicuous on the bare tree. The fruits are eaten by wild animals and goats.

The timber is pale reddish-brown, resembling mahogany, strong and durable, valued locally for a variety of uses. Propagation from root suckers has proved more successful than germination from seed, which is strangely erratic.

Toona ciliata *(Cedrela toona)*
Tropical Asia, S. China, Himalayas

Toona Tree,
Indian Mahogany

A large, spreading deciduous tree with a thickset trunk, growing to 15 m. in height, introduced to Kenya as a coffee shade tree up to 1,850 m.; fairly common around Nairobi.

Bark: dark grey, very rough, furrowing and cracking into squares. **Leaves:** compound, very large, up to 90 cm. in length, with 10 to 14 pairs of leaflets; leaflets narrow, up to 15 cm. long, often unequal-sided, tapering to a fine tip at the apex; margin wavy, midrib and veins contrasting light green. **Flowers:** very small, white, bell-shaped, in inconspicuous sprays. **Fruit:** brown capsules, splitting open into dark brown star shapes and releasing small, winged seeds.

Practical notes: fast-growing, best on good red soil with fair rainfall but tolerant of other conditions and considerable drought; best suited to very large gardens or golf courses. The wood is red and soft, and the tree probably does not live to great age.

147

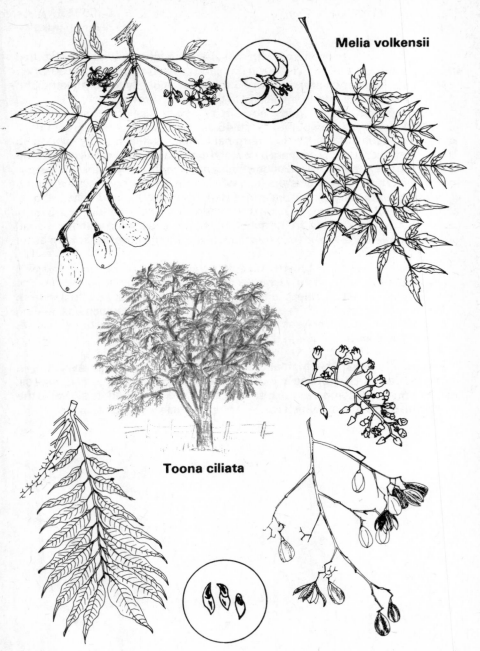

Melia volkensii

Toona ciliata

MELIACEAE

Trichilia emetica *(Trichilia roka)*   **Cape Mahogany**
indigenous   Mururi (Kikuyu)

A handsome evergreen tree with dark, hanging foliage, widely distributed from the coast to 1,850 m. The tree in highland forest is pyramid-shaped when young, later large and spreading, to 15 m. or occasionally to 30 m. in height; in drier savannah the tree is smaller, with thick, corky, greyish bark.

Bark: reddish-brown, fairly smooth or finely scaling to show green underbark. **Leaves:** compound, up to 45 cm. long; leaflets dark green, thick and glossy, usually 4 pairs plus a terminal leaflet; leaflets broadly oval, up to 16 cm. long; midrib very prominent below and extended to an unusual hair-like tip beyond the apex; margin rolled under; stalks and shoots softly hairy. **Flowers:** in inconspicuous axillary clusters, dull white, fragrant, to 3 cm. across, with 5 thick petals and a hairy central column of stamens. **Fruit:** round, velvety brown capsules, 3 cm. in diameter, crimson when ripe and splitting into 3 or 4 sections. The black seeds are attached by thread-like stalks, with each seed almost completely enclosed in a fleshy, brilliant orange covering known as an aril.

The timber is pinkish-brown and soft, darkening with age, polishing well but suitable only for indoor furniture as it is attacked by borer beetle. The specific name 'emetica' refers to the long-recognised use of an infusion from the bark as a purgative. The seeds contain a high quality oil which has healing properties on cuts and bruises and can be used to make soap, but seeds are extremely poisonous, although the toxin is unknown.

Practical notes: the highland forest form is increasingly available in nurseries; fairly fast-growing in well-watered sites, preferring good forest soil. Makes a fine, spreading avenue tree. The large, drooping leaflets swivel in the wind in an unusual way, which can be a helpful guide to recognition.

149

Trichilia emetica

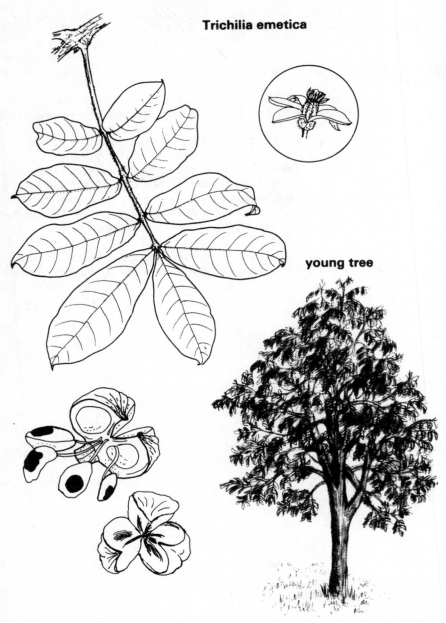

young tree

MELIACEAE

Turraea spp.

The only genus in this family with simple rather than compound leaves, represented by a dozen indigenous species of small trees or shrubs. The fruit capsules of all Turraea contain several black seeds, each of which is partly covered with a fleshy red or yellow aril.

Turraea robusta *(Turraea volkensii)*
indigenous

Honeysuckle tree
Mutinene (Kamba)

A small tree to 9 m with creamy-white flowers, widely distributed from sea-level to 1,850 m.; common in Machakos and Kitui districts and also found in the Nairobi area.

Bark: grey; young branchlets densely hairy. **Leaves:** shiny dark green, softly hairy beneath, less so above; broadly oval, to 15 cm. in length; apex rounded, stalk short. **Flowers:** in dense clusters, creamy-white, yellowing with age, faintly fragrant, 2.5 cm across with narrow, strap-like petals and the prominent orange staminal tube characteristic of the family. **Fruit:** round but flattened capsules, about 1.5 cm. across, green drying brown, distinctive when split open, resembling small woody stars on the ground under the tree.

The common shrubby species at forest margins around Nairobi is **Turraea mombassana,** with small leaves and conspicuous upright white flowers, which are usually solitary in the leaf axils but produced in considerable numbers.

151

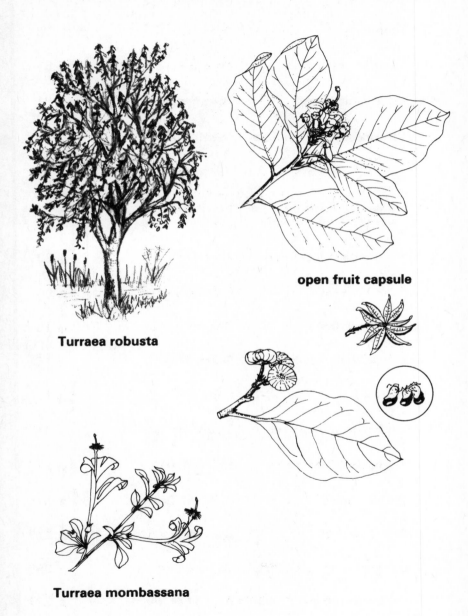

Turraea robusta

open fruit capsule

Turraea mombassana

COLOUR PLATES

153

PLATE I

Kigelia africana   **Sausage Tree**

PLATE II

BIGNONIACEAE

Tecoma stans
- page 35

PLATE III

CAESALPINIOIDEAE

Bauhinia variegata

Orchid Tree

- page 53

PLATE IX

Delonix regia   **Flamboyant**

Acacia elatior **River Acacia**

PLATE XI

Acacia xanthophloea   **Fever Tree**

Ficus sur   **Cape Fig**

PLATE XIII

PALMAE

Hyphaene compressa   **Doum Palm**

Erythrina abyssinica

**Flame Tree,
Red Hot Poker Tree**

PLATE XV

Tipuana tipu   **Pride of Bolivia**

PLATE XVI

Grevillea robusta   **Silky Oak**

PLATE XVII   RUTACEAE

Calodendrum capense   **Cape Chestnut**

PLATE XVIII

Brachychiton acerifolium

Australian Flame

MIMOSOIDEAE Acacia Sub-family of Leguminosae

LEGUMINOSAE, the pod-bearing family, is the third largest of all families of flowering plants, with some 17,000 species distributed worldwide in a variety of habitats. The family is of major economic importance as a source of food, fodder, timber and other products.

This enormous family is divided into three major sub-families, the Cassia sub-family **Caesalpiniodeae,** the Acacia sub-family **Mimosoideae** and the Pea sub-family **Papilionoideae.** However, two botanical features are common throughout. Firstly, the fruit is always a one-chambered pod, called a legume. Secondly, the root nodules contain bacteria which are able to take up nitrogen from the air and incorporate it into the living cells, so that eventually the plant can use it. This remarkable ability to fix atmospheric nitrogen means that legumes will grow in relatively poor soil which itself has little available nitrogen.

As a result several exotic leguminous trees have been widely introduced into Kenya for interplanting with crops, among them *Calliandra, Leucaena, Prosopis* and *Samanea*. These, together with many other species of mainly tropical origin, are classified in the sub-family **Mimosoideae.**

MIMOSOIDEAE

The best-known of the many indigenous genera in this sub-family is the Thorn Tree genus *Acacia.* Kenya has over 60 indigenous species, and they are a familiar and characteristic part of the African landscape. Some are found in very dry conditions, and others where there is a high water table. All indigenous species bear spines or thorns (Greek *akis*: a sharp point) and twice-compound leaves sub-divided into feathery leaflets, which are almost always shed in the dry season. Flowers are regular, often very small, with more than twice as many stamens as petals, and the flower heads are in two distinctive shapes, one a spike and the other a sphere.

The principal exotic species of *Acacia* come from Australia, where they are known as Wattles. By contrast with the indigenous acacias, the exotic species have no thorns. The Australian Black Wattle *Acacia mearnsii* is economically important because of the tannin extracted from its bark, which is used in tanning leather.

The indigenous acacias are described as 'taxonomically difficult', and some species can be very variable. The most distinctive features for identification are probably the seed pods and the thorns, but the bark, the colour and shape of the flower heads and the general appearance of the tree can also help. Differences in the leaves are less easy to distinguish, and have been omitted in most cases.

The summary devised for the following two pages is included for ease of reference, but should not be seen as more than a rough guide.

Members of the Mimosoideae sub-family in Kenya include *Acacia, Albizia, Dischrostachys, Enterolobium, Newtonia.*

154

Summary Guide to the commo

Name	Detailed texts	Usual shape and size	Bark

Group A — the smaller Acacias

	Name	Detailed texts	Usual shape and size	Bark
a.	Acacia brevispica		Usu. scrambler or to 3m.	Grey; twigs zig-zag
b.	A. drepanolobium	page 157	Usu. shrub or c. 3m.	Grey to black, rough
c.	A. hockii		Usu. tree to 6m.	Greenish, peeling, to rough dark brown
d.	A. mellifera		Usu. shrub or small tree	Pale grey-brown, usu. smooth N.B. few broad leaflets
e.	A. nilotica	page 159	Usu. tree to 6m.	Dark, rough, fissured
f.	A. reficiens		Obconical shrub or c. 4m.	Grey to brown, fissured
g.	A. senegal		Usu. tree 4 to 12 m.	Yellow-brown, peeling
h.	A. seya!	page 161	Usu. tree 4 to 12 m.	Green-white, occ. orange-red, powdery
i.	A. stuhlmannii		Usu. spreading bush	Reddish-brown; shoots hairy

Group B — the larger Acacia trees

	Name	Detailed texts	Usual shape and size	Bark
j.	A. abyssinica		to 20 m., flat crown	Dark brown, rough
k.	A. albida	page 163	to 30 m., spreading or upright.	Dull grey; branchlets whitish
l.	A. elatior		to 40 m., riverine	Brown to black, fissured
m.	A. gerrardii		to 15 m., flat to irregular	Dark grey-brown, fissured
n.	A. kirkii	page 165	to 15 m., layered	Bronzy-green, peeling
o.	A. lahai		to 15 m., flat-topped	Grey to dark brown, ¡ rough
p.	A. polyacantha	page 167	to 20 m., upright	Yellow to grey, fissured
q.	A. sieberiana		to 18 m., umbrella	Grey to brown, rough or flaking
r.	A. tortilis	page 169	to 20 m., spreading	Grey to black, fissured
s.	A. xanthophloea		to 25 m., tall, spreading	Green-yellow, smooth, powdery

155

	Spines (in pairs unless indicated)	Flowers (heads round unless indicated)	Pods
a.	Hooked prickles, single, scattered	Creamy-white	Straight, thin, flat, to 15 cm.
b.	Hooked or straight; ant galls	Creamy-white	Narrow, curved, to 7 cm.
c.	Straight, weak, to 2 cm.	Orange-yellow	Narrow, curved, to 15 cm.
d.	Hooked prickles, black-tipped	*Spikes to 4 cm. White or cream	Short, wide, papery, to 8 cm.
e.	Straight, slender, short or to 8 cm.	Golden yellow	Thick, fleshy, variable, to 17 cm.
f.	Hooked prickles, grey brown	White or cream	Straight, narrow to 8 cm.
g.	Hooked prickles, in threes	*Spikes to 10 cm. White to cream	Straight, wide, to 15 cm.
h.	Straight, to 8 cm., sometimes absent	Bright yellow, large	Curved, narrow, shiny, to 20 cm.
i.	Straight, to 5 cm.	White, pinkish	Usu. straight, thick, hairy, to 9 cm.
j.	Short, straight, sometimes absent	White, buds reddish	Straight, rough, to 12 cm.
k.	Straight, to 2 cm.	*Spikes to 14 cm. Creamy-white	Orange, large hoops and spirals
l.	Short brown and straight white, some to 9 cm.	White to pale yellow	Usu. straight, oblong, to 12 cm.
m.	Usu. short, stout, straight or hooked	White or cream	Curved, to 22 × 2 cm.
n.	Straight, diverging, small or to 8 cm.	White, buds reddish	Straight, constricted, to 9 cm.
o.	Straight, small or to 7 cm.	*Spikes to 7 cm. White to yellowish	Short, wide, shiny, to 7 cm.
p.	Hooked, prickles, sometimes absent	*Spikes to 12 cm. Creamy-white	Straight, thin, to 18 cm.
q.	Straight, to 10 cm., often absent	White to pale yellow	Curved, thick, hard, to 21 cm.
r.	Short, hooked, and long straight to 8 cm.	White or cream	Spirally twisted, or rings
s.	Straight, diverging, to 10 cm.	White or pale pink	Usu. straight, constricted, to 13 cm.

156

MIMOSOIDEAE

Acacia spp.   **Thorn Trees**

Acacia brevispica   **Wait-a-bit Thorn**
                                                          Mwikunya (Kikuyu)

A low shrub or small tree, often scrambling, very widespread in thickets, bushland and forest margins from sea-level to 2,100 m., regenerating rapidly after clearing.

Bark: grey; young stems hairy and characteristically zig-zag. **Spines:** small single prickles, mostly hooked, scattered along the stems on longitudinal ridges. **Flowers:** in round heads on 3 cm. stalks, creamy-white, borne on branching stalks to 10 cm. long. **Pods:** usually straight, to 15 cm. but often smaller, dotted with small reddish glands; mature pods thin purple-brown with a raised area over each seed, splitting on the tree.

Acacia drepanolobium   **Whistling Thorn,**
                                                          Ant-galled Acacia

A shrub or gregarious tree to 6 m., abundant on poorly-drained black-cotton and clay soils or on stony ground from 600 to 2,500 m.; common in the Nairobi National Park and easily recognised by swollen black galls at the base of larger spines, which are hollow and inhabited by ants.

Bark: dark grey to black, rough, finely fissured. **Spines:** in pairs of two kinds, small hooked prickles or straight, grey-white, to 7 cm. **Flowers:** in round heads, creamy-white, fragrant, appearing before the leaves; much eaten by giraffe. **Pods:** narrow, sickle-shaped, to 7 cm., reddish-brown or black, splitting on the tree with the seeds hanging out on thread-like stalks.

The young galls, pods and leaves are eaten by game, and the bark and roots have medicinal uses. The wood is hard, widely used for fuel and charcoal.

Acacia hockii   Mugaa (Kikuyu)
                                                          Luaa (Masai)

Usually a spindly tree to 6 m. but occasionally twice that, often with a sparsely rounded crown, very widespread in wooded grassland and savannah to 2,100 m.; often associated with overgrazing.

Bark: greenish-brown, thinly peeling and papery, becoming rough dark brown; branchlets reddish-brown, sticky and hairy. **Spines:** in pairs, straight and rather weak, usually less than 2 cm., sometimes absent. **Flowers:** in small round heads, orange-yellow. **Pods:** narrow, strongly sickle-shaped, to 15 cm., reddish-brown with black dots, splitting on the tree with the seeds hanging out on thread-like stalks.

The name of the Ololua Forest near Ngong comes from the Masai name. Branches are used for making bomas, and the bark for making rope.

157

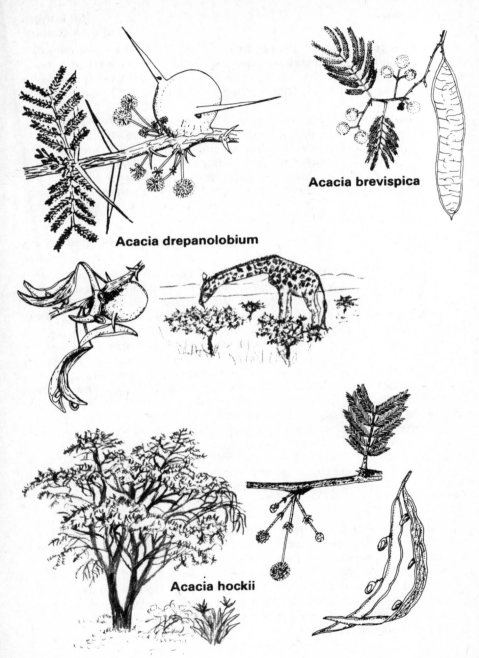

Acacia brevispica

Acacia drepanolobium

Acacia hockii

Acacia mellifera

Hook-thorn
Muthia (Kamba)

Usually a spiky, spreading shrub to 2 m., less often a tree to 8 m., often gregarious, widespread in very dry areas in Northern Province but also found from Ngong to Magadi, in Nairobi National Park and in Kilifi district. The leaves are unusual and distinctive, not feathery, with only 2 or 3 pairs of broad blue-green 2 cm. leaflets.

Bark: generally pale grey-brown, mostly smooth.   **Spines:** hooked prickles, in pairs, grey with black tips, abundant and highly effective.   **Flowers:** in closely-packed spikes to 4 cm., white or cream, attracting many bees and sunbirds (*'mellifera'*: bearing honey).   **Pods:** short, wide, tapering abruptly at both ends, rarely to 8 cm., pale brown to straw-coloured, thin to almost papery.

A devastatingly thorny species, rapidly forming impenetrable thickets. Pods, twigs, leaves and flowers are much eaten by game and stock. The wood makes good fuel and excellent charcoal.

Acacia nilotica *(Acacia arabica)*

Egyptian Thorn, Scented-pod Acacia
Mgunga (Swahili)

An exceedingly variable species, seldom exceeding 6m., often bushy, with the crown flat or umbrella-shaped, common in dry coastal areas in sand or alluvial soil; also found on heavy black-cotton or poor soils in arid areas.

Bark: brown, becoming blackish, rough and deeply fissured; young shoots typically red-brown and hairy.   **Spines:** in pairs, slender, sharp and whitish, to 8 cm. but usually much smaller, often pointing downwards.   **Flowers:** in round heads, bright golden yellow, fragrant.   **Pods:** straight or curved, to 17 x 2 cm. The coast subspecies is narrow, black and shiny when mature, sometimes sticky, constricted, with a raised boss over each seed. The common species inland is green and fleshy when young, darker with age, usually velvety. Pods have a fruity odour and break up on the ground.

Fast-growing in favourable conditions, the leaves and pods providing good fodder. The tree bears full leaf in the dry season, but is often very thorny. Infusions from the bark, leaves and roots are widely used in traditional medicine. The wood is hard, tough and termite-resistant, with many farm uses.

Acacia reficiens

False Umbrella Thorn
Eregai (Turkana)

A shrub or tree to 7 m., mostly flat-topped and shaped like an inverted cone, branching near the base; locally common in dry grassland in Northern Province, Teita district, Ukambani and Kora.

Bark: grey to brown, vertically fissured.   **Spines:** hooked prickles, in pairs, grey brown.   **Flowers:** in round heads, white or cream.   **Pods:** straight, narrow, reddish-brown, hairless, to 8 cm., marked with longitudinal veins.

The bark yields a strong fibre, and the foliage is eaten by game and stock where little else is available.

159

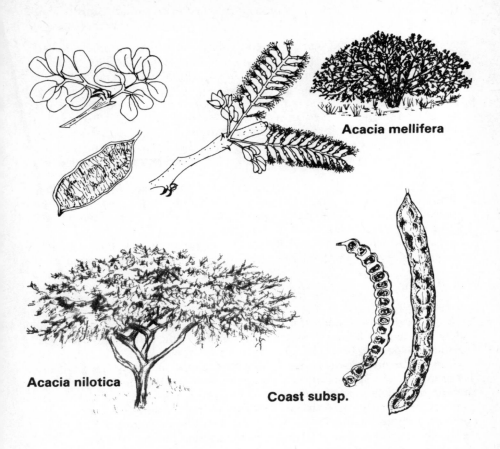

Acacia mellifera

Acacia nilotica

Coast subsp.

Acacia reficiens

Acacia senegal

Three-thorned Acacia, Sudan Gum Arabic
Kikwata (Swahili)

A shrub or tree to 12 m., slow-growing, very variable, usually low-branched and rounded when young, flattened when mature, often forming thickets; widespread in dry grassland in Northern Province, Machakos and Kajiado.

Bark: waxy yellow-brown to red-brown, peeling yellow and papery. **Spines:** broad-based prickles in threes, the central one hooked downwards and the lateral ones curved upwards; occasionally solitary. **Flowers:** in spikes to 10 cm., white or cream, fragrant, scattered, usually appearing before the leaves. **Pods:** variable, flat, oblong, to 15 cm. but usually shorter, tapering to both ends, furry grey-yellow, later papery brown, with prominent veins and few seeds.

This species is drought-resistant, valuable in dryland agroforestry and for erosion control. Foliage and pods are a protein-rich fodder, much eaten by rhino, camels, sheep and goats. The hard wood is used for poles and fuel, and the root fibres for fishnets.

In Sudan and northern Kenya the tree is tapped for gum arabic, a valuable additive used in beer, confectionery, pharmaceuticals and other industries.

Acacia seyal

White Thorn
Musewa (Kamba)

A gregarious, irregularly flat-topped tree to 12 m., sometimes shrubby, widely distributed in dry grassland in Central, Rift Valley and Northern Provinces, especially on black-cotton, alluvial or stony soils.

Bark: distinctive, powdery, pale greenish-yellow to almost white, occasionally orange-red. **Spines:** in diverging pairs, straight, white, stout, to 8 cm., sometimes smaller or absent altogether. Some varieties may bear ant-galls. **Flowers:** in profuse, large round heads, bright yellow, fragrant, usually appearing before the leaves. **Pods:** narrow, sickle-shaped, to 20 cm., shiny red-brown, slightly constricted between the seeds, splitting on the tree.

The tree produces an edible medium-quality gum, widely used in traditional medicine to treat colds, dysentry and stomachache.

Acacia stuhlmannii

Munga (Swahili)

Usually a low, spreading bush, sometimes a rather variable tree to 6 m. shaped like an inverted cone, common on badly-drained soils at the coast and scattered in other areas up to 1,600 m. Young shoots, stalks and pods are covered with golden hairs, which later turn grey.

Bark: reddish-brown, sometimes peeling. **Spines:** in pairs, straight, pale brown, up to 5 cm. **Flowers:** in round heads, white with mauve anthers, appearing pinkish. **Pods:** thick, almost inflated, straight or slightly curved, to 9 cm., hard, dark brown, densely hairy.

Young trees are planted to establish cover on swampy soils.

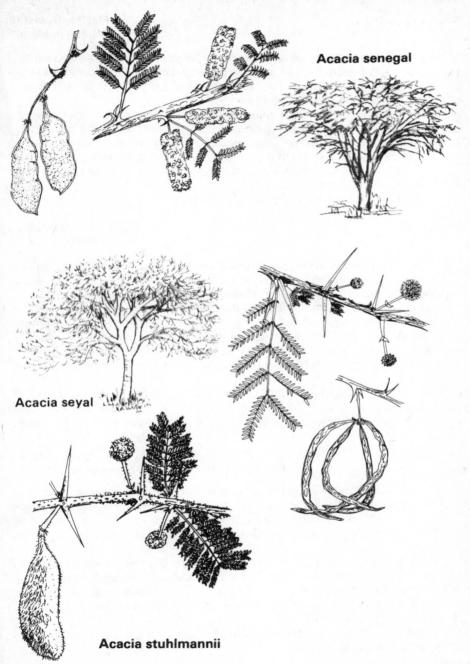

Acacia senegal

Acacia seyal

Acacia stuhlmannii

162

Acacia abyssinica

Flat-top Acacia
Mugaa (Kikuyu)

A large acacia to 20 m. with very feathery foliage and branches ascending steeply to a very flat crown, occurring at the edges of highland forest down to Limuru and Muguga and in wooded grassland from 1,800 to 2,400 m.; common in Western and Nyanza Provinces.

Bark: brown to almost black, rough and fissured. Young trees have papery, peeling bark.   **Spines:** in pairs, pale grey, straight, usually less than 2 cm.; sometimes absent.   **Flowers:** buds reddish, flowers in round heads, white when fully open.   **Pods:** rough grey-brown with dark dots, straight or nearly so, to 12 x 1 cm., prominently veined, splitting on the tree or on the ground. The seeds lie obliquely in the pod.

A fine ornamental tree, fairly fast-growing.

Acacia albida

Apple-ring Acacia
Olasiti (Masai)

One of the tallest of the acacias, sometimes to 30 m. with a high, spreading crown, widely distributed from 550 to 1,800 m., often riverine in dry areas or where the water table is near the surface; common in Rift Valley and Coast Provinces and widely used in dryland agroforestry.

Bark: dull grey, fissured and scaling; branchlets zig-zag, whitish.   **Spines:** in pairs, straight, to 2 cm., often pointing downwards.   **Flowers:** in slender spikes to 14 cm., creamy-white, attracting bees.   **Pods:** distinctive, smooth bright orange, thick, to 25 cm., concave, sickle-shaped or contorted into hoops and spirals.

This species has a deep taproot system, fast-growing even in poor soils if groundwater is adequate. The tree is nitrogen-fixing; leaves are retained in the dry season and fall in the rains, and both leaves and pods are excellent fodder.

Acacia elatior

COLOUR PLATE X

River Acacia
Muswiswa (Kamba)

A tall riverine acacia, which may reach 40 m. with a large trunk and feathery, hanging foliage, found only in the arid areas of northern and eastern Kenya from 180 to 1,100 m., the main subspecies not known elsewhere, sometimes locally common on sandy river banks, as in Samburu Game Reserve.

Bark: brown to almost black, deeply fissured.   **Spines:** of two kinds, short brown spines, sometimes curved, alternating with long, straight white spines, which may reach 9 cm. and have a swollen base.   **Flowers:** in round heads, white to very pale yellow.   **Pods:** brown to purplish-brown, narrowly oblong, straight or nearly so, to 12 cm.

The branches are used for bomas and firewood, and a decoction from the bark used to treat diarrhoea.

163

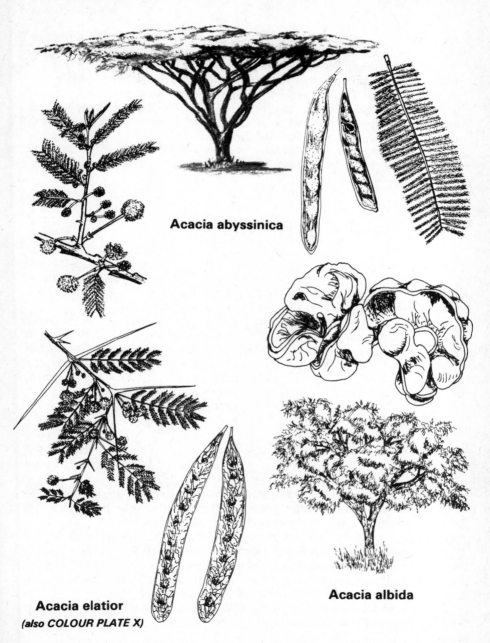

Acacia abyssinica

Acacia elatior
(also COLOUR PLATE X)

Acacia albida

Acacia gerrardii

Gerrard's Acacia
Muthii (Kamba)

A tree to 15 m., occasionally shrubby, with a rather sparse umbrella-shaped or irregular crown, widely distributed in wooded grassland from 1,300 to 2,100 m., including Nairobi and Machakos districts.

Bark: dark grey-brown to black, rough and fissured; branchlets covered with grey velvety hairs. **Spines**: in pairs, stout, sometimes hooked, mostly to 1 cm. **Flowers**: in profuse round heads, white or cream, attracting many insects. **Pods**: sickle-shaped, fairly narrow, to 22 x 1 cm., smooth grey-brown with darker dots, finely hairy, often thickly clustered.

A fast-growing species, attractive in flower. Decoctions of the bark are widely used in traditional medicine to treat coughs and sore throat.

Acacia kirkii

Kirk's Acacia
Ol-erai (Masai)

A handsome, distinctive acacia to 15 m., flat-topped when young, layered when mature, with branches radiating from low down the stout trunk, occurring in riverine woodland, grassland and areas of seasonal drainage from 1,500 to 1,900 m., mainly in Central and Southern Provinces.

Bark: bronzy-green, peeling thinly in yellow-brown scrolls to reveal bright greenish-yellow underbark. **Spines**: in pairs, often widely diverging, straight, small or to 8 cm., greyish-white. **Flowers**: buds reddish-pink, flowers in round heads, creamy white when fully open, fragrant. **Pods**: young pods pink and sticky, mature pods brown, straight or nearly so, to 9 cm., fairly broad, constricted between the seeds with a raised boss over each seed.

Acacia lahai

Red Thorn
Oltepessi (Masai)

A conspicuously flat-topped acacia to 15 m., occurring in grassland and woodland in cool upland districts from 1,500 to 2,500 m.; common in the Rift Valley, for instance towards Kericho. A few have been planted in Nairobi.

Bark: grey to dark brown, rough and fissured; branchlets dark brown and hairy. **Spines**: in pairs, straight, pale grey, small or to 7 cm. **Flowers**: in spikes to 7 cm., white, cream or pale yellow, the flower branchlets covered with red glands. **Pods**: broad, straight or curved, to 7 x 3 cm., shiny brown, splitting on the tree to release many flat, round seeds.

The wood is red and very hard, heavy and durable, useful for fence posts, bridge timbers and heavy construction work.

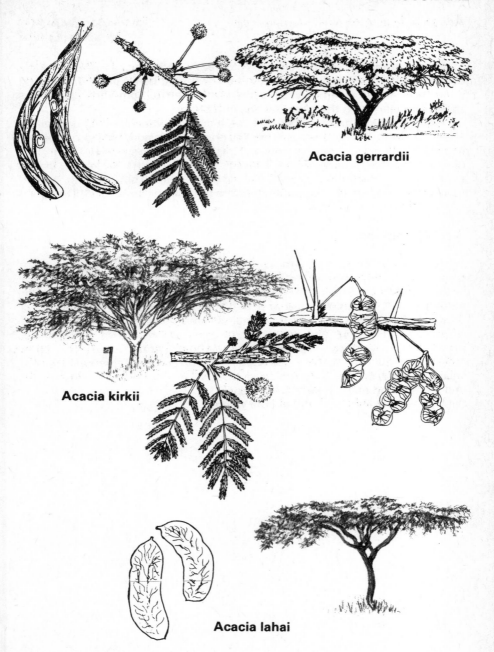

Acacia gerrardii

Acacia kirkii

Acacia lahai

166

Acacia polyacantha *(Acacia campylacantha)*

Falcon's Claw Acacia
Musewa (Kamba)

A fast-growing, upright acacia with feathery foliage, to 20m., widely distributed from 200 to 1,800 m.; common near river banks around Thika and Tana River and in swampy valleys in western Kenya. Some fine specimens have been planted in the central areas of Nairobi.

Bark: yellowish to grey, fissured, variable, sometimes flaking or scaling. The trunk and branches may bear hooked prickles on woody bosses. **Spines:** in pairs, small hooked prickles, pale or dark. **Flowers:** in spikes to 12 cm., two or more together, creamy-white, fragrant, flowering with new leaves; flower stalks hairy. **Pods:** long, straight, flat, tip pointed, to 18 cm., smooth, brown.

The wood is very resinous and therefore termite-resistant, useful for fence posts and farm implements.

Acacia sieberiana

A tall, spreading tree to 18 m., with an umbrella-shaped or irregular crown, occurring in wooded grassland from near sea-level to 1,850 m. in Rift Valley, Nyanza and Coast Provinces. The more spreading varieties found at higher altitudes have branchlets covered with hairs, while the lower altitude variety does not. Some trees are found in the Nairobi area, but may have been planted.

Bark: usually grey and rough, sometimes yellow-brown and flaking, especially on branches. **Spines:** in pairs, whitish, straight, to 10 cm., often absent over much of the tree. **Flowers:** in round heads, creamy-white or pale yellow. **Pods:** curved, thick and hard, to 21 x 3.5 cm., yellow-brown, smooth and shiny when mature, very slow to split.

The wood is light, soft and of little value.

Acacia polyacantha

Acacia sieberiana

168

MIMOSOIDEAE

Acacia tortilis *(Acacia spirocarpa)*   **Umbrella Thorn**
Mgunga (Swahili)

A familiar, spreading tree to 20 m. with a flat or umbrella-shaped crown, very widely distributed up to 1,800 m. in woodland, grassland and semi-desert areas; conspicuous in northern districts, often along rivers, also found in Nairobi National Park; sometimes a low shrub, for instance near Magadi.

Bark: grey to black, rough and fissured.   **Spines:** of two kinds, distinctive, small hooked prickles intermixed with straight, whitish spines to 8 cm. long; sometimes one long and one short spine in the same pair.   **Flowers:** in small round heads, creamy-white.   **Pods:** pale brown, very distinctive, spirally twisted ('tortilis') and contorted, sometimes curled into rings.

A hardy acacia of great character, occurring from North Africa to South Africa, almost always evergreen, with hard red wood that makes excellent firewood and charcoal. The spreading root system makes it a good sand stabiliser, and the pods and leaves are much eaten by game and stock, particularly goats.

Acacia xanthophloea   **Fever Tree, Naivasha Thorn**

COLOUR PLATE XI   Murera (Kikuyu)

A large, graceful tree reaching 25 m. or more, gregarious in high groundwater areas beside lakes or rivers from 600 to 2,000 m., often in black cotton soil; now also widely planted in and around Nairobi.

Bark: distinctive, greenish-yellow, smooth and powdery, fissured in large trees.   **Spines:** in diverging pairs, straight, whitish, to 10 cm., very numerous in young trees.   **Flowers:** in round heads, white or tinged with pink in Kenya, yellow from southern Tanzania through to South Africa.   **Pods:** yellowish-brown, straight or slightly curved, to 13 cm., flat and narrow, slightly constricted between the seeds, at which points the pods break into segments.

The specific name is derived from Greek, *xanthos:* yellow; *phloos:* bark or skin.

Because these trees grow in low-lying swampy areas where mosquitoes breed, the early pioneers were convinced that the trees themselves were the cause of malaria. They are immortalised by Rudyard Kipling's description in 'The Elephant's Child: "the great grey-green, greasy Limpopo River, all set about with fever trees".

Trees are very fast-growing and attractive as ornamentals. However older trees become brittle, and being shallow rooted in soft ground tend to fall or drop large branches in high winds.

169

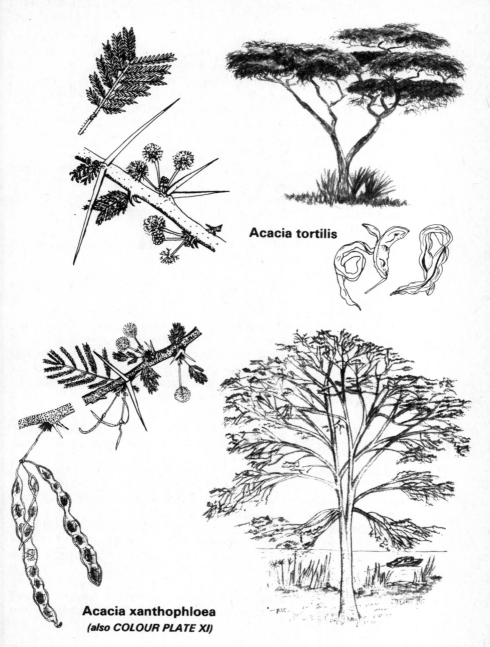

Acacia tortilis

Acacia xanthophloea
(also COLOUR PLATE XI)

170

Acacia mearnsii *(Acacia decurrens var. mollis)*
Australia

Black Wattle
Muthanduku (Kikuyu)

A rounded or rather shapeless tree to 12 m., commonly planted in the highlands up to 2,500 m. and widely naturalised; in Western Kenya also grown in commercial plantations and farm woodlots.

Bark: grey, becoming black and fissured, splitting and curling, producing a brown, resinous gum. The bark may contain up to half its weight of tannin. **Leaves:** to 24 cm. long, with numerous pairs of side ribs; leaflets dull green, extremely small and feathery, less than 4 mm. long. **Flowers:** pale yellow, in small round heads on branched stalks. **Pods:** straight to twisted, to 10 cm., jointed between the seeds, drying dull brown.

Practical notes: a fast-growing, fairly short-lived tree with hard, strong timber, generally useful for fencing and implement handles and excellent for firewood and charcoal. Will grow on poor or black-cotton soils, but shallow-rooted, a greedy feeder, falling easily; not drought-resistant.

Acacia melanoxylon
South Australia

Australian Blackwood

A tall, conical timber tree to 35 m., planted in cooler, wetter upland areas like Limuru and Kericho, usually above 2,300 m.

Bark: dark grey, much fissured. **Leaves:** dense, grey-green, juvenile foliage with feathery leaflets, mature leaves actually expanded leaf-stalks, lance-shaped, slightly curved, to 10 cm. long. **Flowers:** creamy-white, in small round heads. **Pods:** curved, twisted, about 12 cm. long, with hanging, shiny black seeds surrounded by an orange aril.

A very fast-growing tree producing hard, valuable timber. However, in Kenya replanting has been discontinued due to attack by blight.

Acacia podalyriifolia
Australia

Golden Wattle,
Queensland Silver Wattle

An attractive ornamental tree to 12 m., conspicuous in flower around Nairobi and in the highlands up to 2,500 m.; in places naturalised.

Bark: grey, dark and cracking with age. **Leaves:** seedlings with feathery juvenile leaflets which soon fall; expanded leaf stalks, silvery-white, oval to oblong, finely tipped, to 5 cm. long; leaves, young stems and young pods covered with a blue-grey bloom. **Flowers:** golden-yellow, round heads in profuse, upright terminal clusters. **Pods:** flat, somewhat twisted, raised over the seeds, to 8 cm., splitting to show a coppery interior.

Practical notes: an attractive, fast-growing but short-lived tree; best planted away from flower beds, as the roots are shallow. Older trees break and fall easily in wind and rain.

171

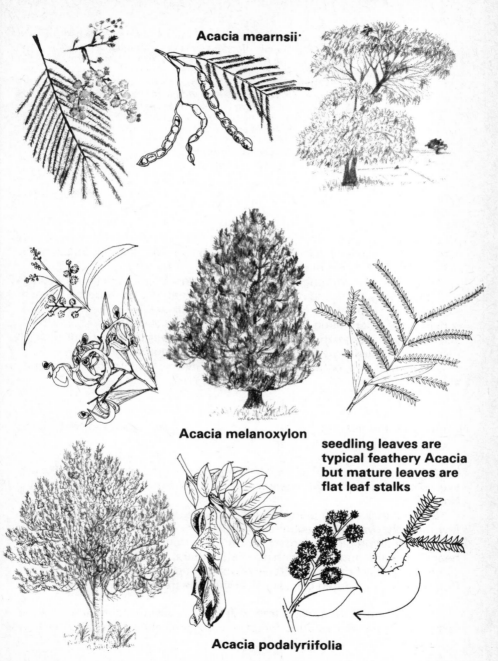

Acacia mearnsii·

Acacia melanoxylon

seedling leaves are
typical feathery Acacia
but mature leaves are
flat leaf stalks

Acacia podalyriifolia

172

Albizia spp.

A genus of over 100 species, named after an Italian nobleman called Filipo degli Albizzi who introduced them to cultivation 200 years ago. The genus is distributed throughout the tropics, and today plantations of Albizia in South-east Asia are a major source of blockboard and plywood, the trees there being among the fastest growing hardwoods in the world.

In Kenya there are about 13 indigenous species. They bear neither spines nor thorns, and the flowers are always hemispheres of small flowers, each with many conspicuous long stamens joined into a tube, at least at the base. A few flowers in the centre of the white or pink 'powder puff' heads are larger and differ in shape from the other flowers. The fruit are straight flat pods containing round, flattened seeds. The leaves are twice-compound, usually with large glandular nectaries on the leaf stalks.

The leaflets are the best guide for distinguishing the species.

Albizia amara   Bitter Albizia
indigenous

A shapely deciduous tree, often rounded, to 10 m. but often smaller, widely distributed in wooded grassland at lower to medium altitudes; also indigenous to India, Sri Lanka, and much of Eastern and Central Africa.

Bark: dark brown, roughly fissured.   **Leaves:** bright pale green, leaflets numerous, very small and narrow, with a fine, feathery appearance. Branchlets and leaves are more or less covered with distinctive soft, golden hairs, conspicuous when young.   **Flowers:** small pale pink or white heads, to 2.5 cm. across.   **Pods:** large, thin, to 20 x 3 cm., bulging over the few seeds, margin thickened, purplish when young, later dark brown and papery.

A beautiful tree, occasionally planted in Nairobi; well worth encouraging as an ornamental.

Albizia grandibracteata   Large-leaved Albizia
indigenous

A deciduous tree to 20 m. with a flattened or layered crown, originally from Western Kenya and the Kakamega forest, now extensively planted around Nairobi.

Bark: pale grey or brownish, fairly smooth.   **Leaves:** leaflets distinctive, few, broadly oval but unequal-sided, the pairs increasing in size with the curved terminal pair the largest, up to 6 cm. long.   **Flowers:** in colourful heads, predominantly pink, with dark red anthers.   **Pods:** flat, fairly small, to 12 cm. long, pale brown, lightly veined, usually tipped with a small blunt point. Dense clusters are often conspicuous when the tree is bare.

Practical notes: a striking tree in flower, widely available in nurseries; fast-growing on well-watered forest soil, but producing many suckers from surface roots.

173

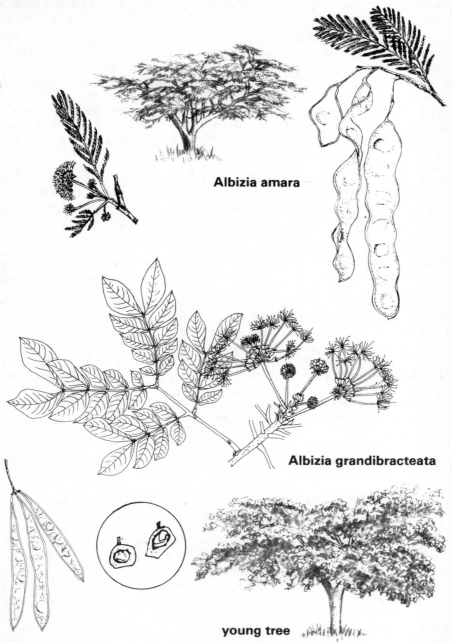

Albizia amara

Albizia grandibracteata

young tree

Albizia gummifera
indigenous

Peacock flower
Mukuruwe (Kikuyu)

A spreading deciduous tree, often flat-topped, usually to 15 m. but in wetter forest up to twice that; the most widespread Albizia in Kenya, occurring from hills at the coast to Marsabit, Kakamega and Central Province.

Bark: greyish, usually smooth. **Leaves:** glossy dark green, leaflets up to 12 pairs, 1 to 2 cm. long; almost rectangular with one outer corner rounded and the base characteristically parallel to the leaf stalk; midrib diagonal. **Flowers:** in typical hemispherical clusters, pale pink and white, the pale staminal tubes topped with tufts of bright red anthers. **Pods:** thin, papery, to 17 x 3 cm. but often smaller, glossy pale brown with a raised margin, often in profuse clusters.

An attractive, graceful shade tree and soil stabiliser, once an important ceremonial meeting tree amongst the Kikuyu and Kalenjin and significant in traditional medicine. Bark extracts were used to treat fevers like malaria, and crushed pods to treat stomach pains. Deserves wide planting.

Albizia lebbeck
Tropical Asia

Siris Tree, Women's Tongue
Mkingu (Swahili)

A graceful deciduous tree, to 15 m. but usually smaller, planted at the coast and at Kisumu, also throughout the tropics, in places naturalised.

Bark: grey, rough. **Leaves:** leaflets oblong, fairly large, apex rounded, hairless, only 3 to 11 pairs, to 5 cm. long. **Flowers:** greenish-yellow, short-lived. **Pods:** shiny yellow-brown, to 30 cm. long, bulging over the seeds. The seeds rattle in the wind inside the pods, giving rise to the somewhat uncomplimentary common name.

The wood is hard and heavy, with a fine grain, much prized for cabinet work. The leaves and pods are used for fodder.

Albizia schimperiana
indigenous

Long-podded Albizia

A tree to 20m., very similar to *Albizia gummifera* but the crown usually more umbrella-shaped than flat, the flowers white and the leaflets rounded, occurring in the highlands of central and southern parts of Kenya; often the most common Albizia in the Kiambu, Kabete and Karen areas of Nairobi.

Bark: smooth, pale grey to brownish; branchlets bear velvety brown hairs. **Leaves:** leaflets usually less than 2 cm. long, obliquely oblong but with rounded rather than angular corners. **Flowers:** white or creamy, in loose, conspicuous heads; stamens white, not protruding; flower stalks hairy. **Pods:** numerous, persistent, dull brown with a thick margin, to 30 x 6 cm. but often smaller, containing many large seeds.

175

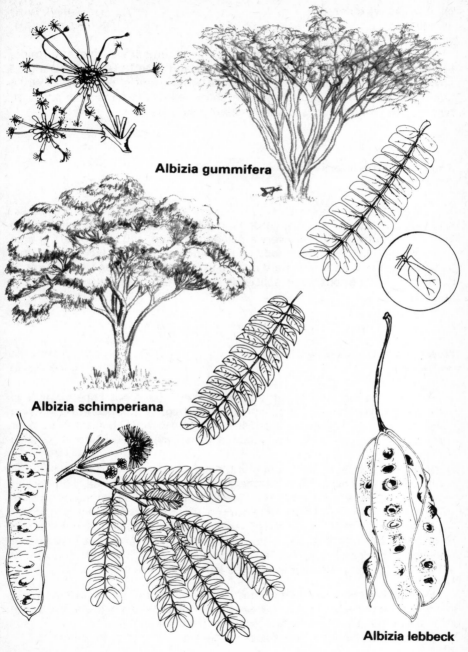

Albizia gummifera

Albizia schimperiana

Albizia lebbeck

MIMOSOIDEAE

Dichrostachys cinerea
indigenous

Sickle bush
Mubilisia (Kamba)

A small, spiny, acacia-like tree to 6m., sometimes thicket-forming, occurring in various habitats in wooded grassland up to 1,500 m. The hanging flower spikes are two-coloured, the top half bearing long pink, mauve or white filaments and the lower half bearing short yellow stamens. The pods are twisted and contorted into strangely-shaped clusters.

Enterolobium contortisiliquum
South America

A small, feathery-looking tree to 6 m. with heavy, rather gnarled branches, occasionally found in streets, gardens and golf-courses around Nairobi. The leaflets are light grey-green, very small and pointed, and the flowers sparse white puff-balls. The seed pods are distinctive, purple-black when ripe, thickened and twisted into a hard ring up to 6 cm. in diameter, with the seeds rattling inside. The pods do not split open; the seeds are released only when the pod rots.

Newtonia buchananii *(Piptadenia buchananii)*
indigenous

Newtonia
Mukui (Kikuyu)

A spreading forest tree with a layered, rather flat-topped appearance, to 15 m. but on river banks to 40 m. with a clear, straight trunk, occurring in forest valleys in Central Province, eastern Mt. Kenya and in the high mist forests near Taita and Machakos; very conspicuous along the Embu-Meru road, also riparian in Nairobi forests.

Bark: smooth, light grey, containing resin; older trees with strongly fluted buttresses. **Leaves:** leaflets feathery, numerous, very small, light green young growth contrasting with dark green mature leaflets; young branchlets rusty brown with dense hairs. **Flowers:** erect, creamy-white fading to brown in axillary spikes to 15 cm., often densely clustered. **Pods:** straight, flat and thin, to 30 x 2 cm. but usually 15 cm., dark brown when mature, splitting down one side to release unusual winged seeds up to 7 cm. in length. Clusters of young, pale green pods high in the tree look almost like blossoms.

Practical notes: a handsome, shady tree, well worth planting in good forest soil on well-watered sites. Young trees are not yet easy to obtain and need care at first, but growth is moderately fast once established.

There are three other indigenous species, mainly in coastal forest.

177

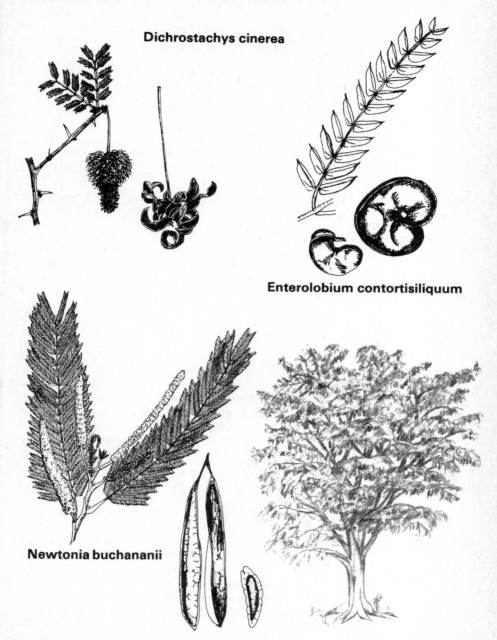

Dichrostachys cinerea

Enterolobium contortisiliquum

Newtonia buchananii

MORACEAE Fig family

A large family of trees and shrubs, widely distributed but primarily tropical or sub-tropical. All trees in this family produce a white latex, although the use of *Ficus elastica* as a source of rubber has been superseded by the commercial rubber tree *Hevea braziliensis* in the Euphorbia family.

The family is named after the Mulberry genus *Morus,* of which there is only one uncommon indigenous species. The two main exotic species grown commercially in Kenya are *Morus alba* from China, where the leaves are used to feed silkworms, and *Morus nigra* from Western Asia. Both species produce abundant fruit.

Flowers in this family are small, with the sexes separated. The fruit vary widely, but are usually fleshy.

The family includes two important herbs, Indian Hemp *Cannabis sativa,* a valuable source of fibre despite its reputation as a narcotic drug, and Hops *Humulus lupulus,* the twining herb cultivated for the papery flower heads which give the characteristic bitter taste to beer.

Members of this family in Kenya include *Artocarpus, Milicia, Ficus.*

Artocarpus altilis *(Artocarpus communis)* Breadfruit
Malaya Mshelisheli (Swahili)

An evergreen tree to 20 m., bearing fruit only in the wetter lowlands but also planted in Nairobi as an ornamental. The leaves are huge, shiny dark green, up to 1 m. long, deeply cut and lobed. The fruit are prickly and rounded, to 20 cm. across, yellow when ripe; the flesh is starchy, but reasonably sweet when boiled or roasted as a vegetable.

Artocarpus heterophyllus *(Artocarpus integrifolius)* Jackfruit
India to Malaya Mfenesi (Swahili)

A bushy evergreen tree to 5 m., occasionally to 20 m., generally found at the coast. A splendid specimen also stands in the Nairobi Arboretum. The leaves are glossy, oval, to 15 cm., not divided. Flowers are borne on the trunk or large branches, where the largest known fruit then develops, massive and irregular with a spiky, yellow-green rind, reaching a record 20 kg. in weight and 1 m. in length. The flesh is sweet and edible, but definitely an acquired taste.

Milicia excelsa *(Chlorophora excelsa)*
indigenous Mvule (Swahili)

One of the tallest trees in Kenya, in lowland rain forest growing to 50 m. with a lofty trunk and high crown, occurring at the coast, in Central and Nyanza Provinces and at Meru, but heavily exploited and now sadly rare. The leaves are oval, to 18 cm., with conspicuous veins, the apex pointed and the margin finely toothed. Male flower spikes, on separate trees, are characteristic drooping catkins, to 15 cm. long. The fruit resemble long green mulberries.

The dark, handsome heartwood was prized for fine furniture. Growth is fast for a hardwood, and seeds germinate readily. This attractive, valuable species deserves extensive replanting.

179

Artocarpus heterophyllus

Morus spp.

Milicia excelsa

MORACEAE

Ficus spp.   Fig Trees

This is the best known genus of the family, containing about 900 species, all with simple, alternate leaves and very pointed buds. Their light, soft wood is of little use for timber or firewood, which is one reason for their widespread survival. **Ficus** flowers are very small and lie within the typical 'fig' structure, where they are pollinated by fig wasps that are specific to each species, forming an extraordinarily complex relationship between insect and plant.

Apart from growing as normal trees with extensive root systems, many figs are also epiphytes or begin life as epiphytes. Seeds borne by birds germinate in the forks of other trees, sending down aerial roots to the ground which develop more usual root systems. The growing fig tree envelops the host trunk and the host tree may eventually be smothered and die, giving rise to the name 'Strangler Fig'. The enormous Indian Banyan *Ficus benghalensis* is a huge tree of this type.

The edible Mediterranean Fig *Ficus carica* has been planted commercially in Kenya.

In Kenya there are over 30 indigenous species, but the identification of some of these is difficult even for the experts. Two of the exotics and five common indigenous species are described.

Ficus benjamina   Java Fig, Weeping Fig
India, Malaya, East Indies

A dense evergreen tree to 10 or 20 m. with attractive drooping foliage, widely planted around Nairobi as an ornamental and street tree; in Europe grown as a pot plant.

Bark: grey, with horizontal markings.   **Leaves:** thin, lime green when young, later glossy dark green; narrowly oval, to 8 cm. long, drawn out to a pointed 'drip tip'.   **Fruit:** axillary, often in pairs, about 1 cm. across, turning from orange to dark red, the ripe fruit attracting many birds.

These hardy, fast-growing trees have an extensive root system powerful enough to crack concrete. The upright variety common in Nairobi is proving too large, and such damage has been caused to foundations and road surfaces that many trees have had to be felled.

Ficus elastica   Indian Rubber Plant
South-east Asia

A spreading evergreen tree to 30 m. in its native rain forests, occasionally planted in Kenya from the coast to the highlands and also found as a pot plant; a very popular indoor ornamental in temperate countries. The rather inferior 'India rubber' was collected from the trunk and roots. The leaves are large, glossy dark green, to 30 cm. long, the apex abruptly pointed and the side veins parallel. The very long leaf buds are sheathed in a red membrane, which falls away as the leaf develops.

Other ornamental exotics planted in Kenya include **Ficus religiosa,** the Peepul tree from India, **Ficus nitida,** a useful street tree from South-east Asia, and **Ficus lyrata,** the Fiddle-Leaf Fig from tropical West Africa, which is occasionally planted in gardens.

181

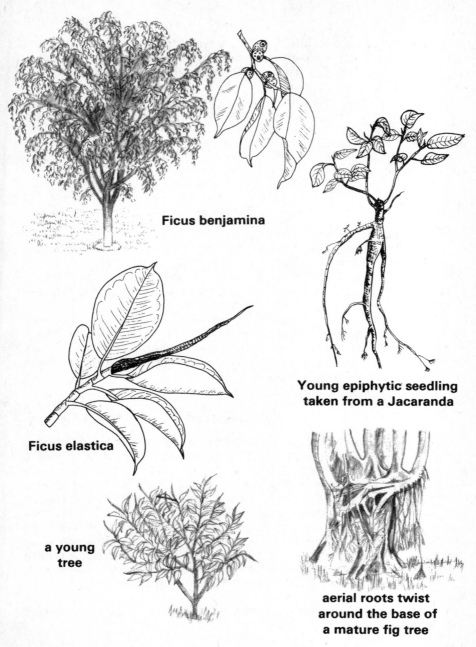

Ficus benjamina

Ficus elastica

**Young epiphytic seedling
taken from a Jacaranda**

**a young
tree**

**aerial roots twist
around the base of
a mature fig tree**

MORACEAE

Ficus lutea *(Ficus quibeba, Ficus vogelii)*
indigenous   Mumbu (Kikuyu)

A spreading deciduous tree to 16 m., often in riverine forest, sometimes epiphytic, occasionally on rocks, occurring in Central, Southern and South Nyanza Provinces up to 2,000 m; common around Thika, also planted in public areas around Nairobi.
Bark: grey-brown.   **Leaves:** elliptic, about 20 cm. long, apex abruptly pointed; paler lateral veins distinct above and below; leaf stalk long, to 12 cm. The leaves arise in dense spirals from rather stout branchlets, which end abruptly in small pointed buds.   **Fruit:** figs axillary, about 2 cm. across, softly hairy and warted, yellow or orange when ripe. Young fruit bear a brown cap, which falls off as the fruit matures.

Ficus natalensis   **Barkcloth Fig**
indigenous   *Illustration at p.* 186   Mugumo (Kikuyu)

A leafy deciduous tree to 30 m., widely scattered in riverine forest and occasionally in drier areas in Kenya from 900 to 1,800 m., but much less common than the very similar *Ficus thonningii. Ficus natalensis* is the commonest fig tree in Uganda, and occurs over most of Africa. The figs are axillary, 8 to 18 mm. across, on stalks 2 to 10 mm. in length, with leafy bracts at the base of the fruit which fall off early and do not persist.

In central Uganda the barkcloth made from this tree was once widely used for ceremonial clothing and wall hangings, and is still used for burial wrappings. The bark from mature trees was beaten with mallets until a 50 cm. strip became a cloth over 2 m. wide; the cloth was later sun-dried to a rich dark brown and stencilled with patterns.

Ficus sur *(Ficus capensis)*   **Cape Fig**
indigenous   *COLOUR PLATE XII*   Mukuyu (Kikuyu)

A large, handsome deciduous tree to 25 m., the crown generally rounded and the trunk often buttressed, widespread in riverine forest or well-watered grassland from the coast to 2,100 m.; common in Central and Nyanza Provinces, and occurring over much of Africa, in Zanzibar and in the Yemen.
Bark: smooth, grey to pale grey, coarser with age.   **Leaves:** large, broadly oval, to 20 x 13 cm.; upper surface usually smooth, margin often widely toothed, sometimes entire or wavy; veins very prominent below; stalk grooved and flexible, to 6 cm.   **Fruit:** in heavy clusters on branches arising from older wood; figs rounded, usually to 3 cm. but occasionally to 5 cm. across, like small apples on short stalks, orange or red when mature, often densely covered with short hairs. The ripe figs are edible but insipid and rather gritty, and are often full of insects.

An infusion from the bark was used by the Masai as a cure for stomach ache and diarrhoea.

183

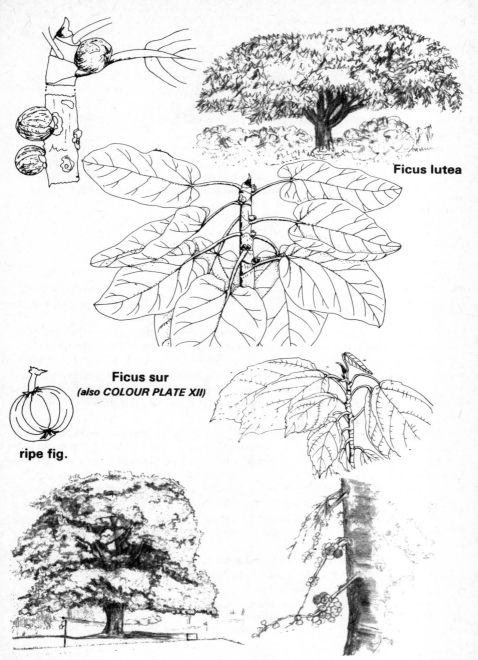

Ficus lutea

Ficus sur
(also COLOUR PLATE XII)

ripe fig.

MORACEAE

Ficus sycomorus *(Ficus gnaphalocarpa,*
Ficus mucoso)

indigenous

Sycomore Fig

Mukuyu (Kikuyu)

A large, buttressed, spreading tree to 21 m., widely distributed near rivers
and in drier woodland from the coast to 1,850 m. and common for instance
along the Athi River in the Nairobi National Park. This is the Biblical sycomore
of Egypt and the Middle East, and is readily identified by its rough, rounded
leaves and yellow bark.

Bark: distinctive, yellow to creamy brown, smooth, cracking with
age.   **Leaves:** broadly oval to almost circular, about 15 x 10 cm.; upper surface
rough and harsh to the touch, margin wavy, occasionally roughly toothed, base
rounded or heart-shaped; stalk short, to 3 cm., covered with dense white hairs.
The leaves dry exceptionally fast after falling.   **Fruit:** in leaf axils or in dense
clusters on main branches and trunk; figs pear-shaped, about 3 cm. across,
yellow or reddish when ripe, often slightly furry. The figs are much eaten by
birds, monkeys, baboon and hyrax.

Ficus thonningii *(Ficus eriocarpa)*
indigenous

Wild Fig, Strangler Fig

Mugumo (Kikuyu)

A large deciduous tree to 21 m., often buttressed or multi-stemmed from
the growth of aerial roots, widespread in upland forest or open grassland in
central, southern and western regions from 1,000 to 2,400 m. and also
common in most of Africa. This is the usual species of the Nairobi area, the
key botanical difference between this and the very similar *Ficus natalensis*
being the two small 4 mm leafy bracts at the base of the figs, which in this
species are persistent and do not fall off.

Bark: thin, grey and smooth.   **Leaves:** very variable, generally oval, to 12 cm.
cm. but often smaller; apex mostly rounded, sometimes notched, base rounded
or tapering; young leaves pale and hairy below.   **Fruit:** in axillary clusters on
terminal branches, often prominent when the leaves have fallen; figs small,
rounded, to 1.5 cm. across, stalk absent or very short; smooth or warted, yellow
or purple-red when ripe, attracting many birds, small mammals and monkeys.

A very important ceremonial meeting tree among the Kikuyu and in several
other cultures, widely regarded as the sacred home of ancestral spirits.

Practical notes: both the Mugumo and the Mukuyu grow readily from large
cuttings on a variety of soils, making dignified, shady trees of very large size.
Young plants need protection from browsing animals. They should not be
planted near buildings, as their enormous,·powerful root systems will crack
foundations and suck up moisture.

185

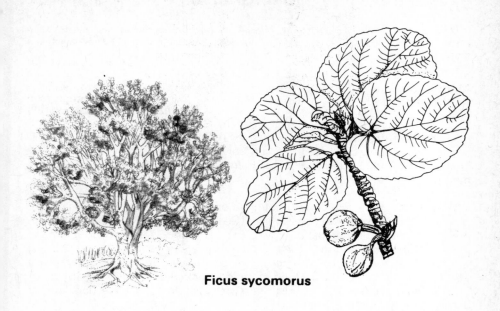

Ficus sycomorus

Ficus natalensis

Ficus thonningii

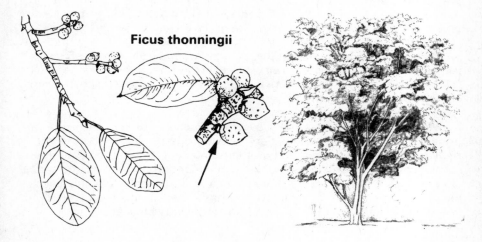

186

MORINGACEAE   Moringa family

A very small family of deciduous trees or shrubs found from the Mediterranean region eastwards to India, with several species from North Africa south to Madagascar. The only genus is *Moringa,* and there are 12 species, all of them fast-growing from seed or cuttings.

Moringa oleifera
India, Arabia

Horseradish Tree
Drumstick Tree
Mzunze, Mrongo (Swahili)

A feathery-looking deciduous tree to 10 m. in height but usually much smaller, commonly cultivated in sandy soils at the coast and at low altitudes. This species is also widely cultivated in India, and has become naturalised in many parts of the tropics.

Bark: grey, thick and corky, peeling in patches.   **Leaves:** soft pale green, twice or thrice compound, the whole leaf 30 to 60 cm. in length; leaflets paired, numerous, variable but usually oval, with a rounded apex, 1 to 2 cm. in length.   **Flowers:** creamy-white fading to yellow, about 2 cm. across, irregular in shape, hanging in long sprays. The flowers are sweet-scented and attract many insects.   **Fruit:** long, hanging, stick-like capsules, to 45 cm. in length, bluntly triangular in cross section, splitting to release dark brown 3-winged seeds embedded in pith.

The name of the tree is derived from the horseradish-like taste of the roots. The leaves and young fruit are popular as a vegetable from South-east Asia to West Africa, and are used in curries. The oil from the seeds, known as Ben oil, is used in salads, skin poultices and for making soap, and the seeds are exported from Sri Lanka for use in the French cosmetic and textile industries.

Recent research has shown that powder ground from this plant is a very valuable water purifier, already widely used in rural areas of the Sudan and the Nile region. It is also used as a cure for scurvy. The tree can be grown from large cuttings, and gives useful shade and fodder.

Moringa stenopetala is one of several indigenous species, a tree to 10 m. in height with bright green feathery foliage from the dry northern areas of Kenya, common near Isiolo and on the islands at Lake Baringo. The tree is conspicuous for its smooth white bark, abundant white flowers and typical long, 3-angled fruit capsules. Modern research suggests that this species may be an even more efficient water purifier, which could prove to be of enormous benefit to rural communities in Kenya and elsewhere.

Moringa oleifera

MYRTACEAE   Eucalyptus family

A large family, principally from Australia and tropical America but named after the only European species, the Myrtle bush *Myrtus communis*, a flowering shrub from the Mediterranean which is also grown in Kenya. The family includes exotic fruit trees such as the Guava *Psidium guajava*, the Rose Apple *Eugenia jambos* and the Java Plum *Syzygium cuminii*, and some outstanding Australian ornamentals such as the Bottlebrush *Callistemon spp.* and the Honey Myrtle *Melaleuca armillaris*, whose white flowers resemble in shape the red flowers of the Bottlebrush, although the feathery, needle-like foliage is different.

However, the most important genus in the family is *Eucalyptus*, of which all species have simple, evergreen leaves, special glands producing aromatic oil and flowers with numerous stamens, often with brightly coloured filaments. 75% of all the trees in Australia are Eucalypts, which include some of the tallest trees in the world.

Eucalypts or Gum trees have narrow, leathery leaves which hang vertically and twist freely, protecting them from strong sunlight. Most mature leaves also have a grey-blue, waxy coating, and produce aromatic, highly inflammable oils. Many species have bright red young leaves, and many produce juvenile leaves which bear no resemblance to mature leaves. The flower bud has a unique 'lid' (Greek 'calypt': a lid or cover) and abundant nectar between the stamens, which attracts many insects and bees. The fruits are woody, bell-shaped capsules containing hundreds of minute seeds, known in Australia as gum-nuts.

Members of this family in Kenya include *Callistemon, Eucalyptus, Eugenia, Psidium, Syzygium.*

Callistemon citrinus var. splendens *(Callistemon lanceolatus)*   **Bottlebrush**
Australia, New Zealand   *COLOUR PLATE VII*

A familiar ornamental tree to 6 m. in height with attractive drooping foliage and vivid crimson brush-like flowers, planted in many parts of Kenya.

Bark: grey, smooth; rougher and furrowed with age.   **Leaves:** narrow, tough, greyish-green, to 8 cm. in length; lemon-scented *('citrinus')* when crushed. Young leaves have a reddish-pink flush.   **Flowers:** showy cylindrical spikes with no obvious petals, attracting sunbirds and bees; stamens very long and protruding; flowers terminal at first, later crowned by a ring of leaves, the shoot continuing to grow after the flowers have formed.   **Fruit:** small woody capsules, in dense clusters, persisting on the tree for many months.

There are several other species and cultivated varieties, some with deep red and some with white flowers. The slightly smaller **Callistemon rigidus** *(Callistemon erectus)* has upright foliage and stiffly erect flowers.

Practical notes: remarkably hardy, tolerant of a wide variety of temperatures and altitudes, thriving even in water-logged black-cotton soil; easily grown from seed and widely available from nurseries. Most species will flower soon after planting, but are fairly slow growing.

Callistemon citrinus
(also COLOUR PLATE VII)

Eucalyptus cinerea
- see page 193

Eucalyptus
juvenile leaves
—to mature leaves

190

MYRTACEAE

Eucalyptus spp.   **Gum Trees**

Fast-growing evergreen fuelwood trees, first planted in Kenya at the turn of the century to supply fuel for the Uganda railway and to drain the mosquito-ridden black-cotton swamps around the new town of Nairobi. There are over 500 species native to Australia, and over 100 have been tried here.

Gum trees regenerate rapidly after cutting or coppicing, but are unsuitable near crops or in seasonal or water catchment areas, as the water loss through transpiration can be extremely high. The Australian micro-organisms that help to decay fallen gum leaves appear to be absent in Kenya and undergrowth is inhibited, with the result that erosion may follow on bare slopes. Generally the trees are shallow-rooted and greedy, and large trees near houses are considered dangerous, as branches or even the whole tree may fall in storms.

The different species are primarily classified by their bark, although the buds, capsules and leaves also assist identification. Two of the most prominent in Kenya are described, with shorter notes on some of the other more common species.

Eucalyptus ficifolia   **Flowering Gum**
South-western Australia

An ornamental tree with the most showy flowers of all gum trees in Kenya, up to 10 m. in height but often smaller, with the crown more or less rounded; common in the wetter districts of the highlands.

Bark: dark, rough and fissured.   **Leaves:** mature leaves alternate, broadly lance-shaped; midrib pale yellow   **Flowers:** large, in terminal clusters, the stamen colour varying on different trees from deep crimson or pale pink to orange or white.   **Fruit:** bell-shaped, the largest of the common species, 2 to 4 cm. long, often in heavy clusters.

The tree is fairly slow growing, and reliable seedlings are difficult to obtain. Grafting is usually necessary to maintain a particular colour.

Eucalyptus saligna *(confused with Eucalyptus grandis)*   **Sydney Blue Gum**
Coastal Eastern Australia

A dense, handsome tree growing to a massive 60 m., the dominant *Eucalyptus* of the highlands from 1,200 to 2,400 m.

Bark: lower bark rough brown, peeling in strips; upper bark smooth, greenish-white.   **Leaves:** tough, linear, often sickle-shaped, to 20 cm. in length.   **Flowers:** small, white, 4 to 8 flowers in each group. The bud cover is a short, pointed cone.   **Fruit:** small capsules, 5 mm. long, with protruding valves.

Eucalyptus saligna is confused with *Eucalyptus grandis,* the two having been exported from Australia under the same name for over 120 years. They are now recognised as distinct, although closely related and likely to hybridize; both are extremely fast-growing, excellent fuel and good general purpose timber. In Kenya many tea companies, major users of wood fuel in tea factories, plant only the true *E. grandis* because the timber has a straighter grain, splitting more easily into firewood, and is ready to cut in only 10 years.

191

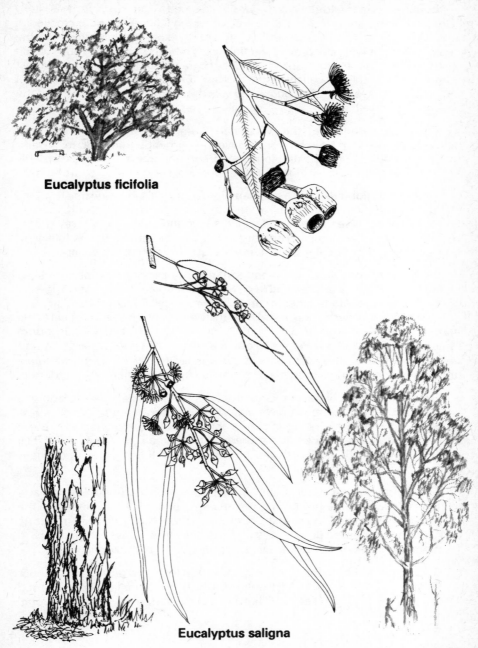

Eucalyptus ficifolia

Eucalyptus saligna

Eucalyptus camaldulensis *(E. rostrata),* the Red River Gum from Eastern Australia: a spreading tree to 40 m. with drooping foliage, growing crooked in early life but a useful source of fuel on dry soil in plantations at the coast.   **Bark:** lower bark brown and flaking, producing a ruby red gum which was the origin of the name Gum Tree; upper bark smooth, pale grey.   **Leaves:** long, narrow, both surfaces the same colour.   **Fruit:** very small hemispherical capsules, 5 mm. across. The dense red wood is resistant to termites, and the tree coppices well.

Eucalyptus degulpta, the Mindanao Gum from the Phillipines, with several specimens in Nairobi: a decorative, fast-growing tree to 30 m.   **Bark:** distinctive salmon-pink, flaking to reveal green underbark.   **Leaves:** broadly lance-shaped, to 15 cm. or more.   **Fruit:** rounded, very small, to 5 mm. across.

Eucalyptus globulus, the Tasmanian Blue Gum: a fast-growing tree to 40 m., sometimes planted in gardens in the highlands.   **Bark:** peeling in long strips.   **Leaves:** juvenile leaves distinctively rounded, stalkless, grey-green, tending to clasp the stem.   **Fruit:** large, to 2.5 across. The juvenile foliage of this species and of **Eucalyptus cinerea** are used by florists for decoration.

Eucalyptus maculata, the Spotted Gum from Eastern Australia, fairly common in Nairobi: a tall tree with a distinctive, dimpled stem.   **Bark:** jig-saw patterned, flaking into patches of grey, brown or yellow; older bark smooth, greyish white.   **Leaves:** long, narrow, with numerous thin veins parallel to the margin.   **Fruit:** urn-shaped, about 1 cm. long. **Eucalyptus citriodora** *(E. maculata var. citriodora),* the Lemon Scented Gum from Eastern Queensland is a tall, straight tree with smooth bark, distinguished from *Eucalyptus maculata* only by the very strong lemon scent of the leaves when crushed or after rain.

Eucalyptus paniculata, the Grey Ironbark from coastal Queensland and New South Wales: a tall tree, conical when young, hardy but fairly slow-growing, common in the Ngong area, often on black-cotton soil.   **Bark:** distinctive, dark brown, deeply fissured.   **Fruit:** small, to 7 mm. long. The timber is very hard and resistant to decay, useful for poles and heavy construction.

Eucalyptus regnans, the Mountain Ash from Victoria and Tasmania: a giant, fast-growing tree reaching a maximum height of 100 m., planted in the wetter highlands near Eldoret and Elburgon, where the long, straight trunks up to 40 m. in length are cut for use as power-line poles. A 99 m. specimen in Tasmania is currently the tallest living broadleaf tree in the world.

Eucalyptus sideroxylon, the Mugga from Eastern Australia: grows in poor soil, but often with a crooked trunk.   **Bark:** a distinctive, deeply fissured Ironbark, black, appearing almost charred.   **Leaves:** narrow, hanging in long, flattened sprays.

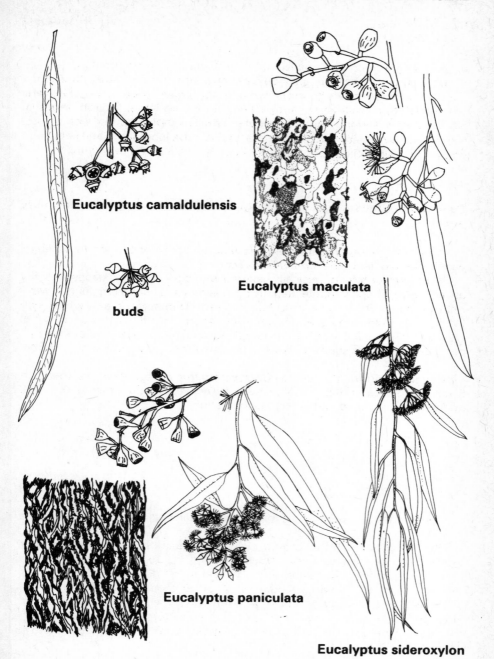

Eucalyptus camaldulensis

buds

Eucalyptus maculata

Eucalyptus paniculata

Eucalyptus sideroxylon

194

MYRTACEAE

Eugenia jambos   **Rose Apple**
India, Malaysia

An evergreen ornamental fruit tree, growing to a spreading 8 m.
Bark: grey, slightly rough.   **Leaves:** opposite, lance-shaped, to 20 cm.,
dark glossy green above. Young leaves and stems have a pink flush.   **Flowers:**
creamy white or yellowish, up to 10 cm. across, in large, fragrant terminal
heads; stamens white and prominent.   **Fruit:** rounded, up to 4 cm. across,
turning yellow tinged with pink, rose-scented; calyx lobes large and persistent
on the fruit, which is edible and soft when ripe, used for jelly or jam.

Eugenia myrtifolia *(Syzygium paniculatum)*   **Brush Cherry**
Australia

An attractive ornamental tree, growing to 15 m. or pruned to a hedge,
widely planted along the streets of Nairobi.
Bark: grey or brown, vertically fissured with age.   **Leaves:** opposite, shiny
green above, shape variable, usually narrowly oval, about 5 cm. long, always
reflexed; apex stiffly tipped, stalk short, reddish.   **Flowers:** creamy white, with
four petals and sepals and numerous short, white stamens, in small
clusters.   **Fruit:** oval, to 2.5 cm. in length, turning bright pink, edible when ripe
but rather acid. Pink stains from fallen fruit are often prominent under the tree.

Eugenia uniflora, the Pitanga Cherry from tropical America, is sometimes
found as an ornamental. The leaves are attractive, pointed, shiny dark green,
and the fruit is ribbed, red and pleasant tasting.

Psidium guajava   **Guava**
Tropical America   Mubera (Kikuyu)

A small, rather gnarled tree to 8 m. with an irregular trunk, often bearing
abundant fruit.
Bark: smooth, light brown, peeling and flaking; young shoots
four-sided.   **Leaves:** opposite, broadly elliptic, to 15 cm. long; side veins
prominent, giving the leaf a corrugated appearance.   **Flowers:** white, axillary,
2.5 cm. across, growing singly or 2 or 3 together, with numerous
stamens.   **Fruit:** heavy, rounded, to 6 cm. long, the calyx lobes persistent;
often attacked by fruit fly. The delicious pink, white or yellowish flesh
surrounding many hard, angular seeds is popular fresh or stewed, and is rich in
vitamin C.'

195

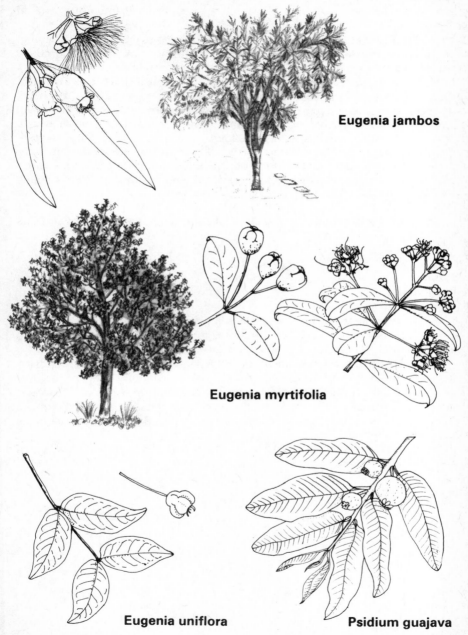

Eugenia jambos

Eugenia myrtifolia

Eugenia uniflora

Psidium guajava

196

MYRTACEAE

Syzygium cuminii *(Eugenia cuminii)*
India, Tropical Asia

Java Plum, Jambolan
Msambarau (Swahili)

An ornamental evergreen tree, growing upright to 15 m. with hanging, glossy foliage not unlike a broad-leaved Eucalyptus; long planted on Mombasa Island, where it has become naturalised, and common in parts of Nairobi.
Bark: brown and fairly rough on the trunk, whitish on the branches.   **Leaves:** opposite, becoming large and oval, up to 20 cm. in length, the apex often tapering to a distinctly pointed tip; smooth glossy green above, strongly aromatic when crushed. Young leaves are narrower, often with a copper flush.   **Flowers:** greenish-yellow, very small, in axillary clusters among the leaves, the stems of the flower head branching at right angles.   **Fruit:** oval, to 3 cm. long, in conspicuous clusters; deep purple when ripe, sweet but slightly astringent, the juice drying the mouth. Purple stains from fallen fruit are often prominent under the tree.

Syzygium aromaticum is the clove of commerce, the dried flower buds being used as the spice.

Syzygium guineense
indigenous

Waterberry
Mukoe (Kikuyu)

A densely foliaged forest tree resembling a a bushy Eucalyptus, usually to 10 or 15 m. but on river banks sometimes to 25 m. or more; a very variable species, widely distributed in Kenya and extending to Southern Africa.
Bark: light brown to grey; cracking and flaking with age.   **Leaves:** opposite, dark waxy green above, broadly elliptic, 6 to 16 cm. in length, often in crowded, untidy clusters. Young leaves and shoots may be purplish-red.   **Flowers:** small, white, fragrant, in dense heads, attracting masses of insects. Insect damage can result in odd gall growths.   **Fruit:** oval, to 3 cm. long, purple-black and edible when ripe.
In traditional medicine, liquid from the pounded bark and roots mixed with water was used as a purgative.

197

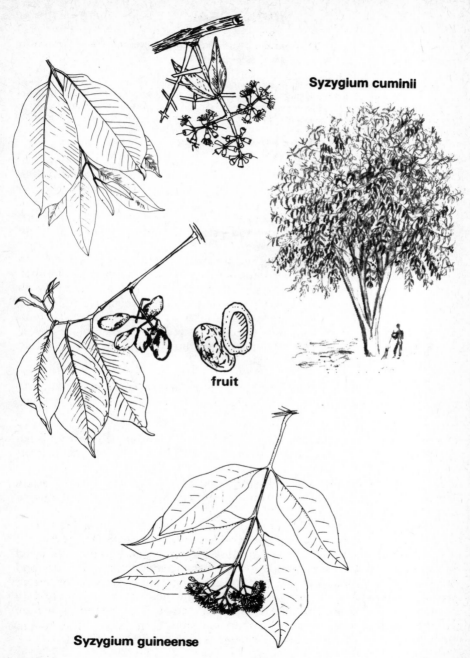

Syzygium cuminii

fruit

Syzygium guineense

OCHNACEAE   Ochna family

A tropical family of trees, shrubs and herbs with 40 genera and over 600 species, centred in tropical South America. The genus Ochna includes 85 species of attractive shrubs and small trees, mostly in tropical and southern Africa.

In Kenya there are about ten indigenous species, but the genus as a whole is easily recognised by its flowers. These have many stamens, and the petals, usually yellow, fall within hours of opening to leave a striking combination of bright red or purple sepals surrounding small black fruit. The swollen tip of the flower stalk below the fruit, known as the receptacle, is also red. The sepals can easily be mistaken for petals.

All species are deciduous, and very slow growing.

Ochna holstii
indigenous

Forest Ochna
Mungarima (Kikuyu)

A variable forest species, reaching 20 m. in the high podo forests of western Kenya but usually seen as an understorey shrub or spindly tree from 3 to 7 m. in woodland at Ngong and Machakos.

Bark: grey-brown, rather rough; branchlets dotted with pale breathing pores. **Leaves:** alternate, shiny green, lance-shaped, 10 to 14 cm. long, apex pointed, base clearly tapering to a very short stalk; veins raised, margin with small regular, spiny teeth. **Flowers:** yellow, 2 to 3 cm. across, on 3 cm. stalks, in clusters arising from short side twigs, the petals falling to leave 5 persistent, spreading sepals which turn pink to purple-red; young sepals blunt-tipped, over 1 cm. long. **Fruit:** soft, to 1 cm. long, in groups of up to nine, black when ripe, hanging from the red receptacle.

Ochna insculpta is a forest tree to 9 m. found above 1,200 m., common at Marsabit, with leaves up to 12 cm. and showy yellow flowers, 2.5 cm. across.

Ochna ovata *(Ochna stuhlmannii)*
indigenous

Ochna, Buttercup Bush
Mungarima (Kikuyu)

A handsome, sturdy shrub or small tree to 5 m., widespread in central Kenya from 600 to 1,900 m.; common around Nairobi in forest margins and rocky bushland.

Bark: pale grey, finely fissured, rougher and darker with age; branchlets covered with dot-like breathing pores. **Leaves:** alternate, oval, to 7 cm. but usually smaller; mature leaves stiff and pointed, glossy dark green with raised veins above, dull and very smooth below; base rounded, margin evenly and finely serrated. Young leaves are soft and drooping, coppery-red turning bright green. **Flowers:** bright yellow, about 1.5 cm. across, in stalked axillary clusters, very fragrant and attracting bees; sepals 5, persistent, unequal, turning to pink or red; young sepals short, less than 1 cm. long. **Fruit:** soft, to 1 cm. long, in groups of up to 4, black when ripe, eaten by birds.

199

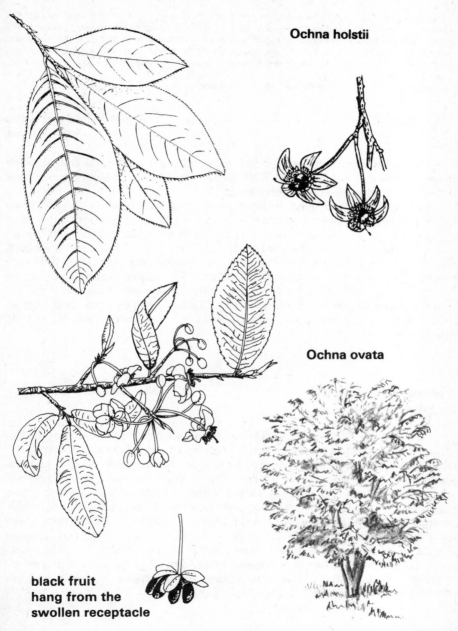

Ochna holstii

Ochna ovata

black fruit
hang from the
swollen receptacle

200

OLEACEAE   Olive family

A family with about 500 species of trees and shrubs, mainly from the northern hemisphere, where two of the major genera are the Ashes *Fraxinus* spp. and the Olives *Olea* spp. The indigenous Wild Olive *Olea europea subsp. africana* is widespread and familiar in the highlands, but there are no indigenous Ashes, although one North American species has been fairly widely planted in gardens and parks. Exotic ornamental shrubs in this family include jasmine, forsythia, privet and lilac.

Members of this family in Kenya include *Chionanthus, Fraxinus, Olea, Schrebera*.

Chionanthus battiscombei *(Linociera battiscombei)*   Small-fruited Ironwood
indigenous   Musharagi (Kikuyu)

A small evergreen forest tree to 8 m. in height, usually occurring at forest edges or beside streams from 1,500 to 1,850 m.; also in the Ngong forest near Nairobi and other remnant forest areas.

Bark: grey to brown, smooth; branchlets dotted with conspicuous breathing pores.   **Leaves:** opposite, oval to elliptic, to 8 cm. long; apex tapering to a blunt tip; texture markedly stiff, darkly glossy above; undersurface paler, with scattered brown dots in the axils of the veins marking curious hairy pockets, said to house mites; margin thickened, sometimes curled under; stalk very short.   **Flowers:** small, fragrant, white, with four narrow strap-like petals, in compact axillary clusters, the four lobes of the calyx covered with dense white hairs.   **Fruit:** ridged oval berries with a single seed, nearly 2 cm. long, purple-black and fleshy when ripe, eaten by birds. The persistent calyx lobes help recognition.

Fraxinus pennsylvanica   Mexican Ash, Green Ash
North America

A spreading deciduous tree to 15 m., fairly widely planted as an ornamental around Nairobi and elsewhere in the highlands from 1,500 to 2,800 m.

Bark: light grey, cracking with age into rough horizontal fissures.   **Leaves:** compound, opposite, up to 30 cm. long, rather crowded at the ends of branches; leaflets 2 or 3 pairs plus a terminal leaflet, spear-shaped, often unequal-sided, up to 18 cm. long; apex tapering, veins conspicuous below, margin irregularly toothed towards the apex. The dark brown leaf buds are very prominent before the lime-green new leaves appear.   **Flowers:** without petals, male stamens purple-brown, female flowers separate, very small, lime-green, both in terminal sprays.   **Fruit:** single seeds with a propeller-shaped wing up to 5 cm. in length, on long slender stalks, drying light brown and hanging in persistent, conspicuous clusters.

201

Chionanthus battiscombei

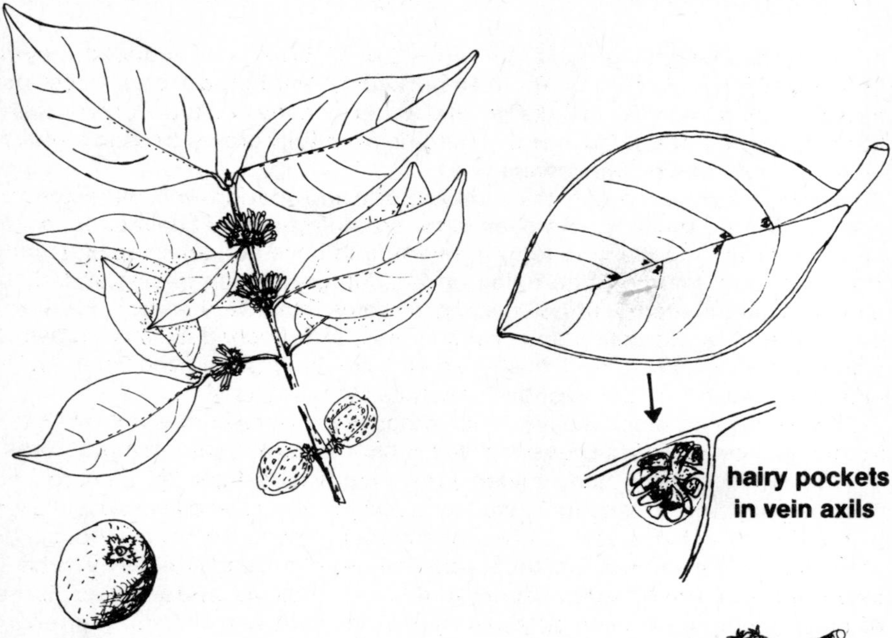

hairy pockets
in vein axils

mature fruit

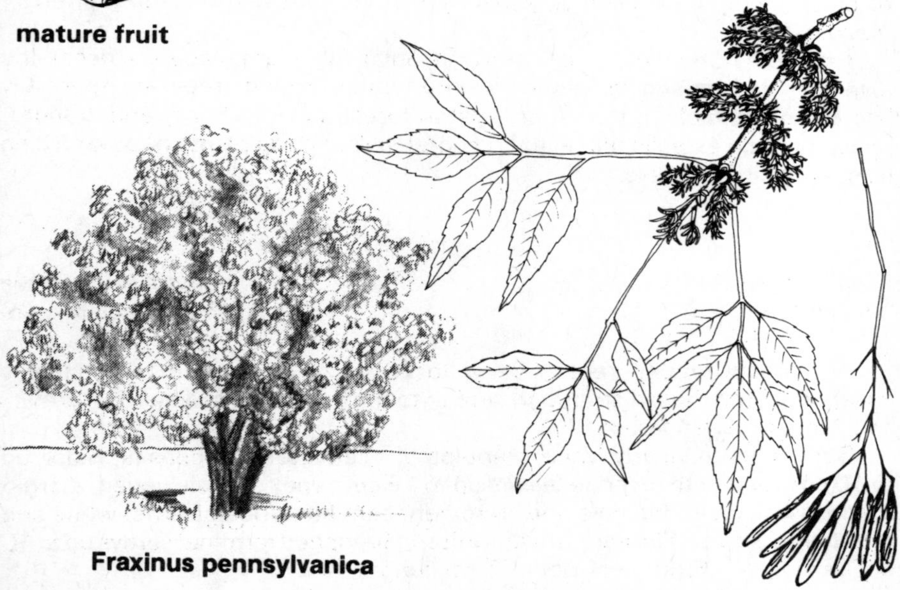

Fraxinus pennsylvanica

202

OLEACEAE

Olea europaea subsp. africana *(Olea africana,*
Olea chrysophylla)
indigenous

**Wild Olive,
Brown Olive,**
Mutamaiyu (Kikuyu)

A handsome grey-green tree with a much-branched, rounded crown, growing to 10 m. or occasionally to 15 m.; widely distributed in drier forest and forest margins from 750 to 3,000 m. and found in many habitats from northern Ethiopia to the Cape of Good Hope, ranging from fully grown trees to stunted, misshapen shrubs on windswept sites.

Bark: dark brown, rough, the trunk crooked and gnarled with characteristic pockets. Young white stems bear large breathing pores. **Leaves:** opposite, narrowly oval, 3 to 8 cm. in length, tapering to base and apex; apex usually sharply tipped, margin often rolled under; dull grey-green above, underside almost white, dusted with powdery gold scales; stalk very short. **Flowers:** small, with 4 white petals and two stamens, in branched axillary sprays to 5 cm. in length. **Fruit:** oval, fleshy, about 1 cm. long, purple and bitter-sweet when ripe, attracting flocks of birds such as Olive Pigeons.

The larger commercial olive which produces olive oil comes only from the Mediterranean variety of *Olea europaea,* which requires winter temperatures.

The wood is very hard, golden brown with dark figuring, planing and polishing to a fine finish; much used for quality furniture and also widely used by the Kamba woodcarvers. It is also a superb firewood, and many thousands of trees were cut down to fuel the steam engines of the early railway. The bark, leaves and roots were widely used in traditional medicine, and smoking pieces of burnt wood were used as a catalyst to ferment and flavour yoghurt or *maziwa-lala.*

Practical notes: fairly slow-growing, but living to great age and deserving extensive re-planting as a useful ornamental. Young trees are gradually becoming available in nurseries; best in forest soil, but hardy and drought-resistant once established, even in poorer soils. Young plants need shielding from browsing animals.

Olea hochstetteri
indigenous

East African Olive
Musharagi (Kikuyu)

A valuable timber tree, growing to 20 m. or more with high, steeply ascending branches; distribution similar to the preceding species, but preferring higher rainfall forest.

Bark: smooth, nearly white, granulated. **Leaves:** stiff, opposite, wider, up to 10 cm. long with juvenile leaves up to 16 cm.; apex sharply tipped, margin markedly wavy, midrib pale and prominent beneath; underside not white and the stalk to 3 cm. **Flowers:** small, white, in branched terminal sprays up to 10 cm. in length. **Fruit:** oval, about 2 cm. long.

203

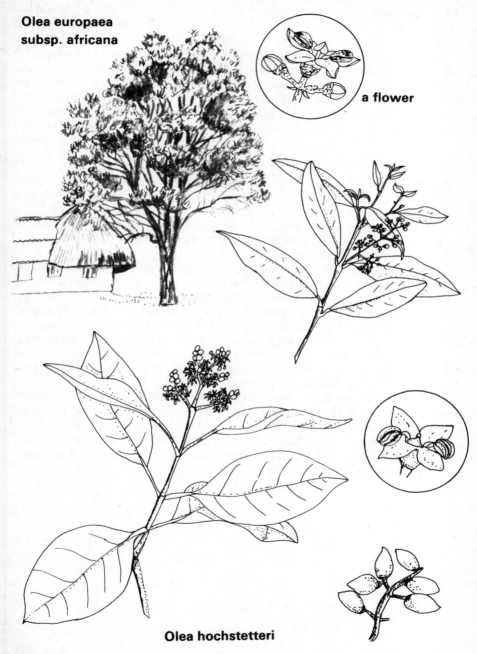

Olea europaea subsp. africana

a flower

Olea hochstetteri

OLEACEAE

Olea welwitschii   **Elgon Olive**
indigenous   Mutukuyu (Kikuyu)

A large timber tree to 25 m. or more from the rainfall forests of the Nyanza Basin from 1,500 to 2,200 m.; now sadly rare.   **Bark:** pale grey to nearly white, vertically fissured.   **Leaves:** opposite, much longer than in the other *Oleas,* to 15x5 cm.   **Flowers**: small, white, in profuse sprays up to 8 cm. long. The timber is pale golden brown with darker streaks, much used for high-class furniture.

Schrebera alata   **Schrebera, Wing-leaved wooden-pear**
indigenous   Mutoma (Kikuyu)

A graceful deciduous tree with light green foliage, to 15 m. or occasionally to 25 m. in height, occurring in open woodland and drier forest from 1,500 to 2,300 m.; common in parts of Nairobi.

Bark: dark grey, cracking with age; inner bark light brown. The trunk is prominently fluted.   **Leaves:** compound, leaflets 2 pairs plus a larger terminal leaflet up to 12 cm. long; apex broadly tapering, with the tip sometimes rounded and notched; leaf stalk characteristically winged ('alata').   **Flowers:** creamy white marked with purple, very sweetly scented, about 1.5 cm. across, the throat powdered with brown and the 2 stamens yellow, in much-branched terminal heads.   **Fruit:** pear-shaped capsules, about 3 cm. long, often in clusters of 4 or 5; light brown and persistent when mature, splitting open on the tree, containing many papery-winged seeds.

The wood is pale brown with dark markings, hard and heavy, making excellent firewood. The bark and leaves are reputed to have anaesthetic properties and can be chewed to relieve headaches and toothache.

Practical notes: an elegant, attractive tree, fairly fast-growing in good forest soil. The leaves fall with the rains but are replaced almost immediately. Young plants are gradually becoming available in nurseries.

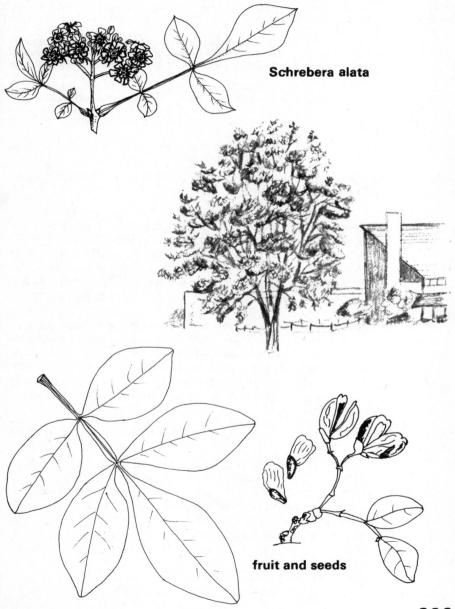

Schrebera alata

fruit and seeds

PALMAE   Palm family

Palms are an ancient and distinctive family of *Monocotyledons*, the class of plants that includes the grass, lily, banana and orchid families. There are over 2,700 species, most of them originating in tropical America and Asia, the main groups being Feather Palms, Fan Palms and Fish-tail Palms, named according to features of the leaves.

The fruits are often rich in food store, and at least three species have world-wide economic importance. These are the Coconut palm *Cocos nucifera*, the Date Palm *Phoenix dactylifera* and the Oil Palm *Elaeis guineensis* from Central Africa, which although uncommon is also indigenous to Kenya.

Compared to Asia and America, there are very few African palms. In Kenya there are only 6 indigenous species, the best known being the Wild Date Palm *Phoenix reclinata*, the Borassus Palm *Borassus aethiopum* and the Doum Palm *Hyphaene compressa,* with its unusual branching stems. However, a large number of exotic species have been planted as eye-catching ornamentals; all grow from seed, and many make attractive indoor decoration.

Members of this family in Kenya include *Archontophoenix, Borassus, Caryota, Chrysalidocarpus, Cocos, Hyphaene, Phoenix, Roystonea, Syagrus, Washingtonia.*

Archontophoenix alexandrae   Alexandra Palm, King Palm
Tropical Asia, Queensland

A handsome rain-forest palm, growing to 20 m. but usually smaller. **Trunk:** grey and closely ringed, resembling layers of brickwork; very slender, to 15 cm. in diameter, sometimes swollen at the base. **Leaves:** 8 to 12, feathery and arching, to 3.5 m. long, rising from a smooth green cylinder known as the crownshaft; leaflets 50 or more, each about 50 x 4 cm., with the underside scaly silver-grey. **Flowers:** creamy white, in distinctive tangled clusters up to 75 cm. in length. **Fruit:** small, coral-red, pointed, about 2 cm. long.

Archontophoenix cunninghamiana, the Piccabeen Palm from Eastern Australia is very similar and grows to 8 m., with the trunk to 20 cm. in diameter the base rarely swollen. **Leaves:** leaflets broader, about 10 cm. in width, green on both sides. **Flowers:** lilac, on pendulous stalks to 1 m. long. **Fruit:** very small, globular, to 15 mm. in diameter, on stalks resembling necklaces with red beads. This is a quick-growing palm, preferring full sun, often known in nurseries as *Seaforthia elegans*.

Borassus aethiopum   Borassus Palm, African Fan Palm
indigenous   Mvumo (Swahili)

The tallest of the indigenous palms, to 25 m. in height, sparsely scattered along the coastal belt; very slow-growing. **Trunk:** grey, older trees developing a strange swelling above the middle of the trunk; young stems clad with persistent dead leaves. **Leaves:** very large, fan-shaped, up to 4 m. long and 3 m. across, deeply divided into numerous segments. **Flowers:** male and female on different trees, male trees producing very large pollen-bearing catkins. **Fruit:** large, round, orange, about 15 cm. long, the pulp fibrous but edible.

The sap is fermented into an excellent palm wine and the leaves are used for weaving. This palm is also found in India, where it has a variety of uses.

207

Archontophoenix alexandrae

Borassus aethiopum

Caryota urens, the Fishtail Palm from tropical Asia is occasionally found in Nairobi, notably by Parliament Buildings. The strange, wedge-shaped leaflets resemble a fish's tail.

Chrysalidocarpus lutescens, the Butterfly Palm or Areca Palm from Madagascar, is a feather palm which has been widely planted in airport gardens and other public areas. The clump of slender stems marked with horizontal ridges grows to 8 m., with glossy leaflets spaced along graceful, arching leaf stalks which arise from prominent cylindrical crownshafts.

Cocos nucifera   **Coconut Palm**
Tropics   Mnazi (Swahili)

A familiar coastal palm growing to 30 m. at sea-level, its origins hazy, possibly in Polynesia and possibly in tropical America.
Trunk: grey-brown, slender, often bent by the wind, swollen at the base, with stem roots often visible.   **Leaves:** 20 to 30, in large terminal tufts, the leaf base surrounded with a brown, net-like fibre; leaves heavy, to 6 m. long, leaflets numerous, narrow, sharply pointed.   **Flowers:** dense, creamy yellow, on branched stalks, up to 300 male flowers at the tip and 12 to 20 female flowers at the base, which develop into the fruit.   **Fruit:** heavy, hard-shelled nuts, the outer coat green, turning to yellow or brown. The inner fibrous husk is the coir used for making ropes, and the fleshy white meat, high in oil content, can be eaten raw or dried to make copra.

The hollow centre contains a clear, sugary milk which develops into the white flesh. The milk is a refreshing drink, and is so sterile that it has been used for emergency transfusions. The sap, tapped from the flower stalk, can be fermented to an alcoholic brew. Leaf fronds are woven into an attractive roofing thatch known locally as *makuti*.

Practical notes: grown entirely from seed, the shoots sprouting from the largest of the three 'eyes' on the shell. Prefers light sandy soil and tolerates salt; some have been planted around Lake Victoria, but grow to only half their height at the coast. The tree produces its best yield between 12 and 60 years of age, and will live to over 100 years.

Chrysalidocarpus lutescens

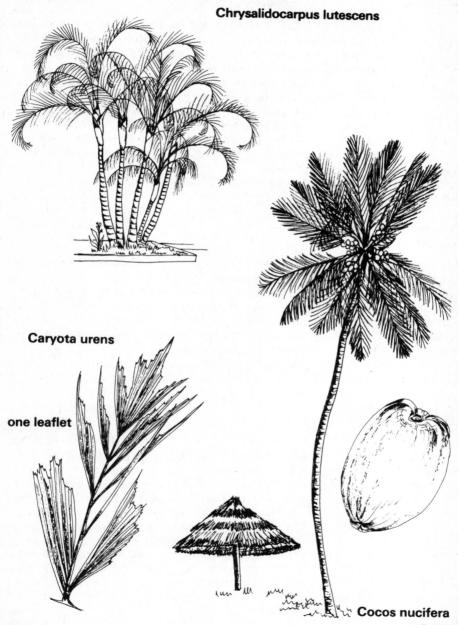

Caryota urens

one leaflet

Cocos nucifera

Hyphaene compressa *(Hyphaene multiformis, Hyphaene thebaica)*　**Doum Palm**
indigenous　　　　　　*COLOUR PLATE XIII*　　Mkoma (Swahili)

An unusual branching palm with the stems dividing regularly, to 15 m. in height, common at the coast, also in northern and eastern areas where it is usually riparian, marking out the course of rivers. Young plants are low and shrubby, often in thickets covering a wide area.

Leaves: fan-shaped, on long spiny stalks, in rather sparse terminal clusters. Dead leaves often persist around the higher stems.　**Fruit:** orange, 8 to 10 cm. long, irregularly pear-shaped with two flattened faces, in heavy clusters, sometimes eaten by Turkana children but usually eaten by baboons and elephants. The elephants swallow the whole fruit and so distribute seeds.

The sap makes a very strong, course brew, and finely woven baskets and mats are made from young leaves.

The similar species *Hyphaene coriacea* is found only at the coast. The fruits are slightly smaller, less than 6 cm. in length.

Phoenix canariensis　　　　　　　　　**Canary Palm**
Canary Islands

A thickset ornamental palm to 15 m., widely popular in Mediterranean resorts and hardy enough to grow in cooler upland districts like Limuru.

Trunk: stout, very rough, covered with a pattern of diamond-shaped scars from old leaf stalks.　**Leaves:** 5 to 6 m. long, in a graceful arching crown; leaflets glossy, numerous, stiff and very regular. The leaflets are smaller at the tip of the leaf stalk, and are reduced to spines at the base.　**Fruit:** small, yellow, in large clusters on female trees only, not edible.

Phoenix roebelenii, the Pygmy Date Palm, is sold as an indoor plant, seldom exceeding 1 m. in height.　**Leaves:** 40 cm. in length; soft, shiny dark green.

Phoenix reclinata　　　　　　　　**Wild Date Palm,**
indigenous　　　　　　　　　　　　**Senegal Palm**
　　　　　　　　　　　　　　　Mukindu (Kikuyu)

A gregarious palm growing to 8 m. in dense clumps beside swamps and rivers from the coast to 3,000 m.; also grown as an ornamental.

Trunk: slender and supple, about 25 cm. in diameter, sometimes bent over ('reclinata'), covered in very rough leaf scars.　**Leaves:** to 2.7 m. long, rising from a fibrous leaf sheath; crown markedly downturned; leaflets narrow, folded, to 30 cm. in length, stiff and sharply pointed.　**Flowers:** male and female on different trees.　**Fruit:** yellow-brown, about 2 cm. long, edible.

The leaves are widely used for baskets and mats, and the roots for dye.

Phoenix sylvestris, the East Indian Wine Palm, does well in Nairobi and is distinguished by the fine powder covering young shoots.　**Leaves:** to 4 m. long, leaflets, delicate, greyish-green.　**Fruit:** reddish, about 2 cm. long. The sap is sugary, used for making wine.

211

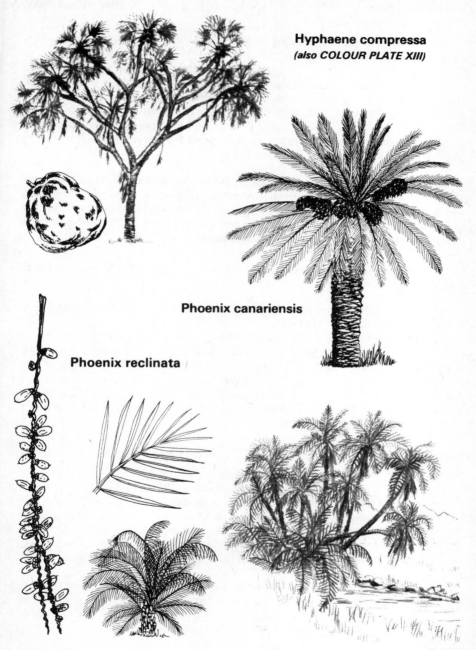

Hyphaene compressa
(also COLOUR PLATE XIII)

Phoenix canariensis

Phoenix reclinata

Roystonea regia   Cuban Royal Palm
Cuba, Central America

A tall, striking palm, growing to 25 m. with a prominent, glossy green crownshaft up to 2 m. in length.

Trunk: light grey, smooth, ringed, swollen at the base and sometimes also higher up.   **Leaves:** to 6 m. long, arching downwards; leaflets soft, narrow, about 75 x 2 cm., growing in 4 rows in different planes, giving a ragged appearance.   **Flowers:** held within erect bright green envelopes at the base of the crownshaft, which split to allow long stalks of pale yellow flowers to emerge.   **Fruit:** brown and black, rounded, about 1.5 cm. across; edible, rich in oil and carbohydrates, used for stock feed.

Roystonea oleracea, the Caribbean Royal Palm, is even taller, with the crown of leaves less drooping than the preceding species.   **Leaves:** shorter, to 4 m. long: leaflets broader, only in one plane, giving a flatter, more symmetrical appearance. The flower stalks have a wavy, zig-zag form. The growing point is the gourmet delicacy known as 'cabbage palm'.

Syagrus romanzoffianum *(Arecastrum romanzoffianum)* Queen Palm, Feather Palm
Brazil, South America

An erect, feathery palm up to 15 m. in height, grown at altitudes up to 2,150 m. and common in Nairobi.

Trunk: slender, grey and smooth, 20 to 30 cm. in diameter, distinctly or indistinctly ringed.   **Leaves:** to 6 m. long, in a graceful, loosely arching crown; leaflets narrow, soft, dark shiny grey-green, to 1.5 m. in length but usually smaller, growing singly or in tufts.   **Flowers:** yellow, in long clusters between the leaves.   **Fruit:** orange, edible, roundish, to 2.5 cm., in dense clusters.

The Queen Palm is fairly slow-growing, and is often sold as a pot plant under the name *Cocos plumosa.*

Washingtonia filifera   Desert Fan Palm, Petticoat Palm
California, Arizona

A striking fan palm to 25 m., prominent along Uhuru Highway in Nairobi.

Trunk: dark grey, very straight, up to 1 m. in diameter, often swollen at the base, with a conspicuous petticoat of dead leaves.   **Leaves:** grey-green, fan-shaped, very large, up to 2 m. across, deeply divided into 5 or more segments which bear thread-like fibres ('filifera') along the margin.   **Flowers:** white, on long branched stalks.   **Fruit:** oval, about 1.5 cm. long, black when mature.

Washingtonia robusta, the Mexican Fan Palm, is no more robust despite its name, but is probably faster-growing. In warm temperate climates it reaches 33 m. with a more slender, tapering, brownish trunk and less of a petticoat of dead leaves. The leaf margins do not bear loose fibres.

213

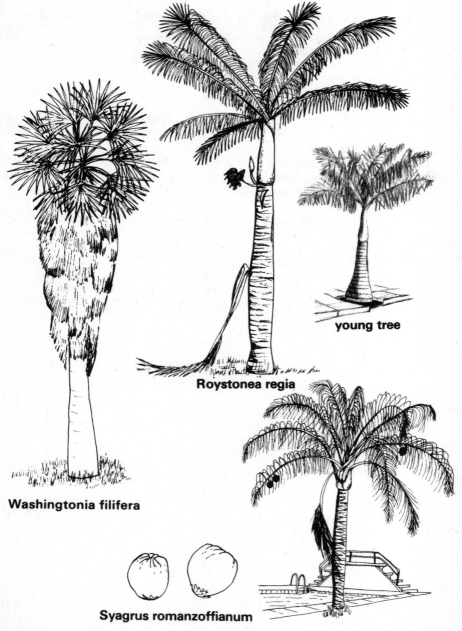

young tree

Roystonea regia

Washingtonia filifera

Syagrus romanzoffianum

214

PANDANACEAE   Screw pine family

A restricted family with only one genus but hundreds of species, found at the water's edge on the tropical shores of the Indian Ocean and the Pacific Islands. Their common names are associations from their appearance, because these trees are neither pines nor palms, all being held out of the water by stiff aerial roots.

The commonest species on the Kenya coast is *Pandanus kirkii,* although there are a few other similar indigenous species, one of them on riverbanks in central Kenya.

Pandanus kirkii
indigenous

Screw Pine, Walking Palm
Mkadi (Swahili)

An unusual, decorative tree to 10 m. in height, found on the strand just above the high water mark, often in association with Casuarinas and indigenous palm trees. Stilt roots arising from the lower trunk anchor the tree in the sand.

Leaves: dark, strap-like, up to 90 x 5 cm., in stiff terminal whorls; margins and midribs very spiny.   **Flowers:** male flowers very small, white, fragrant, in hanging spikes up to 10 cm. long, concealed by leafy bracts; female spikes smaller, greenish.   **Fruit:** conspicuous, resembling a hard pineapple, about 20 cm. long, orange when ripe. Fallen fruit are often seen on the beach.

Dried leaves are used for weaving mats and baskets, and in many areas were used for thatch. The well-known grass skirts of the Pacific islands were often made from split Pandanus leaves.

Pandanus kirkii

PAPILIONOIDEAE   Pea sub-family of Leguminosae

A sub-family of particular importance, as the seeds and pods of many of the herbaceous species are worldwide sources of human and animal food, such as peas, beans, lucerne and groundnuts.

With modern emphasis on agroforestry, various nitrogen-fixing tree species are also increasingly important in Kenya. These include the indigenous *Sesbania sesban* described in the text, the widely planted *Leucaena leucocephala* from Central America and the indigenous *Lonchocarpus eriocalyx,* known in Swahili as *Msomari,* a savannah tree with fragrant violet flowers and a reputation as an excellent bee tree.

The typical pea flower has five petals, often brightly coloured, forming a 'butterfly' shape, with the big upper petal known as the 'standard' flanked by two pairs of petals of different shapes, the 'wings' and the 'keel'. There are ten stamens, which are often enclosed by the two partly joined lower petals which form the keel. Leaves of this sub-family are usually compound, sometimes trifoliate.

Members of the sub-family in Kenya include *Calpurnea, Castanospermum, Craibia, Dalbergia, Erythrina, Millettia, Ormocarpum, Sesbania, Tipuana.*

Calpurnea aurea *(Calpurnea subdecandra)*   **East African Laburnum**
indigenous   Muchingiri, Mwethia (Kikuyu)

A small deciduous flowering tree, rarely over 5 m., common in forests on the Mau, Laikipia and elsewhere from 2,100 to 2,500 m.; also along streams down to 1,500 m., and planted in the Nairobi area as an ornamental.

Bark: pale brown, darker with age.   **Leaves:** compound, leaflets oblong, fresh lightgreen, 5 to 15 pairs plus a terminal leaflet, up to 2.5 cm. in length; apex rounded, with a hair-like tip; softly hairy below, less so above.   **Flowers:** attractive, yellow, about 2.5 cm. across, in dense heads on hanging stems up to 20 cm. in length.   **Fruit:** flat, straight, pale brown pods up to 12 cm. in length, with a narrow wing along one edge, persisting on the tree.

Castanospermum australe   **Moreton Bay Chestnut**
Queensland, Australia

An evergreen tree to 20 m. in height, often with low, hanging branches, found as an ornamental in Nairobi and the highlands, rarely at the coast.

Bark: grey, finely fissured.   **Leaves:** large, compound, leaflets glossy and rather wavy, 5 to 7 pairs, narrowly oval, up to 10 cm. long; apex tapering to a point.   **Flowers:** striking orange-red, about 2.5 cm. long, in short sprays, arising from older woody branches.   **Fruit:** thick cylindrical pods, to 23 cm. long, brown when mature, containing 2 to 5 large, rounded seeds about 4 cm. across, edible when roasted but not very palatable.

Castanospermime, extracted from the nuts, is of particular interest to scientists and is currently being tested for its possible effect on the AIDS virus.

This species is planted in Kenya only as an ornamental, but in Australia it is a valuable timber for furniture. Fairly fast-growing from seed or cuttings.

217

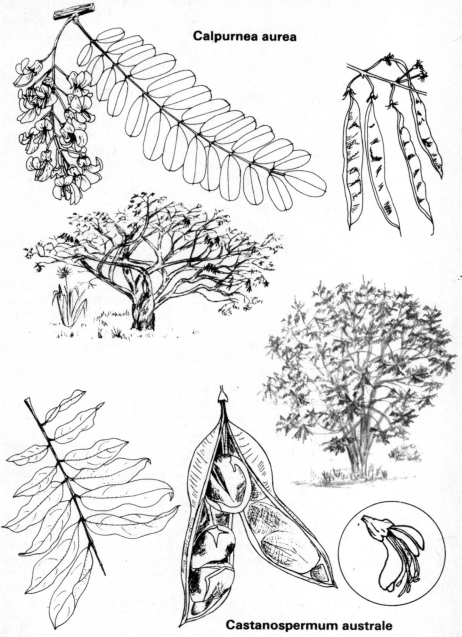

Calpurnea aurea

Castanospermum australe

Craibia brownii *(Craibia elliotii)*
indigenous

Craibia
Mukubu (Kikuyu)

A dense evergreen tree, eye-catching in flower, to 12 m. in height, usually with a short, straight trunk branching to form a rounded crown; occurring in forest and forest margins in Nyanza, Rift Valley and Central Provinces, including the Nairobi area.

Bark: grey, smooth, very thin, flaking slightly with age. **Leaves:** compound, 3 to 7 alternate leaflets plus a terminal leaflet, each 5 to 10 cm. long; dull dark green, very smooth; apex tapering, base rounded, midrib prominent beneath; leaflet stalks wrinkled and flexible, leaf stalks shortly swollen at the base. **Flowers:** showy, white tinged with pale pink, sweetly scented, in short, compact sprays, sometimes covering the tree and leaving a pink carpet of fallen flowers. **Fruit:** dark brown pods, about 6 cm. long, splitting on the tree with an explosive 'crack' to release shiny light brown seeds, 2 cm. in length.

The tree is extremely slow-growing, with hard, white wood.

Dalbergia melanoxylon
indigenous

African Blackwood, 'African Ebony'
Poyi (Trade name)
Mpingo (Swahili)

A much-branched spiny shrub or small tree to 7 m. with a heavily fluted bole and an irregular crown, scattered in low altitude savannah and woodland below 1,300 m. in areas like Kibwezi and Kitui; also found in similar habitat from Ethiopia to Southern Africa. *Dalbergia melanoxylon* is believed to be the ebony of ancient Egypt, and was probably introduced there from Sudan. Its wood is harder than *Diospyros mespiliformis* in the family Ebenaceae, which is also referred to as African Ebony.

Bark: smooth, greyish-yellow, darker, rougher and flaking with age; branches short and twisted, bearing woody spines. **Leaves:** compound, clustered on small hard branchlets; leaflets dark green, small and variable, usually about 1.5 cm. long. **Flowers:** small, white, sweet-scented, in short branched sprays. **Fruit:** thin flat pods, to 7 cm. long.

The heartwood is a beautiful purplish black, very hard and durable, making it a very valuable timber in East Africa. Some flawless pieces are exported to make woodwind instruments such as clarinets, but the lower-grade pieces are greatly in demand for woodcarvings for the tourist industry. The artistic use made of the bends and hollows by the Makonde and Kamba carvers is widely renowned.

The increasing scarcity of this species, which takes many decades to mature, is a matter of national concern.

219

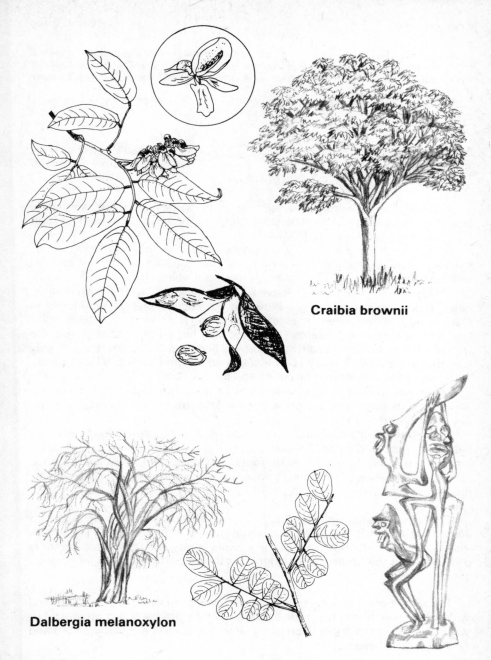

Craibia brownii

Dalbergia melanoxylon

PAPILIONOIDEAE

Erythrina spp. **Coral Trees**

A widespread tropical and sub-tropical genus of trees or shrubs with large trifoliate leaves and showy flowers, often brilliant scarlet or orange. The trunks are mostly gnarled and rugged-looking, with vicious thorns. A number of species are found in Africa, Central America, Australia, Southern Asia and Hawaii.

In Kenya there are five indigenous species, one of them very widespread, and several exotics.

Erythrina abyssinica *(Erythrina tomentosa)*   **Red Hot Poker Tree,**
indigenous   **Flame Tree, Lucky Bean Tree**

COLOUR PLATE XIV   Muhuti (Kikuyu)

A deciduous flowering tree with a short trunk and stout, spreading branches, usually 6 to 12 m. in height, widely distributed in open woodland and grassland from sea-level to 2,000 m.

Bark: brown, thick and corky, deeply fissured, often bearing blunt, woody spines. **Leaves:** trifoliate, the terminal leaflet the largest; leaflets broadly rounded, up to 15 x 15 cm., with 3 prominent veins rising from the base; branchlets and undersides of leaves densely covered with brownish-grey hairs, especially when young. **Flowers:** spectacular orange-red blossoms like feathery red hot pokers, in erect heads up to 15 cm. long over much of the tree; very attractive to sunbirds. Flowering is rather erratic, usually when the tree is bare of leaves. **Fruit:** furry brown pods, up to 10 cm. long, deeply constricted between the seeds. The seeds are bright red with a black patch, rounded and shiny, popular as curios and for necklaces.

The seeds contain minute amounts of a curare-like poison, but there is no danger in handling them and they are so hard that they are unlikely to have any ill-effects even if swallowed.

Many traditional beliefs surround this tree. Among some tribes it was the basis of a curse, and others believed that the wood should never be burned for fear of attracting lightning. Both roots and bark were believed to have medicinal properties, and the soft, easily carved wood was used for mortars, drums and beehives.

Erythrina lysistemon from South Africa is usually smaller than *Erythrina abyssinica,* and its leaflets are broadly triangular in shape, tapering to the apex instead of rounded. The colour of the flowers varies, but the most commonly propagated is the brilliant red variety. **Erythrina caffra** is a similar, slightly smaller species.

Practical notes: striking trees, easily grown even from large cuttings and widely available from nurseries. In good soil they are fairly fast growing, but will also succeed in dry or even rocky sites. All species are soft-wooded and relatively short-lived.

221

Erythrina abyssinica
(also COLOUR PLATE XIV)

leaves

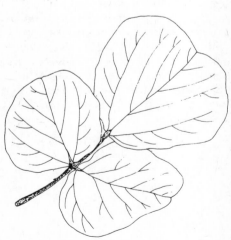

Erythrina lysistemon

Erythrina abyssinica

Millettia dura
indigenous

Millettia
Muhatia (Kikuyu)

A deciduous flowering tree with a sparse, spreading habit, growing to 12 m. in secondary scrub and forest margin areas of Central Province from 1,500 to 2,000 m.; fairly common around Nairobi.

Bark: grey, smooth, with fine vertical fissures. **Leaves:** compound, leaflets dull green, up to 12 pairs plus a terminal leaflet, up to 5 cm. long, often unequal-sided; apex pointed, often with a hair-like tip. Young leaflets and leaf stalks are covered with short, rust-coloured hairs. **Flowers:** lilac, in dense clusters up to 20 cm. in length. **Fruit:** thick flat pods, up to 25x2 cm., bluntly pointed, hanging singly or in small clusters, splitting with an explosive 'crack'.

The wood is tough and resistant to termites, making good poles and handles for garden tools. There are several other species, mainly at the coast.

Practical notes: moderately fast-growing in forest soil, sometimes flowering in three years; hardy and drought-resistant. Formerly planted as a coffee shade tree; now available as an ornamental from many nurseries.

Ormocarpum trachycarpum *(Ormocarpum mimosoides)*
indigenous

Caterpillar pod

A small deciduous shrub or rather shapeless tree, rarely exceeding 3 m. in height, found in open savannah and rocky areas in Machakos and Meru districts and around Nairobi.

Bark: rough, dark brown. **Leaves:** compound, clustered on dwarf side shoots; leaflets grey-green, very small, less than 1 cm. long; apex rounded, with a hair-like tip. Leaf stalks, flower stalks, veins and leaf margins all bear dark, bristle-like hairs. **Flowers:** mauve, heavily veined, 1 or 2 flowers borne on short axillary stalks, the petals persisting in conspicuous dry, pale brown clusters as they fade. **Fruit:** unmistakeable small pods, 2.5 cm. long, covered with yellow-brown bristles and resembling small, hairy caterpillars.

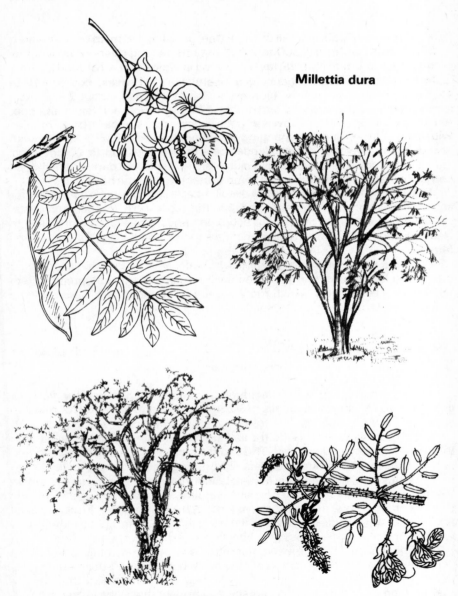

Millettia dura

Ormocarpum trachycarpum

Sesbania sesban *(Sesbania aegyptiaca)*
indigenous

Sesbania, River Bean
Mwethia (Kikuyu)

A deciduous shrub or small or small tree, growing to 8 m. in or near water; widely distributed from 1,300 to 2,000 m., often along rivers or in swampy ground, particularly in Nyanza; fairly common in waste ground around Nairobi.

Bark: reddish-brown, producing a useful fibre. **Leaves:** compound, to 12 cm. long; leaflets narrow, blue-green, 10 to 25 pairs, about 2 cm. long, folding at dusk; apex rounded and notched. Young shoots and leaf stalks bear white, spreading hairs. **Flowers:** pale yellow, the standard petal mottled with dark maroon, usually hanging in sprays up to 15 cm. in length with few or many flowers. **Fruit:** slender pale brown pods, up to 20 cm. long, often curved or twisted, hanging in clusters. The seeds are dark, bean-shaped and prolific, and rattle in individual compartments inside the pods.

The wood is light and soft, but an excellent source of firewood and useful for light construction. In traditional medicine the roots were crushed to a paste, said to be an excellent remedy for scorpion stings. The leaves were used to treat swellings, and are a soap substitute as well as a valuable fodder and fertiliser.

Practical notes: very fast growing from seed; easy to establish in anything from waterlogged clay to dry, eroded soil, developing a deep taproot system which helps soil fertility. Much money spent on nitrogen fertilisers could be saved by intercropping with this species.

Tipuana tipu *(Machaerium tipu)*
Bolivia, Brazil

Tipu Tree, Pride of Bolivia

COLOUR PLATE XV

A large, spreading, semi-deciduous shade tree with yellow flowers, growing to 20 m. but occasionally to 30 m.; widely planted around Nairobi and elsewhere in the highlands.

Bark: reddish-brown on the trunk, fissured and flaking with age; bark on the branches grey and cracked. The sap from cut branches is blood-red and sticky. **Leaves:** compound, leaflets light grey-green, on short stalks, 10 to 14 pairs plus a smaller terminal leaflet; leaflets narrowly elliptic, up to 5 cm. in length; apex rounded, often notched. **Flowers:** small, profuse, 5 crinkly yellow petals, orange at the centre, in loose terminal sprays. **Fruit:** unusual and distinctive, a single seed with a flat wing to 6 cm. long, light yellow-green when young, looking like blossoms, later becoming hard, grey and fibrous.

Practical notes: fast-growing, tolerating a wide variety of conditions and flourishing even in black-cotton soil, quickly becoming a substantial, well-rounded tree. Widely available in nurseries and deservedly popular for avenues, large gardens and golf courses, but probably not living to great age.

225

Sesbania sesban

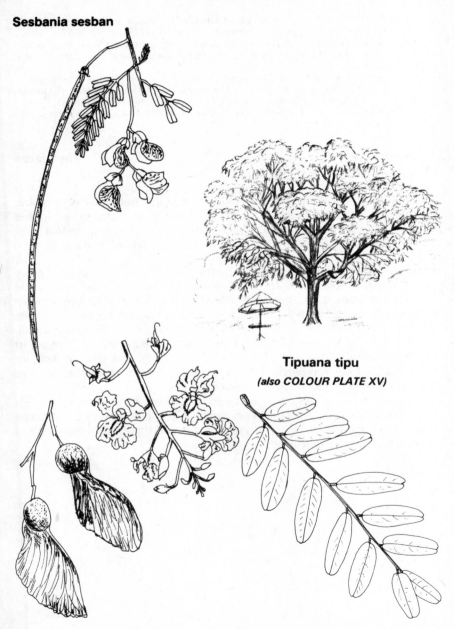

Tipuana tipu
(also COLOUR PLATE XV)

PHYTOLACCACEAE   Phytolacca family

A small family of 125 species of trees, shrubs, climbers and herbs, most of them native to tropical America and the West Indies. The Common Pokeweed *Phytolacca americana* is a striking garden plant in the U.S.A., the berries producing a powerful red dye used as a colouring for food and wines. The roots have medicinal properties, although all parts of the plant are more or less poisonous.

Two species are common in Kenya, widely distributed in higher rainfall areas. The exotic tree species is described below, and the other is the indigenous shrub or climber *Phytolacca dodecandra,* listed as a weed because it is notoriously poisonous to humans and to grazing animals alike. The juice was used in traditional medicine to treat tapeworm and to induce abortion, but overdosing has had fatal results.

Phytolacca dioica   **Phytolacca**
S. America, Brazil to Argentina

A spreading, semi-deciduous tree, to 10 m. in height but generally smaller, planted as an unusual ornamental around Nairobi and elsewhere in the highlands. The trunk is uniquely swollen at the base, which may grow to 4 m. in diameter, spreading overground so that the tree appears to be standing on a mound.
Bark: grey, rough and gnarled with age; young branches fleshy green.   **Leaves:** simple, alternate, typical of the family, appearing as terminal whorls; each smooth, oval, somewhat recurved, to 15 cm. in length, margin edge appearing white, midrib extending to form a distinct tip; young leaves fresh light green, leaf stalks and midribs tinged with red.   **Flowers:** small, creamy-white, with many stamens arising from 5 green sepals, hanging in handsome terminal catkins up to 15 cm. in length, the tree striking in flower.   **Fruit:** shiny red-black, berry-like, with several lobes, hanging in clusters; irregularly produced after flowering.
The tree is reputed to grow rapidly to its preferred height but is fairly aggressive in gardens, with root suckers appearing readily above the soil. Older trees give the appearance of great age, but this is difficult to confirm as the pithy trunk forms no growth rings.

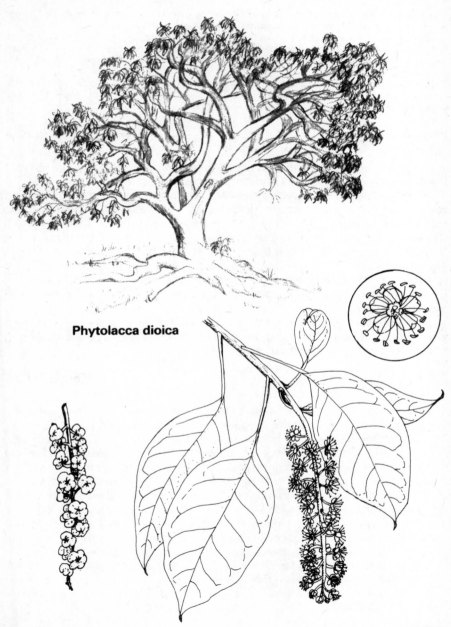

Phytolacca dioica

PINACEAE   Pine family

Although mainly native to the northern hemisphere, pine trees range from the Arctic Circle to the equator, and are the world's principal source of softwood timber.

Pines are evergreen, resinous trees with needle-like leaves and woody cones. They are fast-growing, surviving in heat, cold and drought, and also make excellent windbreaks. In gardens they are less popular as the trees are greedy, with the acid content of the litter of fallen needles suppressing grass.

In Kenya some 16 species have been introduced, of which three are now of major importance for timber and for wood pulp for making paper. *Pinus patula* now represents nearly 30% of all plantation trees in Kenya, and *Pinus radiata* some 10%.

Pinus patula   Mexican Weeping Pine
Mexican

A pine tree to 35 m. with light green 'weeping' foliage and a long, straight trunk; branches more or less horizontal, turning up at the tips.

Bark: grey to dark brown, irregular but usually fairly smooth; bark on younger branches papery and reddish-brown.   **Leaves:** long slender needles, soft but hard-tipped, 15 to 23 cm. in length, in bundles of 3. **Cones:** female small, hard red spheres, up to 1 cm. across, clustered, taking 2 years to mature into cones; male on the same tree, short terminal catkins, yellow to orange-brown, producing clouds of dust-like pollen. Mature cones are shiny, pale brown, up to 10 cm. long with an oblique base, in whorls of 2 to 5, remaining on the tree for many years. Seeds develop below the cone scales and are released over a long period.

The timber is light brown, soft and brittle, widely used for boxwood and wood pulp. This species is fast-growing and easily established, although young trees may suffer from rodent damage.

Pinus radiata *(Pinus insignis)*   Monterey Pine
California, U.S.A.

A pine tree to 50 m. with bright blue-green, tufted foliage and upcurved branches, developing an open, irregular crown as it matures.

Bark: rugged, thick, dark brown, deeply fissured with age.   **Leaves:** soft, sharply tipped, 10 to 15 cm. long, in bundles of 3, forming dense tufts.   **Cones:** mature female cones very large, glossy grey-brown, up to 15 cm. long with an oblique base, in whorls of 3 to 6, remaining on the tree for many years.

The timber is soft and rather brittle. This is one of the fastest-growing of all pines and is planted worldwide as the mainstay of the paper-making industry, but unfortunately no longer planted in Kenya following heavy attack by the fungus Diplodea and by woolly aphids. In 1969 further planting around Nairobi was prohibited and trees within the city boundary had to be felled.

Pinus caribaea, the Cuban Pine, has been successfully planted in Kwale district and the Shimba Hills.   **Bark:** thick, deep red, deeply fissured.   **Leaves:** dark green needles up to 30 cm. long, in bundles of 2, 3 or more. The timber is resinous with prominent ducts, strong and of good quality.

229

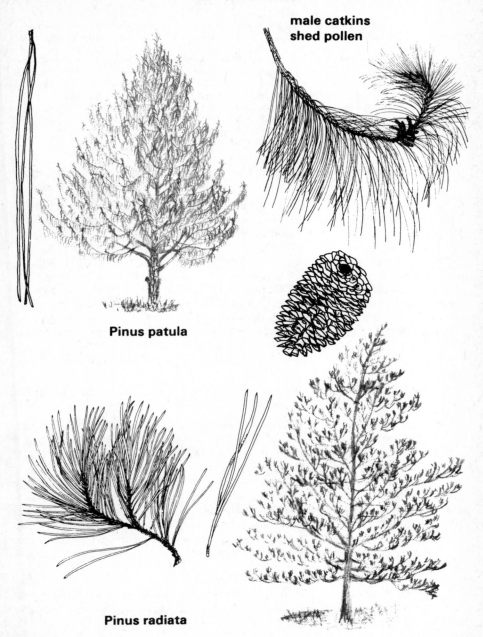

male catkins
shed pollen

Pinus patula

Pinus radiata

PODOCARPACEAE   Podo family

A small coniferous family of about 100 species, mainly from the southern hemisphere. There are the only conifers indigenous to the southern half of Africa. All species are resinous, with linear evergreen leaves, related more to Yews and Junipers than to Pines although they are called 'pines' in Australia and New Zealand. In South Africa they are known as Yellow-woods.

In Kenya there are two principal indigenous species of the genus Podocarpus, both valued as quality softwoods under the same trade name Podo. The pale, straight-grained timber is easy to work and polish, widely used for interior carpentry and an important source of plywood.

Male and female trees grow separately; male flowers resemble small hanging catkins, while female trees bear cones which develop into fleshy, berry-like fruit containing a single seed. The leaves are spirally arranged and rather crowded towards the ends of branchlets, with juvenile leaves often very much larger than mature leaves.

Podocarpus falcatus *(Podocarpus gracilior)*   **Podo, East African Yellow-wood**
indigenous   Muthengera (Kikuyu)

A large evergreen forest tree to 25 m. or even larger in upland rain forest, with a straight, cylindrical bole, very desirable for timber, occurring naturally in a varied but somewhat restricted range from 1,500 to 2,400 m. **Bark:** grey to dark brown, cracking and scaling into irregular rectangles. **Leaves:** tough, narrow, shiny dark green, 2 to 5 cm. in length, tapering gradually to the apex. Juvenile leaves are larger and paler, giving an attractive bright green flush. **Cones:** male catkins axillary, yellow-brown, to about 2 cm. long, solitary or in bunches of 3 together. **Fruit:** hard, rounded, about 2 cm. long, very slow to develop, green with a dull purple bloom, sometimes turning yellowish; outer shell thin and woody, inner flesh much eaten by monkeys and birds such as hornbills.

The Masai used an infusion from the bark to treat stomach-ache.

Podocarpus latifolius *(Podocarpus milanjianus)* **Podo, East African Yellow-wood**
indigenous   Muthengera (Kikuyu)

A similar species, to 35 m. in height, widely distributed from 900 to 3,150 m., often dominant in the forests of Mt. Kenya and occurring also at lower altitudes; found through Central Africa down to the Southern Cape. The trunk may be very large and buttressed in older trees. **Bark:** reddish-brown to grey-brown, narrowly fissured, peeling in long, fibrous strips. **Leaves:** longer and wider than in *P. falcatus,* 2 to 15 cm. in length, tapering abruptly to a sharp tip. Juvenile leaves are larger still. **Cones:** male catkins axillary, pinkish, about 5 cm. long, solitary or in pairs. **Fruit:** rounded, about 1 cm. long, paired or solitary, green to purple with a grey-blue bloom, the stalk below more or less swollen, red or purple in colour when ripe.

Practical notes: both are handsome trees, widely planted in the highlands as ornamentals. Best in good forest soil; fairly slow-growing, but requiring only moderate rainfall and hardy once established.

231

Podocarpus falcatus

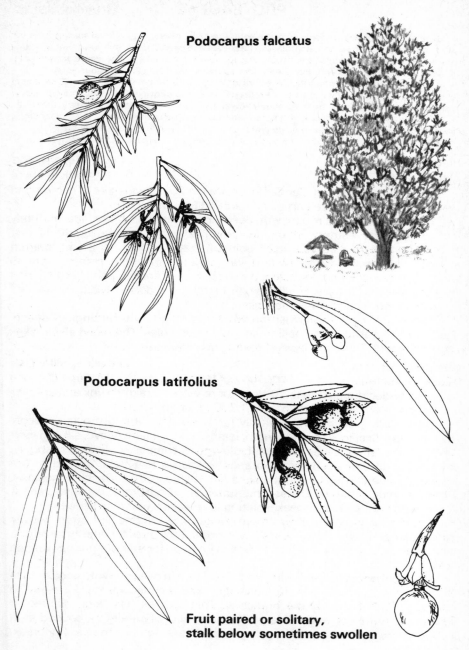

Podocarpus latifolius

Fruit paired or solitary,
stalk below sometimes swollen

232

PROTEACEAE   Grevillea famil,

One of the most notable families of the southern hemisphere, with related species in South America, Southern Africa and Australasia. The shrubs and trees of this family are generally hardy and suited to very dry conditions, with hard or leathery evergreen foliage. The leaves are alternate, and the flowers irregular, with four petals, four stamens and a long, conspicuous style.

The genus *Protea* dominates the Cape flora in South Africa, where there are over 30 species of shrubs and small trees. The 3 species of *Protea* indigenous to Kenya occur on mountain slopes or stony sites, and do not have the same showy flower heads as the ornamental species to the south.

In Kenya the two best known trees in this family are exotics from Australia, the outstandingly successful shade tree *Grevillea robusta* and the commercial nut tree *Macadamia spp.*

Members of the family in Kenya include *Faurea, Grevillea, Hakea, Macadamia.*

Faurea saligna   Beechwood
indigenous   Mutorothua (Kikuyu)

A deciduous shrub or slender forest tree to 20 m., widespread in highland savannah or high forest, particularly around Mt. Kenya.

Bark: almost black, rough, with deep vertical fissures; branchlets minutely hairy.   **Leaves:** leathery, shiny, drooping (*'saligna'* : willow-like); to 12 cm. long, often slightly curved; apex pointed, stalk reddish, to 2 cm., margin wavy.   **Flowers:** dense terminal spikes to 12 cm. in length, creamy white to mauve, honey-scented, attracting bees; calyx hairy and reddish.   **Fruit:** small nutlet: seeds with tufts of silky white hairs; the reddish styles persist, and appear as woolly pinkish-white spikes.

The wood is hard yellowish-brown and mottled, like the English Beech, used for fine furniture, panelling and telegraph poles. The wood also makes good charcoal. There are several traditional ceremonial uses.

Grevillea robusta   Grevillea, Silky Oak
Eastern Australia   *COLOUR PLATE XVI*   Mukima (Kikuyu)

A semi-deciduous tree to 20 m. or more with a straight trunk and angular branches, very widely planted from 1,200 m; often naturalised.

Bark: dark grey, rough, vertically furrowed.   **Leaves:** distinctive, deeply divided, fern-like, to 30 cm. in length; leathery olive-green above, silky silvery-grey below; fallen leaves grey, stiff, slow to decompose.   **Flowers:** showy, numerous, in one-sided golden-orange spikes up to 12 cm. in length. The green pin-head styles uncurl to give a pin-cushion effect. Nectar is copious, often dripping, attracting bees and sunbirds.   **Fruit:** dark capsules, about 1 cm. long with a slender beak, splitting to release two winged seeds.

The timber is pale yellow-brown, tough and durable but often heavily mottled by dark rays. The wood is now increasingly used for quality furniture, and is the closest timber to Beech, used in England for manufacturing wooden toys.

Practical notes: fast-growing from seed, best in deep soil with good rainfall but tolerating poorer soils. Not usually recommended for gardens due to copious leaf fall and brittle branches. This species has been planted in enormous numbers worldwide; in Kenya it was originally introduced as a coffee shade tree, but is now largely grown for fuel, timber and as a windbreak.

233

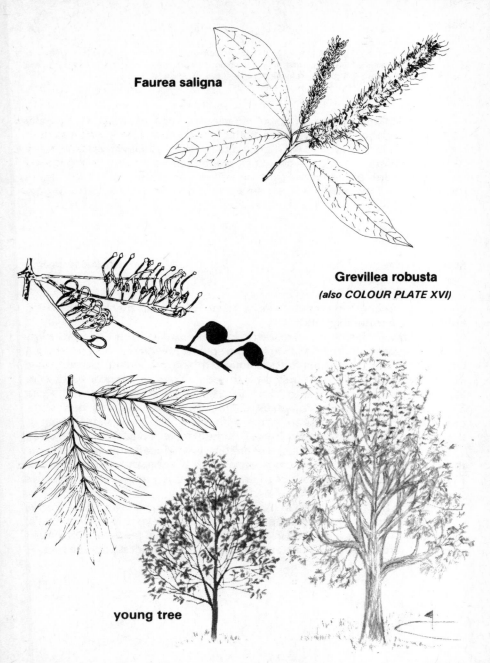

Faurea saligna

Grevillea robusta
(also COLOUR PLATE XVI)

young tree

234

PROTEACEAE

Hakea spp.

A genus of over 100 species, often harsh, spiky shrubs or small trees, mostly from Western Australia. The flowers of the genus are similar in structure to those of *Grevillea robusta,* but the fruit is hard and woody, splitting to release a single flat-winged seed.

Hakea saligna is the principal species planted in Kenya, originally introduced in the highlands as a coffee shade tree and windbreak and occasionally planted around Nairobi as a tall hedge.   **Leaves:** variable, fairly stiff and leathery, about 8 x 1 cm.; apex blunt, stalk very short. Young leaves and shoots are an attractive orange-yellow, and are popular for floral decoration.   **Flowers:** white, very small, about 1 cm. long, in small axillary groups.

Macadamia tetraphylla   Macadamia Nut
Northern Australia

A low-branching evergreen tree to 15 m., planted in the coffee-growing areas of the central highlands.
Bark: grey, fairly smooth.   **Leaves:** in fours, dull to olive green, conspicuously wavy, edged with sharp, forward-pointing spines; juvenile leaves up to 25 x 4 cm., mature leaves smaller; texture tough, midrib prominent below; young leaves and shoots often entirely pinkish-red.   **Flowers:** slender whitish or lilac-coloured axillary spikes, to 25 cm. in length.   **Fruit:** hard, rounded, about 3 cm. across, the husk drying black, containing an exceptionally hard shiny brown nutshell. The kernels are white, with a very high oil content, delicately flavoured and delicious when roasted. The fruit are collected from the ground.
The original species introduced near Thika was **Macadamia ternifolia,** but the main species now grown commercially are **Macadamia tetraphylla** and **Macadamia integrifolia,** both of them recently much improved by selective grafting.
Although 80% of the world's crop is presently grown in Hawaii, Macadamia nuts are becoming an important export from Kenya despite the difficulties of processing. The oil is also used in cosmetics and animal feeds, and the shells used for charcoal, while older trees provide a useful general purpose timber.

Hakea saligna

Macadamia tetraphylla

RHAMNACEAE   Buffalo-thorn family

A largely tropical family with about 850 species of scrambling shrubs, small trees and climbers, many of them armed with strong, hooked spines. The family is named after the Buckthorn genus Rhamnus, which is represented in Kenya by three indigenous species. *Rhamnus staddo* (Kikuyu *Mubura*) is a spine-tipped shrub or small tree not uncommon in highland forest margin areas.

Many species contain substances related to quinine, and the laxative drug Cascara is produced from the bark of the North American Cascara Buckthorn *Rhamnus purshiana*. Other species have soft, edible fruit, and several are fine ornamentals. In this family the leaves are usually simple and the flowers very small, with petals nearly always shorter than the sepals.

Members of this family in Kenya include *Maesopsis, Scutia, Ziziphus*.

Maesopsis eminii   Musizi (Trade name)
indigenous

A large deciduous tree to 30 m. or more, with a straight trunk up to 10 m. high before branching and a rounded crown; originally from the fringes of the Kakamega forest, now widely planted in wetter highland districts for shade and timber and around Nairobi as an ornamental. This is the only species in this unusual tropical African genus.

Bark: pale silvery-grey, vertically furrowed; branchlets covered with breathing pores. **Leaves:** glossy dark green above, opposite or nearly so, narrowly oval, to 14 cm. long; apex tapering acutely, margin distinctively serrated with small, well-spaced teeth; midrib and veins prominent below, stalk short. **Flowers:** small, green, in branched axillary heads to 5 cm. long. **Fruit:** oval, yellow, fleshy, to 3 cm. long, dark purple when ripe, containing a single hard seed; probably eaten and dispersed by hornbills and monkeys.

This is a fast-growing, short-lived tree producing a useful, pale brown timber, one of the few indigenous species used in plantation forestry and also for intercropping.

Scutia myrtina   Cat-thorn
indigenous   Murangari, Mutanda-mbogo (Kikuyu)

A scrambling shrub or small tree to 8 m., with right-angled branchlets armed with solitary, strongly-hooked thorns, grey with shiny brown tips; very widely distributed in forest margins and grassland from sea-level to 2,700 m. This variable species occurs throughout most of sub-Saharan Africa, in the Seychelles and from India across to Vietnam.

Bark: thick, dark and corky in older trees, with vertical fissures. **Leaves:** glossy mid-green above, usually opposite, broadly oval, to 6 cm. long; apex rounded or notched, always bearing a short, stiff point; stalk grooved, very short. **Flowers:** small, creamy-green, bell-shaped, in axillary clusters. **Fruit:** rounded, fleshy, to 1 cm. long, maturing through red to black, edible but rather acid when ripe, much eaten by birds.

237

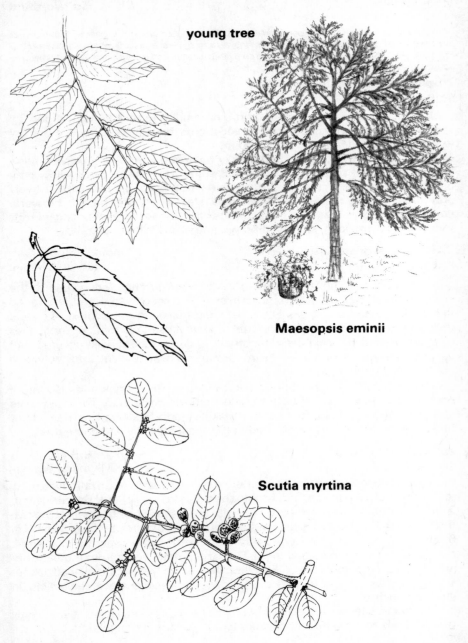

young tree

Maesopsis eminii

Scutia myrtina

238

Ziziphus spp.   Buffalo-thorn

A distinctive genus, both temperate and tropical but most common in dry areas. Most species are armed with spines; branchlets are commonly zig-zag and leaves usually alternate, often with 3 to 5 veins from the base. Several have been cultivated for their edible fruit since ancient times, the Latin name being derived from the Arabic "zizouf".

Ziziphus abyssinica *(Ziziphus jujuba)*
indigenous

A wickedly armed scrambler, shrub or small tree to 7 m. with drooping, tangled branches and scattered recurved thorns, usually found in medium-dry wooded grassland from 400 to 2,200 m.

Bark: grey-brown, rough and deeply furrowed with age.   **Leaves:** fairly thick, broadly oval, usually 5 to 8 cm. long, shiny green above, furry yellow-grey below; base very asymmetric, 3 main veins from base hairy and distinctively prominent below; margin finely toothed, stalk short and hairy.   **Flowers:** small, greenish-yellow, star-shaped, in axillary heads to 2 cm. long   **Fruit:** rounded, to 3 cm. long, shiny red-brown and edible when ripe.

Ziziphus mauritiana *(Ziziphus jujuba)*
indigenous

Indian Jujube, Geb
Mkunazi (Swahili)

A similar, very thorny species, often thicket-forming, widespread at the coast and inland up to 1,400 m., often in disturbed or cultivated land; also found in the Middle East and India, but widely naturalised in the tropics.   **Leaves:** thin, soft, shiny mid-green above, oval to almost round, 3 to 8 cm. long; apex blunt or notched, base almost symmetrical; undersurface densely covered with very short silvery-grey hairs.   **Fruit:** rounded to oval, to 2 cm. long, yellow to black, edible when ripe.

The fruit pulp can be made into a thirst-quenching drink and also into a potent spirit. In Sudan cakes are made from the dried pulp. This species is fast-growing and drought-resistant, making good fodder and an excellent hedge, with hard, heavy wood used at the coast for beds and dhow ribs.

Ziziphus mucronata
indigenous

Buffalo-thorn
Mkunazi (Swahili)

A similar species, widely distributed from the coast to Nyanza Province, up to 2,000 m.; often riparian. The strong, sharp thorns are in pairs, one straight to 2 cm., the other smaller and recurved, with the leaves arising between the two thorns of a pair.   **Leaves:** thin, hairless, the same colour on both surfaces, 3 to 6 cm. long; base rounded, markedly asymmetric, apex tapering to a point, margin with regular rounded teeth. Only the 3 main veins from the base are prominent on the underside.   **Flowers:** very small, yellowish, in heads about 1.5 cm. across.   **Fruit:** dark reddish-brown, very acid and scarcely edible, in stalked bunches.

The wood is tough and elastic. Poultices from roots and leaves were widely used for boils and skin infections, and stomach and chest complaints.

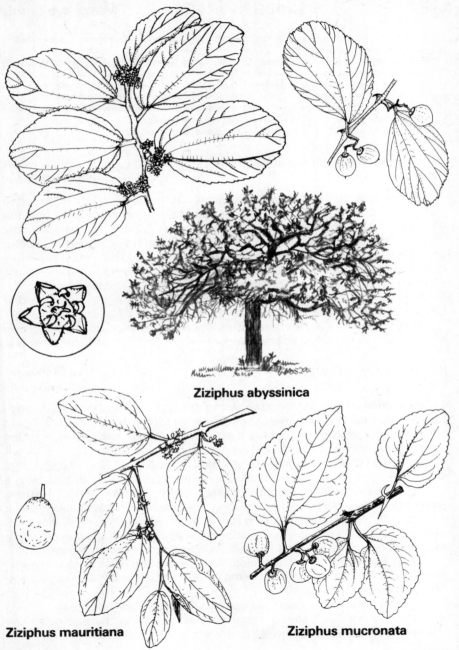

Ziziphus abyssinica

Ziziphus mauritiana

Ziziphus mucronata

RHIZOPHORACEAE   Mangrove family

A widespread family of trees, shrubs and climbers, of which four genera dominate the mangrove swamps of the tropics.

The term 'mangrove' is a unique assembly of unrelated plants which are specially adapted to life in the mud of tidal estuaries and lagoons. The commonest and most important species in Kenya is the Red Mangrove described in the text, but others in the family used for charcoal, poles and tannin are *Bruguiera gymnorrhiza* (Swahili *Msindi*) and *Ceriops tagal* (Swahili *Mkandaa*).

Cassipourea is the largest genus in the family, consisting mainly of trees of inland forests. There are 6 indigenous species, most of which provide valuable timber.

Members of this family in Kenya include *Cassipourea, Rhizophora*.

Cassipourea malosana *(Cassipourea elliotii)*   Pillarwood
indigenous   Muthaithi (Kikuyu)

A tall evergreen tree with a pillar-like trunk, 10 to 40 m. in height, found in wetter forest from 1,700 to 2,600 m., particularly on Mt. Kenya and the Aberdares; also distributed in drier upland forest, including the Nairobi area.

Bark: smooth, greyish, with horizontal lines of breathing pores. **Leaves:** opposite, hard, broadly oval, mostly more than 4 cm. long; margin slightly toothed, apex notched; net veins prominent. **Flowers:** small, axillary, yellowish-green, with many stamens. **Fruits:** small oval capsules.

The wood is almost white, very strong and elastic, once widely used in heavy construction work.

The very similar **Cassipourea rotundifolia** occurs near Nairobi, but grows to less than 10 m. The leaves are rounded, to 4 cm. long, and the margin entire.

Rhizophora mucronata   Red Mangrove
indigenous   Mkoko (Swahili)

The commonest mangrove tree, with a straight trunk to 10 m, confined to coastal mudflats. The tree develops characteristic aerial prop roots up to 2 m. in length which arch over and anchor it in the mud. At high tide the tree appears to be floating on the water, and at low tide perched above the mud on stilts.

Bark: reddish brown to black; branches soft and brittle. **Leaves:** opposite, dark green, cork-dotted beneath, thick and leathery, up to 15x8 cm., with a distinctive hair-like tip. **Flowers:** fleshy, creamy white. **Fruit:** leathery green, cone-shaped berries, to 7 cm. long. The seeds germinate while the fruit is still on the tree. A green seedling root emerges, growing downwards to 45 cm., and eventually the whole torpedo-shaped structure drops and may float away, putting out true roots and leaves within hours of lodging in the mud.

The tree produces excellent building and scaffolding poles known as *boriti,* which are used locally as well as being a major export by dhow to the Middle East, particularly from Lamu.

The wood also makes good fuel and excellent charcoal, and the bark is rich in tannin. These trees play a major part in stabilizing the coastline, and conservation measures require strict enforcement.

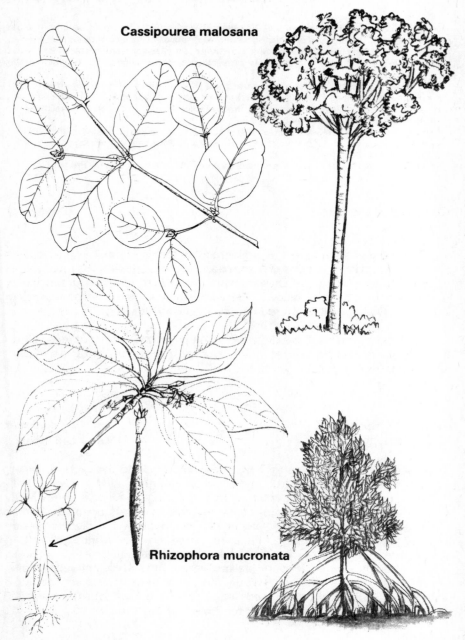

Cassipourea malosana

Rhizophora mucronata

242

ROSACEAE   Rose family

A large, diverse family with over 3,000 species, cosmopolitan but centred in temperate northern regions. The family is of major economic importance because of its many fruit-bearing species, which include plums, apples, pears and loquats as well as soft fruits like blackberries and strawberries. Many varieties of these fruits, often adapted to local conditions, are grown in the Kenya highlands.

The family is named after the ever-popular rose, of which there are now more than 5,000 named cultivated varieties. Rose oil, in the perfume industry often called Attar of Roses, has been distilled for many centuries from rose petals. The family also includes many ornamental trees and shrubs, notably in the genus Prunus.

Flowers of the rose family are characteristically regular and insect pollinated, with numerous stamens. Leaves are usually alternate, simple or compound, almost always bearing growths at the leaf base known as stipules.

Members of this family in Kenya include *Cotoneaster, Eriobotrya, Hagenia, Prunus.*

Cotoneaster pannosa   Chinaberry
S.W. China

An ornamental shrub to 4 m. with graceful, arching branches, sometimes pruned to a hedge. This is one of many species, and is probably the most widely planted in the highlands.   **Leaves:** small, oval, to 3 cm. long, dull green above, pale grey and softly hairy below.   **Flowers:** small, white, in dense, attractive clusters.   **Fruit:** small bright red berries, in showy clusters.

Practical notes: self-seeding but usually grown from cuttings; slow-growing and drought-resistant, suitable for most soils. Very attractive in fruit, and useful for flower arrangements.

Eriobotrya japonica   Loquat
China, Japan   Murungati (Kikuyu)

A dense evergreen tree to 7 m., branching close to the ground, widely planted above 1,500 m. for fruit and as an ornamental.

Bark: grey, rough and powdery with age; young stems pale green, softly hairy.   **Leaves:** dark green, shiny above, in terminal whorls, up to 35 x 10 cm., widest towards the apex; margin slightly toothed, veins well marked; underside covered in fine woolly hairs.   **Flowers:** small, creamy white, fragrant, in woolly terminal clusters.   **Fruit:** yellow, round to pear-shaped, to 3 cm. long, in heavy bunches; young fruit and stalks covered with soft creamy yellow hairs.

The flesh has a sweet acid flavour, and can be eaten raw or stewed into a jelly. However, the dark brown seeds are poisonous, and must be removed. The leaves are long lasting and popular for flower arrangements.

243

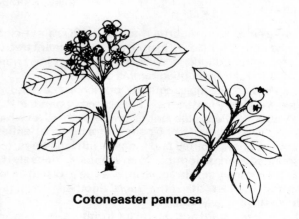

Cotoneaster pannosa

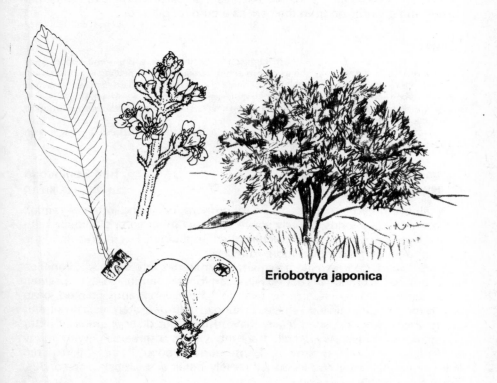

Eriobotrya japonica

ROSACEAE

Hagenia abyssinica *(Brayera anthelmintica)*   **Hagenia**
indigenous   Muthithiku, Mumondo (Kikuyu)

A handsome tree of high mountain forest, to 20 m in height, a species confined to Africa, from 2400 to 3600 m. This is a dominant tree on Mt. Kenya right up to the open moorlands, occasionally found at lower altitudes as at Kericho, Limuru and Kiambu in good rainfall areas.

Bark: reddish brown, flaking irregularly; branchlets covered in silky brown hairs and ringed with hairy leaf scars. **Leaves:** compound, to 40 cm. long, in large terminal tufts; leaflets pale bright green with silvery hairs beneath, reddish and sticky when young, 5 or 6 pairs plus a terminal leaflet, each about 10 cm. long; margin finely toothed and fringed with long hairs; leaf stalk to 12 cm., with expanded wings formed from stipules, densely hairy on the underside. **Flowers:** in large, attractive masses up to 60 cm. in length; female heads pinkish-red, bulkier than the more feathery, orange-white male heads. **Fruit:** small, dry, asymmetric.

The wood is dark red, hard and useful for furniture, but attacked by borers. The dried female flower heads are used as a powerful remedy for intestinal worms, and an infusion from the bark as a cure for diarrhoea.

Prunus spp.

A genus well-known in the northern hemisphere, where cherry, plum and apricot trees produce delicious fruit and are prized as ornamentals, sometimes also yielding beautiful wood. Worldwide there are numerous cultivated varieties; in general the orchard species have their origins in Europe and the ornamental flowering species in Japan or China. All have simple leaves, usually with serrated margins, and the flowers have small petals and many stamens set around a 5-lobed, cup-like calyx.

The only indigenous species is *Prunus africanum*, a useful tree with strong-smelling timber, which also occurs in western and southern parts of Africa.

Prunus africanum *(Pygeum africanum)*   **Red Stinkwood**
indigenous   Muiri (Kikuyu)

A tall evergreen forest tree to 24 m. or more, occurring in better rainfall districts of the highlands, usually above 1,500 m. In forest or plantations the high foliage is open and the branches often pendulous, but in grassland the tree is shorter and the crown more rounded.

Bark: rough, dark, scaling irregularly, sometimes into squares: branches brown and corky, branchlets dotted with prominent breathing pores. **Leaves:** glossy dark green above, broadly oval, to 10 cm. long; apex pointed, base usually rounded, margin with shallow, rounded teeth; leaf stalk typically pink or red, to 2 cm. long. Crushed leaves have a faint but distinct smell of bitter almonds. **Flowers:** very small, fragrant, white or greenish, with many stamens, in short axillary sprays. **Fruit:** rounded, about 1 cm. long, dark red when ripe, appearing two-lobed, extremely bitter and probably poisonous, containing a single oval seed.

(continued)

245

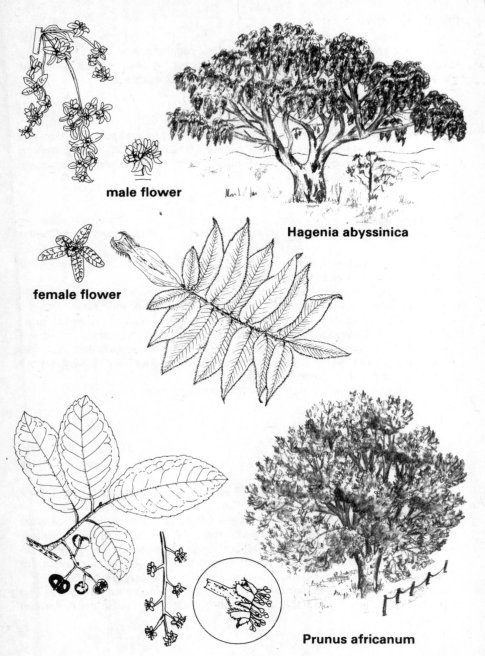

male flower

Hagenia abyssinica

female flower

Prunus africanum

246

ROSACEAE

Prunus africanum (continued)

The heartwood darkens to a dense dark red, and was used for strong furniture, wagons and heavy construction work. It also makes excellent firewood, and unfortunately the tree is now fairly uncommon.

Practical notes: a handsome shade tree, responding well to cultivation and readily grown from seed. Best in well-watered forest soil; fairly slow-growing, but an indigenous tree well worth encouraging for gardens and golf courses.

Prunus puddum (Prunus cerasoides)
Himalayas

Flowering Cherry,
Himalayan Bird Cherry

A fast-growing, deciduous ornamental tree to 8 m. but usually smaller, with a much-branched, sometimes rounded crown.
Bark: easily recognised, shiny copper-brown, peeling in horizontal strips. **Leaves:** shiny mid-green, to 18 cm. long; apex elongated, margin serrated. Young leaves are an attractive bronze colour. **Flowers:** pink, clustered, each flower with 5 petals and 5 pink stamens, appearing before the leaves and often covering the tree at the start of the rains. Flowering is brief, but usually occurs twice a year. **Fruit:** inconspicuous, small oval yellow berries, on long stalks, eaten by birds.
An attractive flowering tree, fairly fast-growing from seed.

Prunus serotina (Prunus capuli)
Mexico, Peru

Wild Black Cherry,
Capulin Cherry

A fast-growing deciduous tree, to 8 m. but sometimes much larger, best above 2,200 m.
Bark: grey-white, vertically fissured; branches dark brown. **Leaves:** smooth, thin and leathery, shiny above, about 10 cm. long; apex elongated, margin serrated; leaf stalk red, about 2 cm. long. **Flowers:** white, fragrant, in sprays up to 15 cm. in length. **Fruit:** small red 'cherries' with a persistent calyx, black when ripe, soft and juicy, rather bitter, making good jam.
Seedlings grow well in highland areas like Limuru and even in Nairobi. The tree planted locally is probably a cultivated variety of the South American species.

247

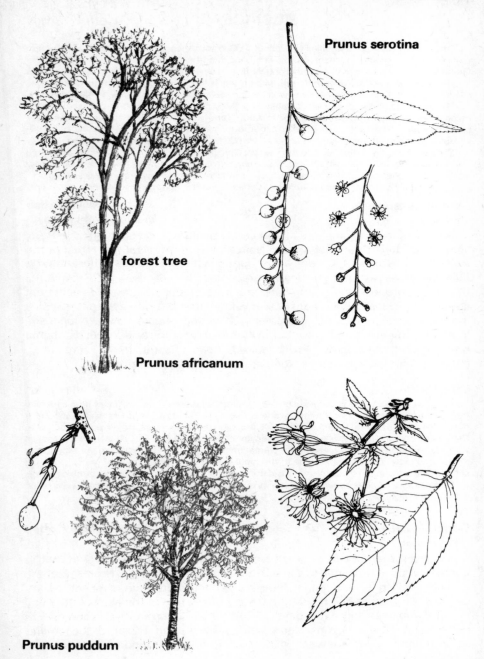

Prunus serotina

forest tree

Prunus africanum

Prunus puddum

248

RUBIACEAE   Coffee family

One of the largest plant families with about 7,000 species, concentrated in the tropics where most species are small trees or shrubs. The family includes the important Coffee genus *Coffea*, the Quinine tree *Cinchona* and plants supplying dyes such as madder and gambier. The name of the family comes from a herb *Rubia tinctorum*, whose roots contain purpurin and alizarin, used as dyes since the time of the Pharaohs. A Kenyan creeper *Rubia cordifolia* yields a traditional brown dye.

The family is common in Kenya, mostly as forest undershrubs, and in general is easily recognised by simple leaves, opposite or in whorls, and well-marked leaf stipules. Flowers are often in heads, and the petals are joined in a tube, often with a hairy throat. Classification into sub-groups is very difficult, and only a few of more than 600 East African species are described.

Ornamentals grown here include the fragrant *Gardenia* from China, an *Ixora* with brilliant red flowers, and the Red Flag Bush *Mussaenda erythrophylla*, whose flowers have one enlarged red sepal. These genera each have indigenous representatives, whose flowers are less striking.

Members of this family include *Canthium, Coffea, Gardenia, Rothmannia, Tarenna, Vangueria.*

Canthium keniensis   Wild Coffee
indigenous   Mubiru-wathi (Kikuyu)

A leafy shrub resembling a large coffee bush or a straggling tree to 8 m., common in forest margins around Nairobi, also in the Arabuko forest at the coast. This is one of a very large genus without obvious differentiating features.   **Leaves:** on right-angled branchlets, broadly oval, to 13 cm. long, thin bright green when young, later dull above, shiny below; side veins not straight, with clear subdivisions; lower vein axils dotted with hairy pits; stipules triangular with a fine tip, prominent on young shoots between opposite leaves.   **Flowers:** small, greenish, in stalked, branching axillary heads; stigma protruding, throat hairy.   **Fruit:** paired, heart-shaped, over 1 cm. long, clustered along the branches, soft black and edible when ripe.

Coffea spp.   Coffee trees

A genus of about 100 ill-defined species, dominated commercially by *Coffea arabica* which now produces some 75% of the total world coffee crop. This species grows wild in the moist evergreen forests of S.W. Ethiopia and on Mt. Marsabit in Kenya. There are other wild species in Kenya, and one rare species has recently been identified in the Teita Hills: all of them represent a valuable source of genes for breeding the plantation trees that provide Kenya's major export crop.

Kiambu District and similar areas in the highlands have a combination of rainfall, soil and climate said to be unsurpassed anywhere in the world for the production of quality Arabica coffee.

Robusta coffee *Coffee canephora*, a variety of which is used for making instant coffee, is found wild in the forests of the Congo Basin and Uganda, and is widely grown in West Africa.

Coffea arabica   Arabian Coffee
indigenous

An evergreen shrub or small tree, capable of growing to 10 m. but in cultivation usually pruned to about 2 m.   **Leaves:** opposite, dark glossy green, broadly oval, to 20 cm. long.   **Flowers:** white, fragrant, in compact axillary clusters. Profuse flowering is triggered by heavy rain at the start of the rainy season, and lasts only a few days.   **Fruit:** fleshy 'cherries', red when ripe, in dense clusters, with two grooved seeds in a silvery skin. These are the familiar coffee-beans, which are washed, dried, roasted and ground into coffee.

249

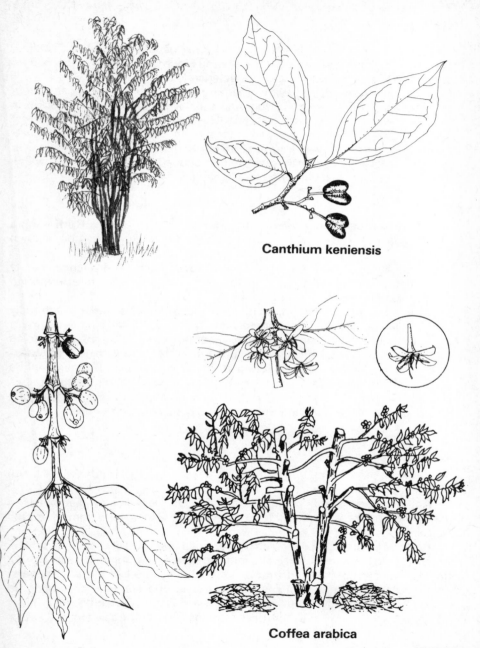

Canthium keniensis

Coffea arabica

RUBIACEAE

Gardenia ternifolia var. jovis-tonantis
indigenous

Large-leaved Gardenia
Mukumuti (Kamba)

A rigid shrub or low-branching tree to 7 m., usually stunted and twisted, found in grassland in western Kenya, around Machakos and at the coast. This is one of 200 species worldwide, characterised by large fruits.

Bark: pale grey, dotted with breathing pores. **Leaves:** opposite or in whorls of 3, on short branchlets, spoon-shaped, wavy, to 12 cm. long; vein axils below dotted with dark hairy pits; stipules brown, membranous, sheathed around the stems midway between the leaf pairs. **Flowers:** solitary, funnel-shaped, creamy white, very fragrant, to 8 cm. across, the petals overlapping in bud, later splaying out. **Fruit:** erect, lemon-shaped, hard, grey-brown, warty, to 8 cm. long, crowned with the persistent calyx.

Rothmannia urcelliformis *(Gardenia urcelliformis)*
indigenous

Forest Rothmannia
Mukombokombo (Kikuyu)

A shapely evergreen tree to 8 m. with low, sweeping branches, widely distributed in highland forest up to 2,000 m., also in wetter forests around Nairobi; sometimes planted in gardens.

Bark: smooth, grey-brown, rough with age; branchlets covered with rusty hairs. **Leaves:** opposite or in threes, broadly oval, to 13 cm. long, lime-green when young, later dark and glossy; apex tapering, stalk less than 1 cm., holding the leaves more or less horizontally; stipules long, thin, falling early. **Flowers:** erect, solitary, broadly trumpet-shaped, to 10 cm. across, 5 creamy-white petals with maroon markings in the throat; stalk absent, calyx tube split, petals in bud overlapping to the right. **Fruit:** erect, egg-shaped, to 6 cm. long, slightly ridged, brown-black and hard when mature, persistent on the tree.

Tarenna graveolens
indigenous

Muthigetu (Kikuyu)

An evergreen shrub or small tree to 8 m., very widely distributed in grassland and forest margins from the coast to 2,000 m.; common around Nairobi.

Bark: pale, greyish; branchlets hairy. **Leaves:** opposite, stiff glossy dark green, drying black; oval, to 15 cm. long; apex tapering, sometimes to a sharp tip; stipules membranous, drying brown, between the leaf pairs. **Flowers:** small, creamy-white, sweet-scented, flat style and stamens protruding, in dense terminal heads about 12 cm. across. **Fruit:** rounded berries, black when ripe, crowned with the ring-like remains of the calyx, containing 2 seeds.

251

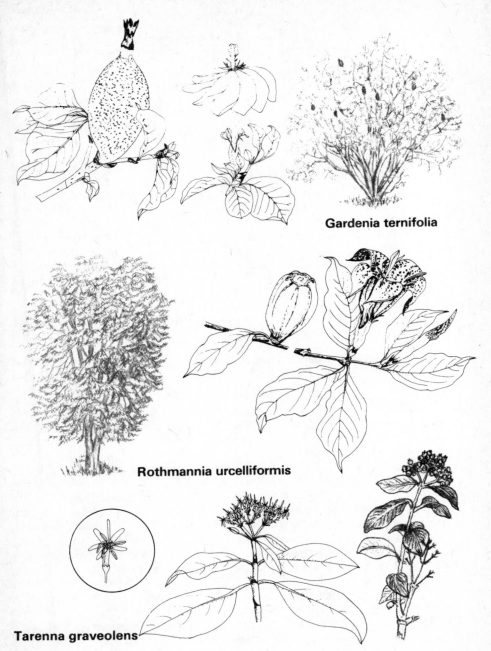

Gardenia ternifolia

Rothmannia urcelliformis

Tarenna graveolens

252

Vangueria spp.   **Wild Medlar**

A tropical African genus of over 20 species. The leaves are large, opposite and often velvety hairy, and the stipules between the leaf pairs are narrow, often united into a sheath, usually falling early. Flowers are in axillary clusters with the adjacent leaves sometimes absent; the fruit are fleshy and often edible.

Vangueria infausta ssp. rotundata *(Vangueria tomentosa)*
indigenous   Muiru (Swahili)

A deciduous shrub or shapeless tree to 8 m., with a short trunk, hanging branchlets and a straggling, twiggy crown, widely distributed in wooded grassland from the coast to the highlands.
Bark: pale grey-brown, peeling in untidy flakes; branchlets hairy. **Leaves:** dull green, broadly oval, to 30 cm. long but generally much smaller; both surfaces velvety hairy; base rounded, veins conspicuous below; midribs, stalks and shoots covered with hairs that may dry yellow or rust-coloured. **Flowers:** small, densely hairy, in crowded, branched heads; petals yellow-green, falling early to leave 5 triangular green sepals, less than 2 mm. long, on the young green fruit; buds pointed, hairy. **Fruit:** rounded, green, glossy, about 4 cm. across, hanging below the leaves, dull orange-brown and soft when ripe. The fruit bear a star-shaped scar from the remains of the calyx, which helps recognition.
The name *infausta* means 'unlucky', and in many parts of Africa the tree is believed to possess evil powers so that the wood will not be used even for fuel.

Vangueria madagascariensis *(Vangueria acutiloba)*
indigenous   Mubiru (Kikuyu)

A deciduous shrub or multi-stemmed tree to 15 m., widespread from the coast to 2,100 m. in scrub or forest margins; common around Nairobi. This species is similar to *Vangueria infausta* but generally less hairy, and occurs also in West and Central Africa; it is cultivated for its fruit in tropical regions from Trinidad to Singapore.
Bark: pale to dark, stems smooth, longitudinally ridged. **Leaves:** large, limp, glossy green, broadly oval, to 28 cm. long but usually smaller; older leaves almost hairless; margin wavy, apex pointed, base sometimes rounded; veins prominent below. **Flowers:** small, few, in hairy-stalked heads; petals greenish-yellow, sepals triangular, less than 2 mm. long. **Fruit:** rounded, green, to 5 cm. across, often in bunches of 5 or 6, brown and edible when ripe.
The fruit have a sharp sweetness, and are popular with children herding goats and cattle. Both roots and leaves have wide uses in traditional medicine.

Vangueria volkensii *(Vangueria linearsepala)* is a very similar tree to 7 m., also common around Nairobi and widespread from Kenya to Ethiopia in evergreen forest, scrub and rocky sites. Leaves and young stems are densely velvety. This species is distinguished by strap-shaped sepals 3 to 8 mm. in length.

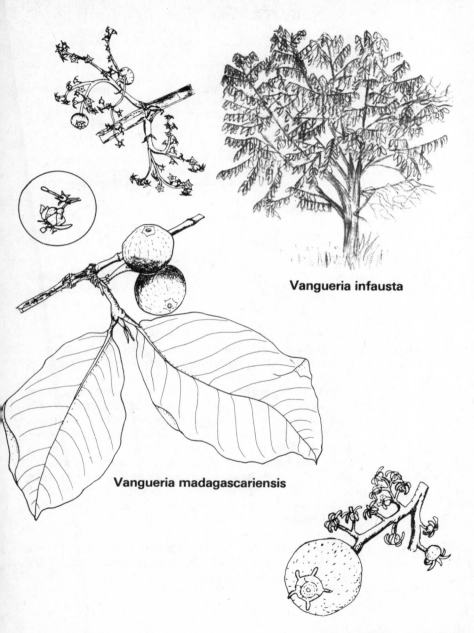

Vangueria infausta

Vangueria madagascariensis

Vangueria volkensii

RUTACEAE   Citrus family

A large family, widespread in the tropics and warm temperate climates, best known for the genus *Citrus* which includes oranges, lemons, limes and grapefruit. The citrus-growing areas are mainly the Mediterranean, South Africa, Australia and Mexico: in Kenya citrus fruit are so far only a relatively minor crop.

The family name is derived from *Ruta graveolens,* the shrub Rue grown in herb gardens in Europe for medicinal purposes. The family has always been important for both medicine and perfumery, and is characterised by glands producing aromatic essential oils: if the leaves are held up to strong sunlight, these glands can often be seen on the blade or along the margin, looking like translucent pinpricks.

The indigenous Cape Chestnut *Calodendrum capense* is one of Kenya's most beautiful flowering trees, especially noticeable in the forests along the Rift Valley Escarpment. Many plants in the family, such as the genus *Zanthoxylum* in Kenya, bear spines or prickles.

Members of this family in Kenya include *Calodendrum, Clausena, Fagaropsis, Teclea, Zanthoxylum.*

Calodendrum capense   **Cape Chestnut**
indigenous   Murarachi, Muroroa (Kikuyu)

COLOUR PLATE XVII

An outstanding deciduous tree to 20 m. in height with a shapely, spreading crown, widespread in evergreen and riverine forest in the highlands up to 2,200 m.; also widely planted as an ornamental. The tree remains bare for some months, and flowering may be profuse but is rather irregular.

Bark: pale grey, smooth; young branchlets and leaves densely hairy, soon becoming shiny and hairless.   **Leaves:** opposite, simple, dark green, broadly oval, rather wavy, to 14 cm. long; apex usually narrowed, midrib and veins prominent below; stalk short.   **Flowers:** large, showy, pink to pinkish-white, in erect terminal heads, 5 strap-shaped petals alternating with 5 sterile stamens of similar shape, pale pink dotted with crimson glands. The unusual stalked ovary is also glandular. The 5 white filaments are as long as the petals, and bear purple-brown anthers.   **Fruit:** knobbly to softly spiny, 5-lobed capsules, to 5 cm. across, brown when mature and splitting open from below to release shiny black, angled seeds.

Practical notes: slow-growing but hardy and drought-resistant once established, often flowering in 6 to 8 years. Best in well-watered forest soil, but succeeding also on drier sites and even in black cotton soil. Very ornamental in groups or for lining avenues. Leaf-fall is fairly heavy.

255

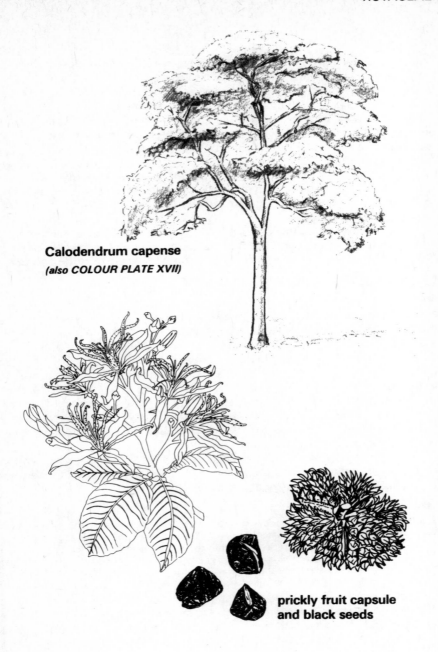

Calodendrum capense
(also COLOUR PLATE XVII)

**prickly fruit capsule
and black seeds**

RUTACEAE

Clausena anisata
indigenous

Clausena
Mutathi (Kikuyu)

An attractive shrub or small tree to 5 m., common in dry forest margins, wooded grassland or regenerating bush from the coast to 2,200 m. Crushed leaves smell strongly of lemon in highland plants, but in the coastal variety smell more like aniseed ('anisata').

Bark: smooth, grey-green, becoming brown and mottled. **Leaves:** compound, small or to 30 cm. long; leaflets mid-green, numerous, more or less narrowly oval, to 2.5 cm. long, set alternately along the main leaf stalks; margin scalloped, apex tapering or notched; gland-dots noticeable; young leaflets and shoots purplish-red. **Flowers:** small, fragrant, creamy-white to yellow, about 1 cm. across, in axillary sprays about 10 cm. in length. **Fruit:** small, shiny, rounded or in 2 sections, about 1 cm. across, turning through pink to dark red, purple-black when ripe.

Infusions from roots and leaves are widely used in traditional medicine, and twigs are used for cleaning teeth in the same way as the Toothbrush Tree *Salvadora persica* (Swahili *Mswaki*) from hotter, drier parts of the country.

Fagaropsis hildebrandtii *(Clausenopsis hildebrandtii)*
indigenous

A deciduous shrub or small tree to 7 m., occurring in dry upland forest around Nairobi and in bushland in Central Province from 1,300 to 1,900 m.

Bark: grey, rough, flaking in squares; branchlets hairy, purple-brown, dotted with pale breathing pores. **Leaves:** compound, to 15 cm. long, opposite but usually seen as terminal clusters; leaflets few, 2 to 4 pairs plus a larger terminal leaflet, each oval, up to 7 cm. long; base often rounded and unequal-sided; undersurface and stalks hairy, margin closely packed with gland dots. **Flowers:** small, greenish-yellow, in hairy terminal heads to 6 cm. long. **Fruit:** small, rounded, to 1 cm. across, abundant, pale green with dark raised gland-dots, soft shiny purple when ripe.

Fagaropsis angolensis (Kikuyu *Mukarakati*) is a similar but taller species, scattered at the edges of highland forests. The yellow-brown timber, sold under the name *Mafu,* was once prized for fine furniture.

Teclea spp.

An Africa genus of about 30 species of evergreen shrubs and trees, all with simple or trifoliate leaves densely dotted with glands and small, fleshy fruit, much eaten by birds and monkeys.

The Kenyan species described are some of the commonest trees of the dry forest areas around Nairobi, and are also found in Central, Rift Valley and Coast Provinces. The dense, dark green leaves are easily recognised once identified. The wood of all species is tough and whitish, used for implement handles, spear shafts and bows.

Teclea nobilis is one of the largest trees in the genus, growing to 12 m. in riverine forest, widely distributed in highland forests in areas such as Kitale, Londiani and Mt. Kenya but everywhere uncommon. The leaves are normally trifoliate but the leaves, stalks and branchlets bear no hairs. The fruit are small, less than 1 cm. long, in dense clusters.

257

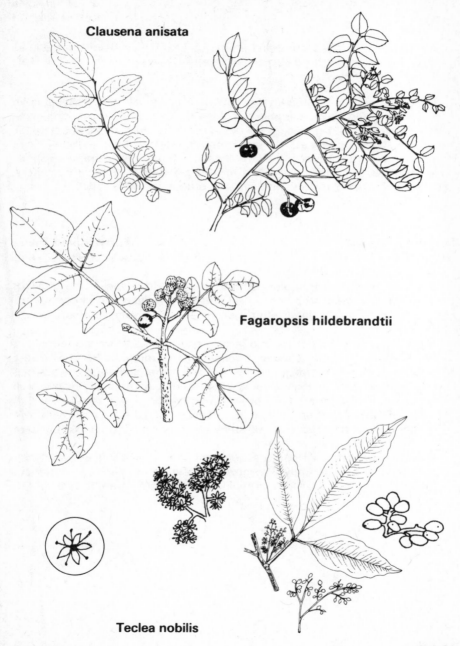

Clausena anisata

Fagaropsis hildebrandtii

Teclea nobilis

258

RUTACEAE

Teclea simplicifolia
indigenous

Teclea
Munderendu (Kikuyu)

A rounded, much-branched evergreen tree 4 to 10 m. in height, sometimes shrubby, widespread in dry forest and wooded grassland from 300 to 2,300 m.; very common around Nairobi.

Bark: dark grey, fairly smooth to granular.   **Leaves:** almost always simple, smooth dark green above, variable but generally oval, 3 to 15 cm. long; apex tapering, usually blunt-tipped; gland-dots very noticeable; side veins parallel, prominent above, looping at the margin; stalk grooved and jointed, over 1 cm. long, set at an angle to form a characteristic 'elbow'.   **Flowers:** very small, fragrant, greenish-yellow, male and female separated, in axillary clusters. **Fruit:** smooth, round, to 1 cm. in diameter, orange-red when ripe.

Teclea trichocarpa
indigenous

Furry-fruited Teclea
Munderendu-wa-ikurari (Kikuyu)

A dense evergreen tree, very similar in size and shape to the previous species but distinguished by its leaves and fruit; widespread in coastal and upland forest and grassland, often near rivers; also very common around Nairobi.

Bark: grey, smooth, flaking into large pieces with age; young branchlets covered with fine hairs.   **Leaves:** trifoliate, the terminal leaflet the largest, narrowly oval, to 10 cm. long; texture thin and rather stiff, with the margins curling up in drought; net veins conspicuous above, midrib hairy below; stalk hairy, to 5 cm.   **Flowers:** small, greenish-yellow or cream, in short axillary clusters.   **Fruit:** oval, over 1 cm. long, velvety when young, green with pale, raised gland-dots, dark red, soft and shiny when ripe, often in dense clusters.

Practical notes: both species are well worth planting as handsome background trees; moderately slow-growing, best in forest soil. Can be difficult to obtain from nurseries, although wild seedlings are common near parent trees.

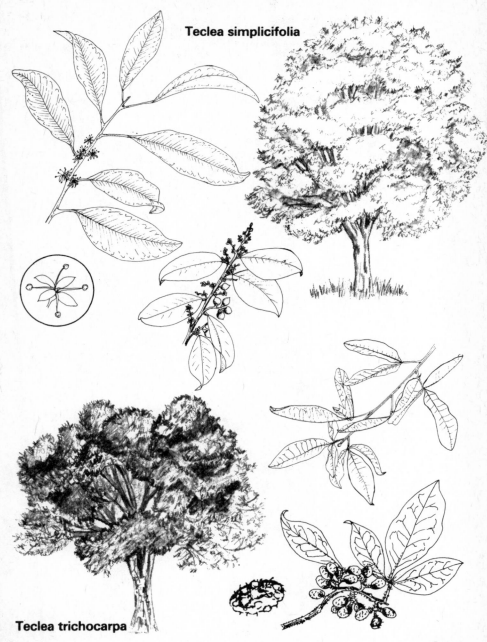

Teclea simplicifolia

Teclea trichocarpa

RUTACEAE

Zanthoxylum spp.

A large genus in tropical and temperate regions, sometimes called 'prickly ashes' because of the shape of the leaves. The trunks are easily recognised, as they are usually covered with conspicuous woody, spine-tipped bosses.

Zanthoxylum usambarense *(Fagara usambarensis)*
indigenous

Knobwood
Muguchua (Kikuyu)

A prickly, much-branched tree to 14 m., often multi-stemmed and rather straggling, not branching for several metres, occurring at forest edges in the highlands from 1,600 to 2,600 m., often in copses near termite mounds; common in the Karen district of Nairobi, often in regenerating forest.
Bark: greyish brown, conspicuously longitudinally furrowed and covered with spiny bosses on the ridges; branchlets with straight or upcurved dark red prickles. **Leaves:** compound, to 24 cm. long; leaflets 2 to 8 pairs plus a terminal leaflet which may be absent, each oval, variable, to 8 cm. long; margin scalloped to serrated, with clear gland-dots; midribs and stalks dark red and thorny. The leaves are strongly aromatic and hot to taste. **Flowers:** small, white to cream, strong-smelling, in branched terminal sprays up to 6 cm. long. **Fruit:** rounded, paired, sharply tipped, about 1 cm. long, half red and half greenish, in conspicuous clusters, breaking open to release several shiny blue-black seeds.

The wood is hard and white, traditionally popular for walking-sticks and 'rungus' or knobkerries. The leaves are used in soup as a treatment for colds and 'flu, and an infusion of the bark is used for coughs and rheumatic pains.

Zanthoxylum gillettii *(Fagara macrophylla)* is a lofty timber tree known as African Satinwood, from the Western Mau and Kakamega forests. The compound leaves are very large, to 1 m. in length, and the leaflets up to 30 cm. long.

Some other species are common, particularly at the coast. The trunks armed with woody spines are always conspicuous.

Zanthoxylum usambarense

SAPINDACEAE   Lychee family

A largely tropical family with about 2,000 species of trees, shrubs and many climbers, named after the Soapberry genus *Sapindus* from Mexico and southern U.S.A. It includes a number of edible fruits, notably the Chinese Lychee *Litchi chinensis,* which is grown as a minor crop in Kenya. Many species have resins or milky juice in their tissues.

In Kenya there are 18 genera, of which the largest is *Allophylus,* a widespread, rather shrubby genus whose often trifoliate leaves can be confused with those of *Rhus spp.* in the Mango family *Anacardiaceae.* However, the spikes of small creamy flowers and the crimson to black fruits of the genus *Allophylus* are distinctive. Useful timber trees include *Allophylus abyssinicus* (Kikuyu *Mushami*) from high mountain forest, and the white-flowered, mango-like *Blighia unijugata* (Kikuyu *Muikuni*) which is sometimes planted in Nairobi for its ornamental, orange-pink fruit. The Akee *Blighia sapida* is a fruit well-known in West Africa and the West Indies.

Majidea zanguebarica (Swahili *Mlanyuni*) is a tall timber tree from Lamu district planted as a leafy ornamental at the coast. The inside of the dry fruit capsules is bright crimson, contrasting with velvety black seeds.

Members of this family in Kenya include *Dodonaea, Filicium, Pappea.*

Dodonaea angustifolia *(Dodonaea viscosa)*   Sand Olive
indigenous   Murema-muthua (Kikuyu)

A thin-stemmed shrub or upright small tree, occasionally to 8 m., widely distributed from sea-level to 2,800 m. in a variety of habitats, often on rocky sites or poor soil.
Bark: dark grey, fissured and peeling; branchlets rusty-red and resinous. **Leaves:** thin, narrow, stiffly erect, up to 10 cm. long, widest towards the tip; light green and sticky when young; apex pointed, base tapering to a short stalk.   **Flowers:** small, with shiny greenish-yellow sepals and no petals, in short, dense heads. Male flowers have pale brown stamens.   **Fruit:** distinctive 2 cm. capsules, usually with 3 papery wings, sometimes inflated, in masses that resemble blossoms, the wings greenish, pale brown or coral pink. The coastal species *Dodonaea viscosa* usually has fruit with only two wings.

The wood is hard and heavy, useful for implement handles. An infusion from the roots has been used from very early times as a reliable remedy for the common cold.

The Kikuyu name, taken literally, means "Defeater of termites."

Practical notes: a quick-growing ornamental or windbreak, easily grown from seed and very hardy; an excellent hedge in dry areas and useful in sand or marshy soil, regenerating rapidly even after burning.

263

Dodonaea angustifolia

Majidea zanguebarica

264

SAPINDACEAE

Filicium decipiens   **Thika Palm, Fern-leaf Tree**
indigenous   Kamiti (Kikuyu)

A shapely evergreen tree, usually to 8 m., occasionally to 25 m., uncommon in forest valleys in the Kamiti district of Central Province, in the Taita Hills and near Meru, but now widely planted in the highlands as an ornamental. This species is distributed from Southern India to South Africa.

Bark: grey, smooth, becoming dark brown, rough and cracking.   **Leaves:** characteristic compound leaves to 30 cm. in length, with conspicuously winged stalks; leaflets resinous, glossy dark green above, 5 to 10 pairs, each long and narrow, to 14 x 2 cm.; apex rounded and notched at the tip, leaflet stalks absent.   **Flowers:** white, very small, in branched axillary sprays up to 12 cm. long.   **Fruit:** small, round, fleshy, purple-black when ripe, eaten by birds.

The botanical name, freely translated, means 'deceptively fern-like'.

Pappea capensis *(Pappea ugandensis)*   **Pappea**
indigenous   Mubaa (Kamba)

A leafy, semi-decidous tree, usually to 6 m., occasionally to 13 m., with a short trunk branching low down to form a spreading, rounded crown; widely distributed at medium to higher altitudes in drier forest and open woodland, often near rocks.

Bark: pale to dark grey, with horizontal markings.   **Leaves:** alternate, often crowded in terminal rosettes; mature leaves dull dark green above, stiff and rather wavy, slightly hairy below; shape variable, averaging 10 cm. in length; margin entire or irregularly and sharply toothed, base rounded and unequal, stalk short.   **Flowers:** small, yellow or greenish, in terminal spikes up to 12 cm. long.   **Fruit:** round, furry green capsules, about 1 cm. across. in tight clusters, splitting on the tree to reveal a bright orange, jelly-like aril covering a single, shiny black seed. The flesh is edible, slightly tart and pleasantly flavoured.

The wood is hard and tough, with a twisted grain, and the leaves are eaten by game and stock. Oil from the seeds can be used for soap and as a lubricant, and is claimed to be a remedy for ringworm. A soup made from the boiled bark was taken for stomach disorders.

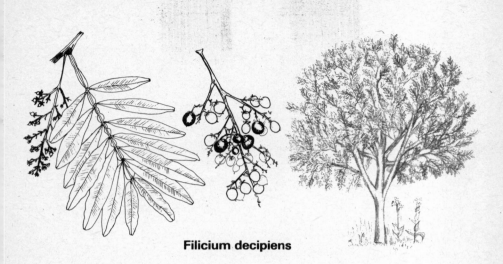

Filicium decipiens

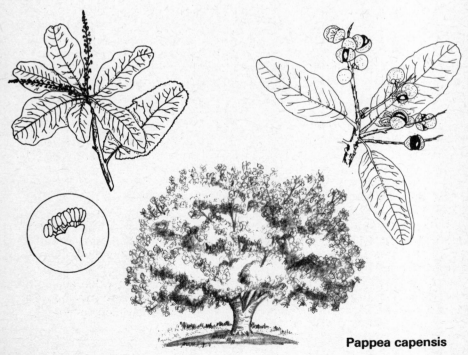

Pappea capensis

266

SAPOTACEAE   Manilkara family

A tropical family of about 800 species, producing timber, latex and edible fruits. Milky latex is present in all species, always in the twigs and usually in the bark. Gutta percha, once a gum of commercial importance and an even better insulator than the rubber which replaced it, comes from a species in South-east Asia. The Central American Sapodilla *Manilkara achras (Sapota achras)* produces chicle for chewing gum as well as the delicious Sapodilla Plum.

An indigenous timber tree in this family, *Aningeria adolfi-friedericii* (Kikuyu *Muna*), was valued for furniture. This species was once common in mountain forest, and remnant trees with small crowns and towering, heavily buttressed trunks can still be seen in tea-growing areas such as Limuru.

Leaves in this family are simple and usually spirally arranged. Flowers are inconspicuous, often nocturnal and pollinated by bats. Both *Manilkara* and *Mimusops* are widely distributed in Africa. Members of the family in Kenya include *Manilkara, Mimusops.*

Manilkara discolor
indigenous

Manilkara, Forest milkberry
Mugambwa (Kikuyu)

A leafy forest tree to 15 m. but twice that on river banks, one of 5 indigenous species, scattered in drier forest from 400 to 2,100 m., including the Nairobi area.

Bark: rough dark brown, flaking in patches with age: twigs dark, often knobbly.   **Leaves:** alternate, usually in terminal whorls, dark green above contrasting ('discolor') with velvety silver-grey below; broadly oval, to 10 cm. long; apex rounded or notched, side veins numerous and distinctly parallel; stalk grooved.   **Flowers:** fragrant, small, creamy yellow, in axillary clusters.   **Fruit:** oval, about 1 cm. long, yellow to red; edible and sweet.

Mimusops kummel
indigenous

Mimusops, Red Milkwood
Mugumo-ciano (Kikuyu)

A densely leafy small tree or shrub, occasionally to 25 m., often riparian, very widely distributed in drier forest and wooded grassland from 500 to 2,100 m., including the Nairobi area.

Bark: dark grey to dark brown, sometimes deeply corrugated: twigs slender, with dense rusty hairs.   **Leaves:** small, smooth, dark and glossy above, in upright bunches; broadly oval, up to 3.5 cm. long; apex rounded or notched, midrib prominent below; stalk short.   **Flowers:** fragrant, creamy-white, flat star-shaped, style prominent, all parts in fours, the petals subdivided, sepals in two rows, rusty hairy; flowers axillary, on long stalks.   **Fruit:** oval berries, about 2 cm. long, hairy, green turning to orange-yellow; style persistent.

267

Manilkara discolor

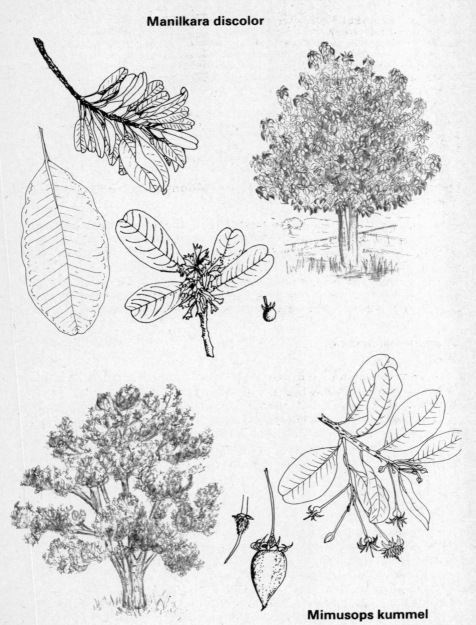

Mimusops kummel

SOLANACEAE   Potato family

A large family of herbs and shrubs, rarely trees, centred in tropical America. Food plants include potatoes, tomatoes, peppers and Cape gooseberries, but as a family *Solanaceae* is extremely poisonous and produces dangerous alkaloids, such as nicotine from the tobacco plant *Nicotiana* and atropine from the Deadly Nightshade *Atropa belladonna*. However, it has long been recognised that these plants also have valuable medicinal properties.

Among ornamentals the evergreen shrub *Brunfelsia calycina* from Brazil is popular, known as Yesterday, Today and Tomorrow. The flowers fade from deep purple to white.

Two common annual weeds in this family are notorious among farmers. The prickly Sodom Apple *Solanum incanum* has purple flowers and round yellow fruit, while the equally widespread Thorn Apple *Datura stramonium* has white flowers and thorny fruit. The seeds of the latter are poisonous enough to cause deaths in both humans and stock if plants are accidentally harvested with the cereal crops they invade.

Members of this family in Kenya include *Datura, Solanum.*

Datura suaveolens *(Brugmansia candida)*   Moonflower, Angel's Trumpet
Peru, Chile

A shrub or small tree to 5 m. with dense, drooping foliage, one of the several species planted as quick-growing ornamentals. **Leaves:** large, mid-green, softly hairy; margin very wavy, apex pointed, base often unequal-sided. **Flowers:** showy, trumpet-shaped, pendulous, to 25 cm. across, with the petals flaring at the mouth. The common variety is white, with others yellow, apricot or pink, sometimes double-flowered. The scent at night is almost overpowering. All parts are both poisonous and narcotic.

Solanum macranthum   Brazilian Potato Tree
Brazil

A common ornamental tree to 10 m., quick-growing but short-lived. Branches and leaves may bear sharp, hooked prickles. **Leaves:** large, up to 30 cm. long, in terminal clusters; rough above and minutely hairy below; margin deeply and irregularly lobed, apex blunt, base very unequal-sided. **Flowers:** star-shaped, with 5 joined petals, to 5 cm. across, in small terminal clusters; petals purple, fading to white, stamens yellow. **Fruit:** large, rather soft berries, to 3 cm. across, yellow when ripe; calyx persistent.

Solanum mauritianum   Asian Bug Tree
South America, Asia

An unarmed shrub or tree to 5 m.; naturalised around Nairobi, common on waste ground, sometimes a troublesome weed. The stalks, branchlets and leaves are covered with soft, whitish hairs. **Bark:** greenish to pale brown, smooth, speckled. **Leaves:** large, grey-green, limp and tapering, to 30 cm. long; leafy stipules prominent at the base of the leaf stalks. **Flowers:** small, star-shaped, pale mauve, in flat heads about 12 cm. across. **Fruit:** small berries, in large clusters on long erect stalks, yellow when ripe and poisonous.

269

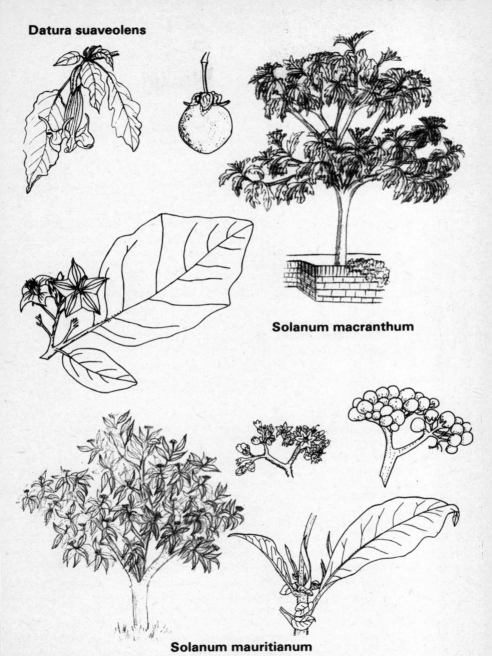

Datura suaveolens

Solanum macranthum

Solanum mauritianum

STERCULIACEAE Cocoa family

A large, mainly tropical family of softwood trees and shrubs, named after the genus *Sterculia* which has several indigenous representatives, mainly in coastal or lowland bush. The Cocoa tree *Theobroma cacao* is native to South America, and the genus *Cola* has its origins in the rain-forests of tropical Africa, although now widely cultivated for the stimulant in its seeds, which is the basis for the world-wide soft drink. There are other indigenous *Cola* species. The genus *Brachychiton* is native to Australia and New Guinea, while the genus *Dombeya* appears in many parts of Africa.

Leaves in this family are simple or palmately lobed, often with star-shaped hairs. The flowers have five petals or none at all, and the fruits are often dry.

Members of the family in Kenya include *Brachychiton, Dombeya*.

Brachychiton acerifolium *(Sterculia acerifolia)* Australian Flame
Queensland, New South Wales *COLOUR PLATE XVIII*

A spectacular deciduous flowering tree with a pyramidal shape, to 15 m. or occasionally twice that, widely planted in the highlands as an ornamental. **Bark:** grey, smooth; rougher with age, bearing scars from detached branches. **Leaves:** large, palmately lobed, up to 30 cm. across, resembling the leaves of a paw-paw; glossy mid-green above, with radiating veins prominent below; stalks very long and slender; crowded towards the ends of branches. **Flowers:** brilliant red, made up of 5 joined sepals, bell-shaped, to 2.5 cm. long, in loose sprays; prolific, often in patches over the tree, later carpeting the ground. The flowers usually appear when the tree is bare. **Fruit:** smooth black capsules, to 10 cm. long, splitting down one side.

Practical notes: fairly fast-growing in good forest soil, but not flowering for up to ten years and then only erratically. Young trees are widely available.

Brachychiton populneum *(Sterculia diversifolia)* Australian Bottle Tree
Eastern Australia

A dark, evergreen tree, usually to 8 m., in drier areas developing a swollen, bottle-shaped trunk, fairly widely planted in Nairobi city and elsewhere as an ornamental shade tree. **Bark:** dark grey, with fine vertical fissures. **Leaves:** variable, thin and dull green, heart-shaped or lobed, usually 5 to 8 cm. in length with a long, pointed tip, crowded towards the ends of branches. The leaf stalks are long and exceptionally slender, so that the leaves shake in the wind like the aspens and poplars of the northern hemisphere. **Flowers:** cup-shaped, to 2 cm. across, pale yellowish-green with rusty red markings within, sometimes hanging in dense clusters. **Fruit:** woody capsules, to 7 cm. long, solitary or in remarkable cartwheels of up to 5 fruits, splitting to release scarlet seeds.

Practical notes: easily grown from seed; slow-growing but potentially useful in harsh, arid areas where other evergreen species may not survive.

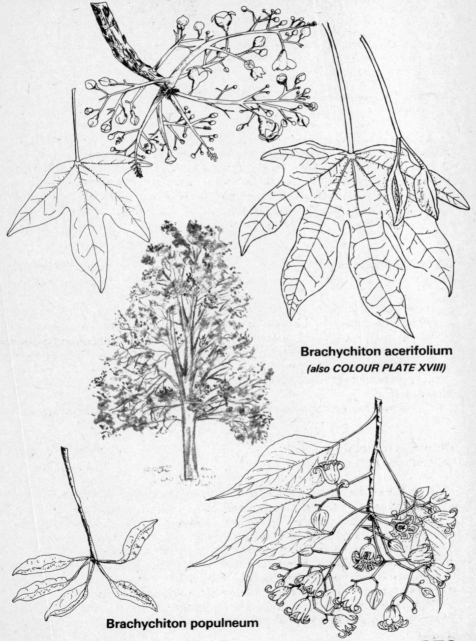

Brachychiton acerifolium
(also COLOUR PLATE XVIII)

Brachychiton populneum

STERCULIACEAE

Dombeya spp.

A distinctive African genus of trees and shrubs with hairy heart-shaped or palmately lobed leaves, and showy pink or white flowers. The 5 oblique, asymmetric petals turn brown and papery, and persist around the dry capsule. There are a number of species, many with fibrous bark which was widely used for cordage and weaving.

Dombeya burgessiae *(Dombeya nairobiensis)*
indigenous

Dombeya
Mukeu (Kikuyu)

A common undershrub, rarely a small tree, widespread in almost all drier upland forest areas. **Leaves:** broadly heart-shaped, velvety hairy, up to 18 x 12 cm.; apex tapering, base rounded, stalk to 12 cm. long; veins prominent below, radiating from the leaf base; margin toothed, sometimes lobed. The leaves are often eaten by insects to a lace-like skeleton. **Flowers:** pale pink or white, 3 to 5 cm. across, on long axillary stalks. **Fruit:** small capsules, covered in soft brown hairs.

Dombeya goetzenii
indigenous

Forest Dombeya
Mukeu (Kikuyu)

A timber tree to 15 m. of wet highland forest above 2,200 m.
Bark: grey, smooth. **Leaves:** felty dark green, thick, heart-shaped but not lobed, up to 30 x 25 cm.; nerves usually red above, vein network very prominent below; apex extended, margin sharply toothed, bases often overlapping; stalk hairy. **Flowers:** pale pink or white, with red centres, in showy clusters on branched, hairy stalks to 30 cm. long. **Fruit:** small, densely hairy capsules.
The light brown wood was widely used as a general purpose timber.

Dombeya rotundifolia
indigenous

White Dombeya
Mutoo (Kikuyu)

A small deciduous tree, usually to 4 m., in dry wooded grassland from 1,400 to 2,200 m., often near termite mounds; common in the Machakos area.
Bark: dark brown, deeply furrowed. **Leaves:** rough, dark green above, often densely hairy; broadly oval to circular, 6 to 18 cm. across, strongly 5-veined from the base; margin irregularly toothed, stalk to 8 cm. The leaves dry very crisp and hard. **Flowers:** snowy white, sometimes tinged with pink, to 2 cm. across, in many-flowered, branching heads; sweet-scented, attracting many bees; buds densely woolly. **Fruit:** small round hairy capsules.
The wood makes good fuel, strong and tough but usually twisted. Deserves encouragement as an attractive, fairly fast-growing ornamental.

273

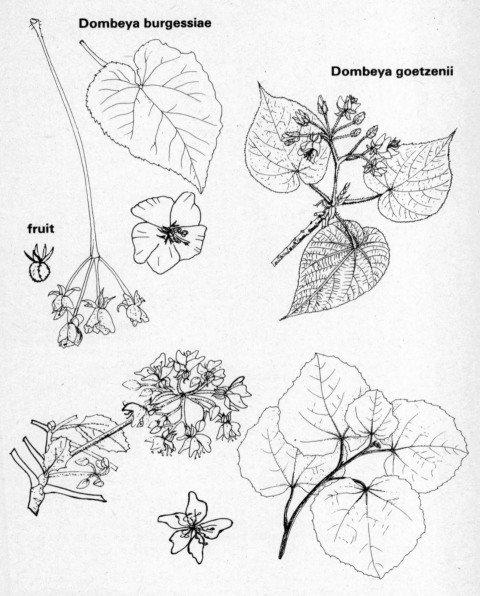

Dombeya burgessiae

Dombeya goetzenii

fruit

Dombeya rotundifolia

STRELITZIACEAE   Strelitzia family

A small tropical family, with conspicuous flowers that splay out from leathery, boat-shaped bracts which hold the flower heads. The family is closely related to the Banana family *Musaceae*, but in the family *Strelitziaceae* the leaves are in two regular ranks, giving an attractive symmetrical shape. Both tree species of the Strelitzia family that are planted in Kenya are exotics, as is the Bird of Paradise flower *Strelitzia reginae*, whose striking orange and blue flowers are well-known to gardeners.

The indigenous representative of the Banana family is the Wild Banana *Ensete ventricosum* from wet upland forest valleys. This dramatic plant has a tall stem up to 12 m. in height composed of strong leaf bases, and is distinguished from the Banana genus *Musa* by having a pendulous terminal flower head up to 3 m. long and by dying after flowering. *Ensete ventricosum* is also indigenous to Ethiopia, where it provides a staple food and valuable fibre, but in Kenya it is better known as an outstanding ornamental bearing bright green leaves with red midribs.

Members of this family in Kenya include *Ravenala, Strelitzia.*

Ravenala madagascariensis   Traveller's Palm
Madagascar

An unmistakable fan-like tree with a trunk to 10 m., planted as an ornamental from the coast to the highlands. Despite its common name this is not a palm but a giant woody herb, as are all members of this family; in its native forests in Madagascar the trunk alone may exceed 30 m. in height. **Leaves:** very large, leathery, on long stalks, growing only in one plane, the bases overlapping to form a fan up to 8 m. across, flaring out at the tips. The leaf blades are often split into narrow strips.   **Flowers:** white, in groups arising from large boat-shaped bracts between the leaf stalks. The nectar attracts birds.   **Fruit:** woody capsules, containing bright blue-coated seeds.

The leaf bases form hollows, which may store up to 2 litres of water. This can be tapped for drinking in case of emergency, which explains the English name for this tree.

Strelitzia augusta *(Strelitzia alba)*   Great White Strelitzia
South Africa

A tree to 10 m. in height with a spindly, woody trunk covered with old leaf bases, native to the forests of the southern Cape but in Kenya planted as an ornamental.   **Leaves:** large, drooping, up to 2 m. long, often split into ribbons; texture shiny, leathery. **Flowers:** petals and sepals white, arising from purplish boat-shaped bracts between the leaf stalks. **Fruit:** 3-lobed woody capsules, containing many seeds.

Practical notes: Both the above species are readily grown from seed or by dividing the suckers; best planted in sheltered positions, as trees exposed to strong winds suffer torn leaves and look untidy.

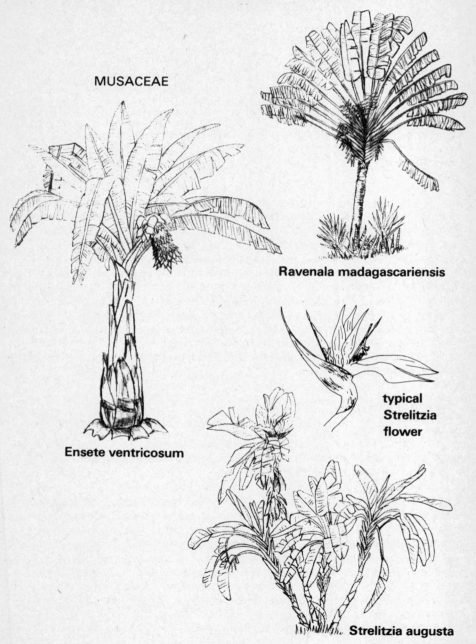

MUSACEAE

STRELITZIACEAE

Ravenala madagascariensis

Ensete ventricosum

typical
Strelitzia
flower

Strelitzia augusta

276

TILIACEAE Jute family

A medium-sized family of trees, shrubs and herbs, best represented in the tropics and regions south of the equator but named after the genus *Tilia,* which includes the Lime or Linden trees from the northern hemisphere. In North America these ornamental timber trees are called Basswood.

Many of the tropical trees and shrubs in this family have fibrous stems, the best known being Jute *Corchorus capsularis,* an annual cultivated in northern India for commercial fibre.

The largest genus is *Grewia,* which occurs in tropical Africa, Asia and Australasia. Kenya has about 30 indigenous species, most of them shrubs, some with white or yellow flowers and others with pink or lilac. The five sepals, often coloured within, are sometimes more prominent than the five petals. All have berries in fruit, with one to four sections, and most indigenous species have asymmetric leaves, with finely toothed margins and three veins arising from the leaf base.

Grewia bicolor
indigenous Mulawa (Kamba)

A much-branched shrub or small tree to 3 m., occasionally to 9 m. in moist valleys, widespread in dry grassland and bush from the coast to 2,000 m., often on rocky ground; common around Machakos, Kitui, Mtito Andei and Isiolo.

Bark: grey brown, sometimes flaking; branchlets speckled with pale breathing pores. **Leaves:** shiny dark green above, contrasting ('bicolor') with silvery-white below; broadly elliptic, up to 9 cm. long but usually smaller; apex rounded or tapering, base rounded; margin finely serrated, veins raised below. **Flowers:** bright yellow, fragrant, 5 reflexed petals and spreading sepals, to 1.5 cm. across, in small axillary clusters; often in profusion. **Fruit:** rounded, usually with only one lobe about 6 mm. in diameter, green and hairy, becoming glossy orange brown, edible when ripe.

The sweet, rather astringent fruit are eaten by children, and the leaves are browsed by domestic stock.

Grewia similis
indigenous Mutheregendi (Kikuyu)

A straggling shrub, occasionally a small tree to 3 m., often a climber entwined with other plants or even prostrate on the ground, common in bush and grassland from 600 to 2,200 m. but not occurring in dry areas.

Leaves: shiny dark green above, broadly oval, almost rounded, about 5 cm. long but often smaller; apex rounded or notched, base rounded, not asymmetric; margin finely serrated, 3 veins from base prominent below; young shoots hairy. **Flowers:** attractive, bright mauve or pink with yellow anthers and mauve filaments, in terminal or axillary groups of 3 to 6 flowers, each star-shaped, about 3 cm. across; 5 petals oblong, sepals acute, underside mauve, as long or longer than the petals. The flowers do not open until late morning. **Fruit:** fleshy berries, deeply 4-lobed although some lobes may not develop; each lobe about 5 mm. across, orange to bright red and edible when ripe; much eaten by birds.

The sticky substance under the bark was used as a cure for sores.

277

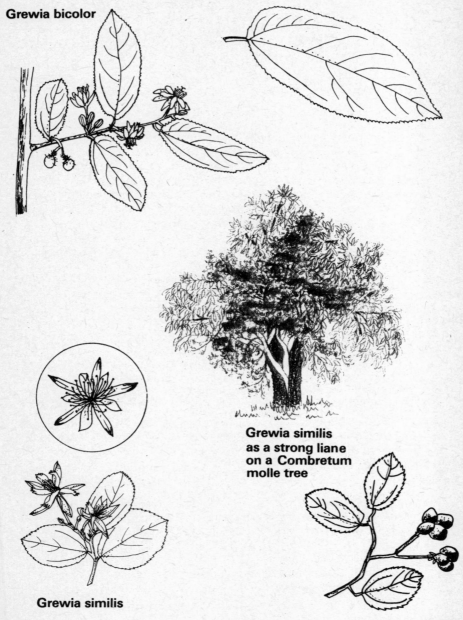

Grewia bicolor

**Grewia similis
as a strong liane
on a Combretum
molle tree**

Grewia similis

ULMACEAE   Elm family

A family of over 150 trees and shrubs, mostly tropical or from temperate northern regions, named after the Elm genus *Ulmus* which does not occur in Kenya. All members of the family have simple, alternate leaves with the blade often unequal-sided, and small flowers with no petals. There are few indigenous species, but these are common and widespread over much of Africa.

Members of this family in Kenya include *Celtis, Chaetacme, Trema.*

Celtis africana *(Celtis kraussiana)*   White Stinkwood
indigenous   Murundu (Kikuyu)

A deciduous forest tree to 12 m. or sometimes to twice that, mainly in high rainfall areas up to 2,400 m.; locally common in the Rift Valley.
Bark: grey, smooth, slightly ringed; branchlets covered with rusty hairs.   **Leaves:** rough dull green above, to 10 cm. long, with 3 to 5 veins from the base; apex elongated, margin serrated over the top two-thirds.   **Flowers:** small, greenish, axillary.   **Fruit:** small, rounded, orange and fleshy.
The wood is yellowish-white and tough, used for implement handles. This is an attractive, spreading tree, easily grown from seed.

Chaetacme aristata *(Chaetacme microcarpa)*   Thorny Elm
indigenous   Muyuyu (Kikuyu)

A scrambling, thorny shrub or much-branched tree to 10 m. with drooping, zig-zag branchlets. occurring in forest and forest margins from 900 to 2,100 m.; not uncommon around Nairobi and in Nyanza Province. This is the only species found throughout Africa.
Bark: pale grey, smooth; trunk and branches armed with sharp spines, often paired and axillary, to 3.5 cm. long.   **Leaves:** leathery, glossy, unequal-sided, to 9 cm. long with a needle-like tip; midrib prominent below, margin serrated or spine-toothed only on juvenile leaves.   **Flowers:** small, greenish, in dense axillary clusters.   **Fruit:** oval, about 1.5 cm long, waxy orange-yellow, bearing two persistent styles.
The wood is yellowish, heavy and difficult to chop, used for making clubs.

Trema orientalis *(Trema guineensis)*   Pigeonwood
indigenous   Muhethu (Kikuyu)

A shrub or spreading tree to 12 m., widely distributed in Africa from sea-level to 1,850 m. in secondary forest or at forest margins in disturbed soil.
Bark: light grey, thin, smooth; branchlets densely covered with short hairs.   **Leaves:** alternate, to 14 cm. long, rough and dull above, softly hairy below; apex elongated, margin neatly serrated throughout; 3 veins clear from the rounded base.   **Flowers:** small, yellowish-green, in dense axillary clusters.   **Fruit:** small, round, fleshy, black when ripe, much favoured by doves and pigeons.

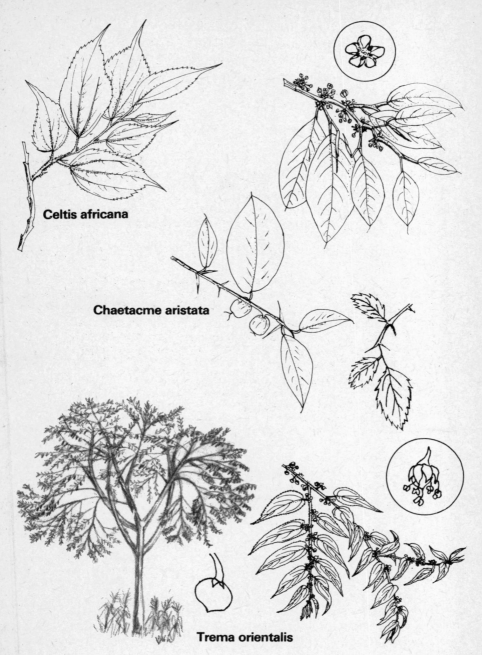

Celtis africana

Chaetacme aristata

Trema orientalis

URTICACEAE •Nettle family

A medium-sized family, widely distributed in both temperate and tropical climates. Some plants contain fibres, and in South-east Asia *Boehmeria nivea* is grown commercially for a fibre known as Ramie fibre.

In Kenya there are over 20 herbs in this family, but only one tree species. Leaves are usually simple, and the leaves, branches and even stems may be armed with coarse, stinging hairs. Despite these stinging hairs the young leaves of several species, notably *Urtica massaica,* are in common use as a vegetable.

Obetia pinnatifida   **Stinging Nettle Tree**
indigenous

A low shrub or tree to 7 m., when it has the habit of a paw-paw, with a tall bare trunk and foliage in leafy tufts; widely distributed but not common, occurring on dry, rocky hillsides like the eastern slopes of Lake Nakuru, Hell's Gate and Mt. Suswa, and in Voi and Taita districts. There is a fine specimen in front of the Nairobi National Museum, although its shape is not typical.

Bark: smooth, grey to yellowish-green, young bark bearing dry leaf remnants.   **Leaves**: large, deeply lobed, to 30 x 25 cm.; margin jaggedly toothed; veins prominent above, lower surface matted with soft white hairs. Stems, branchlets, stalks and leaf veins are covered with stinging hairs which can cause intense, burning irritation.   **Flowers**: small, greenish-white to yellow, drying brown and papery, in much-branched terminal heads.   **Fruit**: small dry nuts, which germinate readily.

The wood is soft and brittle, but a tough rope or weaving cord can be made from the fibres of the stems. An infusion of the leaves was used in traditional medicine as a gargle to relieve toothache.

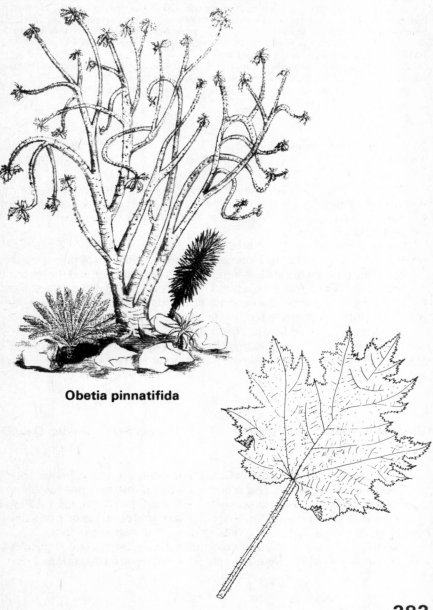

Obetia pinnatifida

VERBENACEAE   Meru Oak family

A large tropical family with over 3,000 species of herbs, shrubs, trees and climbers. Verbenas are small shrubs and herbs containing aromatic oils, well known for herbal teas and medicines; however, the family includes several valuable timber trees such as Teak *Tectona grandis* from South-east Asia and the indigenous Meru Oak *Vitex keniensis*. There are also many popular ornamentals, including the Purple Wreath Vine *Petraea volubilis* and the Chinese Hat Plant *Holmskioldia sanguinea* from the Himalayas.

There are 7 genera indigenous to Kenya, including the willow-like tree *Avicennia marina* of the coastal mangrove belt, which sends numerous air roots up through the mud.

Members of this family in Kenya include *Clerodendrum, Duranta, Lantana, Vitex.*

Clerodendrum myricoides   Butterfly Flower
indigenous   Munjuga-iria (Kikuyu)

An attractive shrub or small tree to 5 m., occurring in wetter scrub or wooded grassland in most districts of Kenya. There are a number of other indigenous woody species and several exotic ornamental climbers and shrubs in the genus *Clerodendrum.*

Leaves: opposite or in whorls, soft, narrowly oval, up to 12 cm. long but often smaller; margin lightly to deeply serrated.   **Flowers:** 4 pale blue-mauve petals outspread like butterfly wings, the fifth petal darker and more rounded; stamens blue, long and protruding. This structure assists cross-pollination by the large carpenter bees and sunbirds that are attracted by the nectar.   **Fruit:** small green berries, black and edible when ripe.

The wood was used by the Wakamba for making arrows.

The flower of this species has been chosen as the emblem of the E.A. Herbarium in Nairobi. This is an attractive ornamental, well worth planting in gardens.

Duranta repens *(Duranta plumieri)*   Pigeon Berry, Golden Dew Drop
Tropical America

An evergreen shrub or tree to 6m., naturalised in parts of Kenya and often planted as an ornamental. The branches are square-stemmed, drooping and sometimes prickly.   **Leaves:** opposite, soft, oval, to 10 cm. long.   **Flowers:** pale mauve, small and trumpet-shaped, in terminal bunches on one side of the flower stalk.   **Fruit:** soft, shiny orange berries, in dense clusters.

The tree is fast growing and drought-resistant, and makes a good hedge. There is also a white-flowered variety. The berries are poisonous.

283

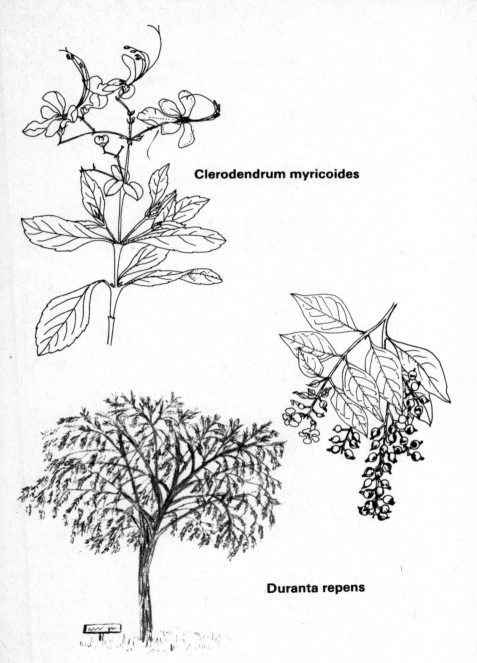

Clerodendrum myricoides

Duranta repens

VERBENACEAE

Lantana camara
Tropical America

Lantana, Curse of India
Mukigi (Kikuyu)

An evergreen shrub to 3 m. in height with square, prickly stems, forming impenetrable thickets, a noxious weed widespread through much of Kenya.

Leaves: aromatic, opposite, oval to rounded, to 8 cm. long; margin serrated, upper surface rough. **Flowers:** small, 5-lobed, in flat, rounded heads about 5 cm. across, in a mixture of shades of pink, yellow and mauve, changing colour with age. **Fruit:** small black berries in round heads, decorative but dangerously poisonous, although not to birds.

Lantana trifolia is an indigenous scrambling species with hairs and not prickles on the stems, leaves in threes, pink to mauve flowers and purple fruit.

There are several drought-resistant hybrids with showy white, yellow, orange or red flowers. These cultivated hybrids, which can be planted as ornamental hedges, are less aggressive than the exotic weed species as they are not self-seeding.

Vitex keniensis
indigenous

Meru Oak
Muhuru (Kikuyu)

A handsome deciduous forest tree, growing to 20 m. but on river banks up to 30 m. or more with a clear straight trunk, occurring in a restricted range from 1,500 to 1,850 m. on the eastern slopes of Mt. Kenya; elsewhere in plantations. This species is now endangered due to the demand for its timber.

Bark: thin pale brown with narrow vertical fissures, darkening with age. **Leaves:** palmate, on long stalks, with a distinctive 5-leaflet pattern; leaflets variable, light green and drooping when young, up to 25 cm. in length; midrib and veins prominent below; stalks, young stems and undersides of leaflets covered in pale, velvety hairs. **Flowers:** small, about 1 cm. long, creamy white with one prominent mauve petal, in branching axillary heads up to 24 cm. across. **Fruit:** rounded, about 1.5 cm. across, shiny green turning black, edible when ripe.

The timber is hard and durable, pale brown with darker heartwood and a handsome wavy grain, much prized for high quality furniture, panelling and veneer but now relatively scarce. The wood yellows somewhat as it ages.

There are a number of other indigenous *Vitex* species, including several at the coast.

Practical notes: apart from its valuable timber, this fine species deserves extensive planting as an ornamental or windbreak. Young trees can sometimes be obtained from nurseries. Growth is moderately slow, but is much improved with good water and forest soil.

285

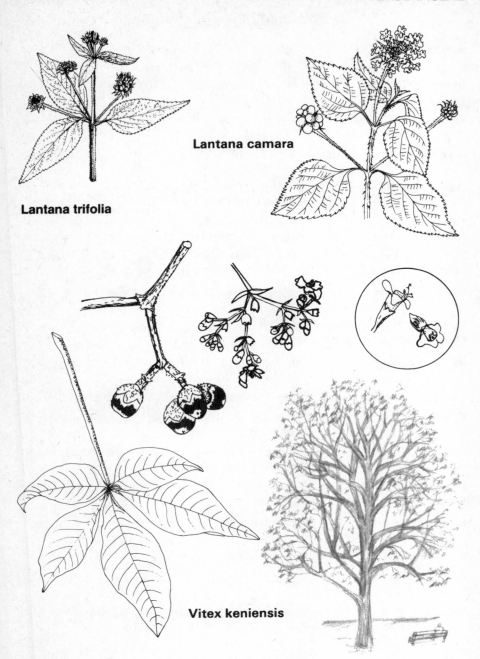

Lantana camara

Lantana trifolia

Vitex keniensis

Selected bibliography

Battiscombe, E. : Trees and Shrubs of Kenya Colony, Government Printer, Nairobi, 1936.

Blundell, Michael : Wild Flowers of East Africa, William Collins Sons & Co. Ltd., 1987.

Brockman, C. Frank : Trees of North America, Golden Press, New York, 1979.

Coates Palgrave, Keith: Trees of Southern Africa, C. Struik (Pty) Ltd., Cape Town, 1981.

Dale, Ivan R. : Introduced Trees of Uganda, Government Printer, Entebbe, 1953.

Dale, Ivan R. & Greenway, P.J. : Kenya Trees & Shrubs, Buchanan's Kenya Estates Ltd., 1961.

Davidson, Lynette & Jeppe, Barbara : A Field Guide to the Acacias of Southern Africa, Centaur Publishers, Johannesburg, 1981.

Heywood, V.H. : Flowering Plants of the World, Oxford University Press, 1978.

Hubbard, C.E. & Milne-Redhead E. et al.: Flora of Tropical East Africa, Crown Agents, London, 1952-

Jex-Blake, A.J. : Gardening in East Africa, Longmans, Green and Co. Ltd., London, 1957.

Johnson, Hugh : Encyclopaedia of Trees, Mitchell Beazley, 1979.

Kokwaro, J.O. : Medicinal Plants of East Africa, East African Literature Bureau, 1976.

: Classification of E.A. Crops, Kenya Literature Bureau, 1979.

Lötschert, Wilhelm & Beese, Gerhard : Tropical Plants, William Collins Sons & Co. Ltd., 1983.

Macoboy, Stirling : What Tree is That? Tiger Books International, 1979.

Perry, Frances : Flowers of the World, Optimum Books, 1972.

Teel, Wayne : Trees and Seeds in Kenya, KENGO, Nairobi 1988.

Williams, R.O. : Useful & Ornamental Plants of Zanzibar and Pemba, Government of Zanzibar, 1949.

FLOWERS

A diagrammatic section through a typical flower

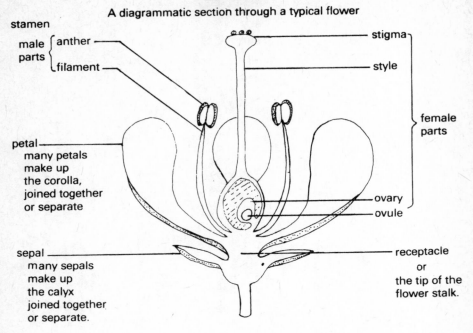

stamen

male parts { anther
filament

petal
many petals
make up
the corolla,
joined together
or separate

sepal
many sepals
make up
the calyx
joined together
or separate.

stigma

style

female parts

ovary

ovule

receptacle
or
the tip of the
flower stalk.

The diagram shows the parts that may be present in a perfect flower. The function of the flowers is to produce seed for the next generation. Pollination takes place when pollen from the anther reaches the stigma and grows down the style to the ovule, where the male and female cells join and set the seed. After this fertilization process, the ovule and the ovary become the basic parts of the fruit.

Parts of a flower vary in size, number and position according to the plant family. Usually it is the petals of a flower that are striking or colourful, but sometimes it is other parts: for instance, an Ochna may have red sepals, and a Bottlebrush has bright crimson stamens.

Although they may sometimes be green and insignificant, flowers are found in all trees other than those from primitive plant families such as the cycads and the conifers. In some families the male and female parts develop separately on the same tree or even on different trees, and in others, parts like petals may be missing altogether.

288

LEAVES

a simple leaf

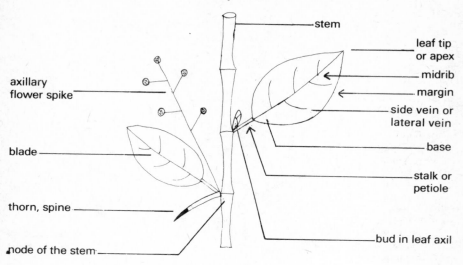

stem

leaf tip
or apex

midrib

margin

side vein or
lateral vein

base

stalk or
petiole

bud in leaf axil

axillary
flower spike

blade

thorn, spine

node of the stem

The diagram shows two simple leaves alternate on the stem. A good example is *Teclea simplicifolia*.

Leaves can also arise in threes, as in *Lantana trifolia*.

Some leaves arise spirally, like *Dracaena steudneri*, or in clusters, like *Maytenus senegalensis*.

Leaves arise or grow out from the stem at the nodes. This is clearly seen in families such as *Rubiaceae*.

Thorns may also arise at the nodes, either in pairs or singly. Examples are *Acacia spp*. or *Ziziphus spp*.

Leafy outgrowths or stipules at the base of the leaf stalk are prominent in certain trees, for instance *Markhamia lutea*. Most members of the *Rosaceae* family have well defined stipules.

compound leaves

A compound leaf is a leaf whose blade is divided up into smaller leaflets.

a simple leaf

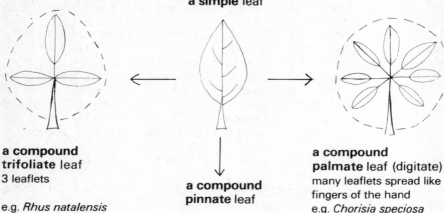

a compound trifoliate leaf
3 leaflets

e.g. *Rhus natalensis*

a compound pinnate leaf

a compound palmate leaf (digitate)
many leaflets spread like fingers of the hand
e.g. *Chorisia speciosa*

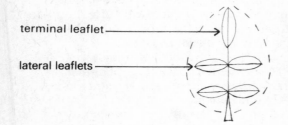

terminal leaflet

lateral leaflets

5 or more leaflets arise on either side of the leaf stalk, resembling a birds' feather (Latin *pinna*: wing)
e.g. *Schreberá alata*.

pinnate compound leaves are very common in our area. Those with very small leaflets have "feathery leaves".

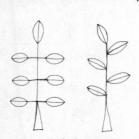

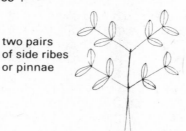

two pairs of side ribes or pinnae

compound pinnate leaves
e.g. *Spathodea campanulata*
   Tipuana tipu.

twice compound leaves (bipinnate)
e.g. *Acrocarpus fraxinifolius*
   Acacia species.

GLOSSARY

alternate : (of leaves) alternating along the stem; not **opposite.**

anther : the main part of the flower **stamen,** producing pollen.

aril : a growth, sometimes fleshy, partly or completely covering a seed.

axil : the upper angle between the stem and a leaf or branch.

axillary : growing from the **axil.**

berry : a soft, juicy fruit with pulp surrounding the seeds.

bract : a small or modified leaf, often just below the flower, which may be brightly coloured and resemble a petal.

calyx : the outer envelope of a bud, protecting the flower, made up of free or joined **sepals.**

capsule : a dry fruit, releasing seed from pores or breaking open when ripe.

catkin : a closely-packed, hanging spike of small flowers, usually of one sex.

compound : (of leaves) a whole leaf made up of similar leaflets; not **simple.**

conifer : an important group of trees bearing woody fruit known as cones, whose seeds are borne on the cone scales.

deciduous : (of trees) shedding all leaves periodically; not **evergreen.**

entire : (of the leaf margin) edge uninterrupted, without teeth or lobes.

evergreen : (of trees) with leaves falling and growing continuously throughout the year; not **deciduous.**

exotic : introduced from outside (Kenya); not **indigenous**

filament : the stalk of the flower **stamen,** supporting an **anther.**

fruit : (botanical) the ripened ovary of a seed plant, with its contents.

genus : see introduction: plural **genera.**

gland : an organ on or within a plant secreting fluids such as oil, resin or nectar.

head : (of flowers) the flowering stalk and the flowers massed upon it.

herb : any plant with soft, non-woody stems; commonly used of culinary or medicinal plants.

hybrid : the offspring of two plants of different species.

indigenous : native or belonging naturally to (Kenya).

leaflet : a single division of a compound leaf.

lenticels : corky cells in pores on the bark which allow the tree to breathe; seen as dots or lines.

naturalised : (of plants) so successfully introduced (into Kenya) that they reproduce naturally.

nectar : sugary fluid produced by some plants, made into honey by bees.

nut : a dry single-seeded fruit with a hard outer covering.

291

pod	:	a dry fruit, usually splitting into two, typical of the Leguminosae family.
pollen	:	small grains containing the fertilising male cells, produced by the **anthers** and stored there until released.
resin	:	sticky fluid produced by certain plants, insoluble in water.
riparian	:	of or growing along river banks.
scale	:	a reduced leaf, often the protective covering of a bud or bulb.
sepal	:	one of the separate, leaf-like, parts of the **calyx**, usually green.
shrub	:	a woody plant branching at or near the base with no defined trunk, usually smaller than a tree.
spine	:	a sharp, rigid outgrowth, deeply attached, not pulling off readily with the bark (cf. **thorn**); sometimes the tip of a branch.
sp., spp.	:	abbreviation for species, and the plural of species.
ssp., subsp.	:	abbreviations for subspecies.
stipules	:	small leafy outgrowths, usually paired at the base of the leaf stalk.
succulent	:	(of leaves or fruit) juicy, watery, containing soft pulp.
thorn	:	a sharp outgrowth which is relatively superficial (cf. **spine**)
trifoliate	:	(of compound leaves) with leaflets in threes.

INDEX

*Names shown in small type are synonyms, or names
which have been superseded.*

293

INDEX

KENYA

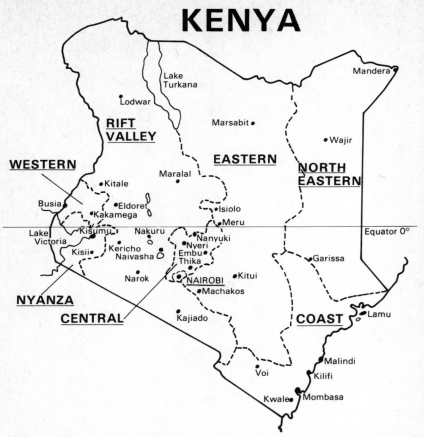

Province	Districts	Province	Districts
NAIROBI	Nairobi	**NYANZA**	Kisii
			Kisumu
CENTRAL	Kiambu		Siaya
	Kirinyaga		South Nyanza
	Murang'a		
	Nyandarua		
	Nyeri	**RIFT VALLEY**	Baringo
			Elgeyo-Marakwet
COAST	Lamu		Kajiado
	Kilifi		Kericho
	Kwale		Laikipia
	Mombasa		Nakuru
	Taita Taveta		Nandi
	Tana River		Narok
			Samburu
EASTERN	Embu		Trans Nzoia
	Isiolo		Turkana
	Kitui		Uasin Gishu
	Machakos		West Pokot
	Marsabit		
	Meru		
NORTH EASTERN	Garissa	**WESTERN**	Bungoma
	Wajir		Busia
	Mandera		Kakamega